HISTORY OF NORTHEAST INDIA

New Research and Perspectives

HISTORY OF NORTHEAST INDIA

New Research and Perspectives

Edited by

Dr. Rusievan Shangpliang

PATHAK PUBLISHER AND DISTRIBUTORS
New Delhi (INDIA)

HISTORY OF NORTHEAST INDIA: New Research and Perspectives

Editor : Dr. Rusievan Shangpliang

ISBN : 978-93-91952-89-1

Price : 1750/-

First Edition: 2024

Published by :
PATHAK PUBLISHER AND DISTRIBUTORS
E-6/33c & 34, Ground Floor, Sangam Vihar
New Delhi-110080
E-mail: pathakppd@gmail.com

In Association with :
RESEARCH INDIA PRESS

Typographic Design by: G. R. Sharma

Printed in India

Contents

Preface & Acknowledgements

For more than a decade now in research, I have come across many works on the history of the communities of northeast India. However, most of these works largely focus on political and administrative developments, identity issues, the beginning and development of Christian missions, etc. In the short span as a researcher I also find many works done in the past contain only descriptive accounts. I felt a need to have a book on emerging problems of research by budding scholars. Hence, I discussed with some of my teachers and fellow researchers of northeast India and the book is the outcome of the same. Purposely, new perspectives and new regions were explored. Therefore, in light of the above, this book aims to present fresh perspectives on the issues relating to the history and historiography of northeast India. It seeks to identify various factors that influence not only socio-cultural changes in the region but also address emerging issues and developments related to its socio-political, economic, and cultural identity.

At the outset, my greatest gratitude goes to the Almighty for His countless blessings. The book is not an outcome of my labour but it has come out successfully due to the contributions of many individuals. Firstly, I am immensely thankful to all the contributors who not only submitted their essays within time but have developed the patience to endure the editing of the volume for two consecutive years till it attains completion. Secondly, the book would not have seen the light of the day without the help and guidance of Prof. A. K. Thakur. My sincere thanks and gratitude go to him for his immense professional guidance which taught me a great deal about research which I have always treasured and have been able to put to use. As my teacher and mentor, he has taught me more than I could ever give him credit for. I am indebted to Dr. Chinmaya Lal Thakur for his readiness to help me many times whenever I called for his valuable suggestions. His objective insights have given the book a good shape and have helped me clear many doubts that I encountered during the editing process.

I also wish to thank my teachers, colleagues, friends and family members for encouraging me at various levels towards the publication of the book. My most sincere gratitude goes to my father Mr. Mlonstarwell Pdahkasiej for his never-ending support and encouragement. His patience and humility inspired me all these years and helped me sustain myself through the good and difficult times of my life. Last but not least, my profound gratitude goes to my wife Georgia and my daughter Rijanai, whose continuing support, immeasurable love, care and affection have made sure that I complete the book despite any odds. I am deeply grateful to the publisher of this book, Pathak Publisher and Distributors, New Delhi for bringing out this volume within a short period.

Shillong — Rusievan Shangpliang
23rd September 2023

Introduction

Rusievan Shangpliang

Studies of societies and their histories consist of a wide range of dimensions including different aspects of human interactions in the social, political, religious, ecological, environmental and economic spheres. Hence, when one studies a particular community, the evolution of history is associated with the progress of that society in terms of identity formation, social values, traditional ethics or norms, modernity and its concurrent dilemmas, and even cultural schisms. Considering the diversity of cultures in northeast India, we must also accept the fact that the societies in this region of the country also have unique developments and histories that tell the stories of not only their progress but also of their "stagnation" and "regress". To understand the basic idea about the importance of collectivism and individualism in the indigenous way of life, we can make use of the opinion of Clifford Greetz who suggests that "becoming human is becoming individual, and we become individual under the guidance of cultural patterns, historically created systems of meaning in terms of which we give form, order, point, and direction to our lives."[1]

In the last few decades, historical studies in Northeast India have gained momentum with numerous works done by scholars both from within and outside the region. With changing times and changes in approach, the studies on history of tribal lives in the region have opened up scope for more research and new findings from different aspects. While dealing with the pre-colonial period, though numerous problems such as lack of sources and written records are being encountered by scholars, nevertheless a substantial amount of brilliant works have been published by scholars of the region which have attracted even researchers from abroad to take interest in the history of northeast India and its communities. Studies on the colonial era find a wider representation due to the availability of official documents and records, as well as the monographs and reports of British administrators and ethnographers. The post-colonial period and the evolution of the modern nation-state of India provide ample scope for scholars to put forward their contributions in a more holistic way on the many aspects of the history of India's north-eastern region. The same is reflected in the growth in research works from the 1970s onwards. The paradigm shift is seen in the emergence of regional history as an area of interest which has provided fresh perspectives on the history of India as a whole. These interests did not mean the rejection of colonial and nationalist paradigms, rather, they suggest that other narratives and histories are also worthy of recognition.[2] Moreover, from the 1990s onwards, social history and the study of material culture have got more acceptances in the framework of historiography since there is an awareness of the need to supplement empirical and quantitative studies with methods suited to society and culture.[3]

However, to date, historical studies and research in northeast India has not been able to entirely come out of the influence of Western tradition especially when it comes to historiographical issues, conceptual frameworks, and methodology. Much of the earlier published works focus on elitist perspectives and have not used approaches such as social history, women studies, subaltern and indigenous narratives to include the contribution of the common people to the history of the region. Therefore, when historians turned to the study of common people, while sometimes using the perspective of 'history from below' and social history, they found the traditional sources and methods unhelpful. In such cases, Robert Harrison remarks that historians turned to different methods, many of them drawn from other social sciences.[4] While in some disciplines the engagement of scholars with government agencies in drafting policies has helped to bring up deliberations on many issues, this has not found its place in many disciplines of social sciences including history.

Generally, history and studies on communities of northeast India still lack many research analysis and techniques that had already developed in the West and in India too. We must accept the fact that the cultural traits of these communities which include the faith that they adopt and practices, the marriage ceremonies, the variety of language and dialects, the development of literature, art, music, and also the traditional administrative system and polity as well as the environmental dimensions among many other aspects have enough histories to their attributes to enable them to earn a place in the history of India and Indian historiography. The key factor for this drawback is because Indian history is suffused by the spirit of nationalism and modernist reform and thus inextricably entangled in the ideological web of national, regional and sectarian politics of South Asia.[5] In addition to these issues, historiography of indigenous societies was influenced by the development strategy of the time in which the historians wrote their histories. Thus, contemporary concerns have always been at the stage of writing the history of these societies.[6] However, the contemporary history of communities of northeast India has rarely been attempted by historians. Taking the diversity of the northeast as a region in terms of communities, languages and cultures on one hand and the prospect that the region offers for broader research on another, comprehensive studies and historical analysis of the region and its societies can be achieved. It is therefore very apt to mention here the views of J. B. Bhattacharjee who opines that there is a "need for a Northeast India regional perspective on researches which should be conducted on the intellectually liberal but methodologically rigorous lines starting from the use of source materials and evidence to the formulation of theories and interpretations of the data."[7]

Arthur Mawrick published his book with a new title *The New Nature of History*[8] and in that year, I joined M.A. and it was mostly after I completed my post-graduate studies that I could realise the importance of the term 'New' in the title of the book. Since its first publication in 1970-71 and subsequent revised editions, the changes in historical studies were incorporated. However, instead of publishing revised editions, Arthur Mawrick provided a new title that added information related to the challenges faced by post-modernism and/or linguistic turns to history.

This volume of edited essays on the history and culture of Northeast India also has 'New' in the subtitle of the book. It is mainly because here the new problems have been studied or the existing problems have been studied from new perspectives. The historiographical progress in other parts of India and the world has encouraged mostly young scholars of diverse streams of social sciences and humanities. Hence, history can be considered as a link of a system in which the social sciences and humanities are interconnected.[9] Although larger parts of oral traditions are used as the main sources when it comes to the writing of histories of pre-colonial communities in northeast India, however, we cannot rule out the dependency on secondary literature when we attempt to re-construct the modern and contemporary history of the indigenous peoples and their society. Based on the background highlighted above, the book aims to address the issues which are directly related to the societies in northeast India. It seeks to identify the various factors which influence not only socio-cultural changes in northeast India but other emerging issues and developments which are related to its identity, religion, politics, and economic progress.

This edited volume brings together works that include new research and findings on different aspects of history in Northeast India. This book starts with the articles on sources of history writing, of course from new perspective. The article of Rosy Yumnam's examines about how collective memories can have stories and myths that a group of people share and where remembrance is reconstructed and represented. Her area of focus is on the ancient written texts known as the *Puya*s and their significance in the history of the Meitei community of Manipur. Another chapter which fits this theme is Rima Sarkar's paper in which an attempt has been made to examine how through the integration of text and image, coins provide insights not only into economics and the 'big history' of state organizations, but also into 'small histories', Thus, the chapter aims to build a conversation between the fields of archaeology and numismatics. Scholars in the 1970s and after have made efforts to locate representations of certain group of people in the previous writings or other sources of history. The following three articles locate various groups and reconstruct historical past of northeast India. Lallianzuali Chhangte discusses the representations of the Mizo community of Mizoram in Colonial Ethnography. She examines the background of the colonial discourse on the Mizo and how these backgrounds affected the representations of the Mizo tribe in their writings. Marhunlang Kharwanlang attempts to study the position of men in the Khasi society as represented in Khasi films. The last paper in this category by Rishababiang L. Nonglait examines the role of women's wings of christian missions in Khasi-Jaiñtia Society in bringing out the efforts of the female members towards the mission and expansion of a church.

Various aspects of traditions of Northeast India are the focus of scholars all over. This book too, finds a number of articles on the same. The emerging trend is the study of traditional health care system, games and sports, and music, etc. The chapter by Adeno N. Kithan deliberates on the traditional medicine men and their methods of healing of the Lotha Naga community. She opines that the repository of medicinal knowledge and the art of treatment passed down for generations created an institution of the medicine men in the Lotha community. Jigme Wangchuk Bhutia's paper is also related to the same. He discusses the role of the traditional healers in Sikkim such as the *Bongthing* for the Lepcha, *Lama* and *Ngakpa* for Bhutia and *Jhakri* or *Dhami* for the Nepali. Relating to the health issues, we also have a joint paper by Sashi Teibor Laloo and Andrew Marwein who deliberate on the response of the people to the emergence of epidemic and plague in Khasi-Jaintia society of Meghalaya. Another aspect of tradition is being brought in the discussion on festivals and sports by Kamei Kabinai where he focuses on the socio-cultural and religious phenomenon of these activities in Rongmei Naga society. Mitchell Reeves Thongni in his chapter reiterates on the impact of Western music on Khasi Traditional Music. Both these papers speak about the changes and impact brought about with the coming of Western culture and Christianity into the hills. Pradeep Kumar Deepak in his paper describes the impact of Indian philosophical values on the indigenous culture of Tripura.

Krishna Kumar Sharma describes the socio-cultural and economic relations influenced by the Nyingma Buddhist tradition of Tibet that were important for the origin and development of the Pemayangtse Monastery in eastern Himalaya. Kabyashree Sarma in her paper studies the acceptance of *tuloni biya* or the tradition of puberty marriage in the Islamic community of Assam. Her attempt is to provide a detailed ritualistic ceremony of the process and try to understand if the concept of *tuloni biya* is fading away. Mahabir Jha in his research paper highlights the establishment, scope and functions of traditional modes of local governance i.e., the Village Development Board (VDB) and the Village Council (VC) in Nagaland, which have evolved from indigenous practices of the Naga communities and later regularised through legislation, facilitating their easy assimilation with the existing village system.

V. Mancy Baite conceptualises the idea of freedom, consciousness and print media by laying out a brief background of the freedom struggle in India. She also highlights events of Indian freedom movements in Manipur in which the role of women is assessed through local print media. Sudev Chandra Basumatary and Junmani Basumatary in their joint paper attempt to study the students' movements among the Bodos as a dynamic force of change which emerged out of relative deprivation theory.

In her paper, Sanshi Upadhya seeks to explore the "history of spaces" in relation to the shifting *Dooar*s region before and after the British occupation. The paper also focuses on the significant changes that occurred which affected the local population's demography, culture, language, and way of life in the *Dooar*s region. Bishnu Kumari Gurung's paper studies British counterinsurgency operations in Northeast India by exploring the methods used by the army during the early twentieth century. It contributes to the broader debate surrounding the use of 'minimum force' by the British and by looking into the Gurkhas' involvement in several conflicts in northeast India. Geri Koyu in his paper presents a semi-biographical work on Late Harkom Scofield Pariat from Meghalaya who served most of his service period in Arunachal Pradesh and contributed to the establishment of administrative centres. Through the paper, an attempt is being made to disseminate the very early perspective of a frontier official on NEFA, its people and the implication of their duty on their life. Christine Zenith Mylliemngap emphasizes on the use of urban legends to bring out the history of vanishing hitchhikers. Her paper is a combination of oral literature and its use in contemporary history highlighting events, memory and experience in broader economic and social settings which are reflected in Khasi society of Meghalaya.

Areas for Further Research

The reconstruction of history of northeast India is an ongoing process. Earlier scholars too have used all available sources; however, they have depended largely on British records and colonial writings. Now it is high time that scholars should make use of indigenous literature in the history writing along with archaeological finds. Individual research papers of various historians have been published highlighting the importance of indigenous literature; however, a consorted effort is required in this regard to critically use them. It will also help, besides history writing, to counter the colonial bias and European prejudices.

The colonial ethnography presented the communities of northeast India as isolated ones, however, the trade practices indicate contrary to it. If the communication networks of pre-colonial and colonial periods are reconstructed along with means of communication through land or river route, it will be very helpful in various ways to highlight the history of northeast India. It is because the region lies at the tri-junction of Tibet/China and Myanmar on the one end and the Great Indian sub-continent on the other. The region was important having its contact from Tibet to the Chittagong Hill Tracts.

Though some historians have worked on the technological past of the people and the kingdoms of northeast India, still there is a tremendous scope for further researches. The technological processes and products are not only indicative of rising production (agricultural and non-agricultural) but also defence and offence mechanisms of the societies. It also reflects various aspects of material culture, aesthetics, philosophy of life, society and polity and several other dimensions of culture.

The reconstruction of historical past has been influenced by a number of philosophers and scholars. They have explained different methods of history writing. Thomas Carlyle, Ralph Waldo Emerson, Leo Tolstoy, Karl Marx and many more are important in this regard. In northeast India, an area of history writing is largely untouched that is biography and history and the histories of urban centres which developed during the British period having a cosmopolitan culture of its own. The contribution of political leaders, freedom fighters, socio-cultural activists in the making of northeast India and their contribution at all India level need to be written impartially without any bias and prejudice; along with the formation of a number of urban centres. These centres show the example of plural-urban conglomeration and some of them served as the centre of awakening and consciousness. A number of luminaries visited these centres and have recorded their reminiscences. All these need to be studied to reconstruct the rich historical past and significant contribution of northeast India beyond the Northeast India.

Notes

1. Clifford Greetz, "The Impact of the Concept of Culture on the Concept of Man", *The Interpretation of Cultures: Selected Essays*, Basic Books, New York, 1973, pp. 46-54.
2. George G. Iggers, Edward Wang and Supriya Mukherjee, *Global History of Modern Historiography*, Dorling Kindersley Pvt. Ltd., New Delhi, 2010, pp. 381-382.
3. *Ibid.*, p. 368.
4. Robert Harrison, "History and Sociology", in Lambert and Philip Schofield (eds.), *Making History: An Introduction to the History and Practices of a Discipline*, Routledge, New York, pp.138-149 (p.143).
5. Partha Chattarjee, "Introduction: History and the Present", in Partha Chattarjee and Anjan Ghosh (eds.), *History and the Present*, Permanent Black, New Delhi, fourth impression 2015 (first published 2002), p.2.
6. Archana Prasad, "Tribal Societies and History Writing in India", in Sabsyasachi Bhattacharya, *Approaches to History: Essays in Indian Historiography*, Primus Books, New Delhi, 2011, p.14. (1-26)
7. J. B. Bhattacharjee, *Lectures in Applied History*, Akansha Publishing House, New Delhi, p.94.
8. Arthur Mawrick, *The New Nature of History: Knowledge, Evidence and Language,* Palgrave, London, 2001.
9. Robert Gildea and Jean-Frederic Schaub, "Has History again become a Branch of Literature?", in Robert Gildea and Anne Simonin (eds.), *Writing Contemporary History*, Bloomsbury Publishing India Pvt. Ltd., New Delhi, 2017, pp.95-120 (p. 120).

List of Contributors

Baite, V. Mancy is a Research Scholar in the Department of History, North-Eastern Hill University, Shillong. Her areas of interest are study and implication of the concept of consciousness to historical revolutions mainly through media platforms like newspapers, radio, films.

Basumatary, Junmani has been teaching in the Department of Political Science, Bodoland University. She has published a number of articles in reputed journals and has co-authored a book. Her areas of interest are public administration, autonomous council, social movements, gender issues, middle class and ecological and environmental issues.

Basumatary, Dr. Sudev Chandra has been teaching in Department of History, Bodoland University since 2008. He has a number of publications in reputed journals, and he is credited with three edited books. His areas of interest are social history, tribal history, history of ecology and environment etc.

Bhutia, Dr. Jigme Wangchuk is currently the Controller of Examinations, Khangchendzonga State University, Sikkim. He also serves as Asst. Professor in History Nar Bahadur Bhandari Degree College. Gangtok, Sikkim. His areas of research include history of Eastern Himalayas, socio-economic history of Sikkim.

Chhangte, Lallianzuali is currently working as Assistant Professor, Department of History, Government Kolasib College, Kolasib, Mizoram. Her area of research interest is on Mizo society and culture.

Deepak, Dr. Pradeep Kumar teaches History at Adwaita Malla Barman Smriti Mahavidyalaya Amarpur, Gomati, Tripura. He is the life member of North East India History Association and Indian History Congress. Some of his works include *Bharat mein Mughalon ka Sainik Abhiyan: 1526-1658 A.D*, *Tripura*, *History of Tripura* and *History of Assam*. His areas of research interest include history of Tripura, military warfare and techniques and history of indigenous people.

Gurung, Bishnu Kumari is a Ph.D. candidate in the Department of History, North-Eastern Hill University, Shillong. She received a study grant from the Indian Council of Historical Research in 2019 and was nominated for a short-term doctoral fellowship from the Indian Council of Social Science Research in 2021. She has authored multiple articles, book chapters and edited the proceedings of the first international conference on History and Archaeology in 2022. She currently holds the position of treasures at the Asiatic Society of Social Science Research (ASSSR) in New Delhi.

Jha, Dr. Mahabir is an Associate Professor & Head, Department of Political Science, Yingli Govt. College, Longleng, Nagaland. His field of specialization is International Law, Public Administration and Human Rights. He has published two books (in 2017 and in 2023). He has presented many research papers in regional, national and international seminars. His works have been published in peer reviewed refereed journals and his chapters have been included in several edited books. He has been conferred with the Meritorious Service Award-2022 by the Department of Higher Education, Govt. of Nagaland.

Kabinai, Kamei is currently a Research Scholar pursuing his Ph.D (Doctor of Philosophy) in the Department of History, North Eastern Hill University, Shillong, India. He specialized in medieval history during his postgraduate studies. His area of interest in research includes traditional society, games and sports, cultural history, post colonialism and Social change. He has to his credit contributed a number of chapters and articles published in edited books, journals and proceedings. He has also presented papers in various national and international seminars, conferences and webinars.

Kharwanlang, Dr. Marhunlang is an Assistant Professor in the Department of History, Mawlai Presbyterian College, Shillong. Her areas of interest are Khasi films and Khasi social history.

Kithan, Adeno N. is a Ph.D. scholar in the Department of History, North-Eastern Hill University, Shillong. She specialises in pre-colonial formations and changes in the colonial period in Nagaland.

Koyu, Geri is a Research Scholar pursuing his Ph.D. on 'History of Military Operation in Arunachal Pradesh (1826-1947)' in the Department of History, Rajiv Gandhi University, Arunachal Pradesh. His areas of interest in research include Modern History and Colonial History. He has presented papers in national seminars/conferences. He is also a Life Member of North East India History Association (NEIHA).

Laloo, Sashi Teibor is in his final year of research, on the topic "Drawing Borders and the Making of Khasi-Jaintia Identity (1772-1972)" in the Department of History, NEHU Shillong He has been awarded the Charles Wallace Short Term Research Grant, 2023. He has also presented papers in a number of national and international conferences and has articles published in edited books, journals and e-journals. His areas of interest revolve around folklore, subaltern history, material culture, partition of 1947 concerning northeast India, archival studies and museology.

Marwein, Gardener Andrew is a Research Scholar in the Department of Cultural and Creative Studies, NEHU Shillong. His topic is "Khasi Indigenous Knowledge System: A Folkloristic Study." His areas of interest in research include material culture, folk beliefs, folk medicine and traditional healing and indigenous knowledge in agrarian practices and traditional architecture.

Mylliemngap, Christine Zenith is Assistant Professor of History at Saint Mary's College, Shillong (India). She has keen interests in the supernatural folk narratives particularly in the evolution of contemporary legends and the interweaving of such narratives in the socio historical milieu. She is a member of the International Society of Contemporary Legend Research (ISCLR) as well as the North East India Historical Association (NEIHA).

Nonglait, Dr. Rishababiang L. is currently teaching history at Nongstoin College, Higher Secondary Section, Nongstoin. Her research interests revolve around, women's history, religious history, cultural and folk history, social history and local histories. She is keen on recognition and promotion of non-mainstream histories. She has a handful of papers, articles and chapters published in edited books, journals and proceedings. She has presented a number of papers at local, national and international conferences and seminars.

Sarkar, Rima is a Research Scholar at North-Eastern Hill University, Shillong. She has completed her M. Phil degree on 2019. She specialized in modern history during her postgraduate. Her area of interest in research includes socio-cultural studies, study on coins and economy. She has to her credit a number of publications on journals and proceedings. She has also presented papers in National and International seminars/conferences.

Sarma, Kabyashree is a B. Ed student and an independent Research Scholar. She has completed her Masters in Ancient Indian History at Gauhati University. She had previously worked as a PGT History under Kendriya Vidyalaya Sangathan. She has presented papers in state-level and national-level seminars and a few of her papers have been published as well. She is presently a contributor to This Day by Ekank - a platform for promoting the history, art, culture and heritage of India across the world.

Shangpliang, Dr. Rusievan teaches history at Synod College, Shillong. He specialized in modern history during his postgraduate studies. His areas of interest in research include Christianity, culture, historiography and material culture. He has authored the book *History of the Seventh-day Adventist Church in Northeast India* (2018). He has to his credit a number of articles and chapters published in peer reviewed journals, edited books and proceedings. He has also presented papers in National and International seminars/ conferences in India and abroad. He is currently the Treasurer of the renowned North East India History Association (NEIHA).

Sharma, Krishna Kumar is a Research Scholar availing the Indian Council of Historical Research (ICHR) Junior Research Fellowship from the History Department, North-Eastern Hill University, Meghalaya. He has taught history at Zakir Husain Delhi College, New Delhi. He specialized in Medieval Indian History in Postgraduate and M.Phil studies. His areas of research interest include Buddhism and the tribal history of the eastern Himalayas. He has published several research papers and presented papers in national and international seminars/ conferences.

Thongni, Rev. Mitchell Reeves is currently working as the Principal of District War Sepngi Christian Higher Secondary School, Dangar, East Khasi Hills District, Meghalaya. His area research interest includes ethics, culture, theology, social issues and apologetics.

Upadhya, Sanshi is a Ph. D. Research Scholar in the Department of History, North-Eastern Hill University. She did her post-graduation from Gauhati University and has a specialization in Modern Indian History. Her area of interest in research includes migrational studies, culture and identity and spatial history. She has also published a number of articles in the journal *Lohit Putra*. She is currently working on the history of spaces including the history of the Gorkha Community in North-East India.

Yumnam, Dr. Rosy is Associate Professor in the Department of English Language Education, The English and Foreign Languages University (EFLU), Shillong, India. She co-edited the book *Language and Discourse: Culture, Literature and Pedagogy in North East India* (2018). Her research addresses language, culture and pedagogy, teaching language skills, production of ELT materials and academic writing.

1

Memory, History and the Claims of the *Puyas*

Rosy Yumnam

Memory studies is a multidisciplinary field where individual memory contributes to broader extents of social memory. The diverse areas may include history, cultural studies, media, anthropology, sociology, philosophy, politics, literary studies and drama, among others. Generally, the emphasis of memory study has been on "how these forms of remembering operate as collective representations of the past, how they constitute a range of cultural resources for social and historical identities, and how they privilege particular readings of the past and subordinate others."[1]In the early times, it was the social thinkers who were fascinated with the concept of memory. Later in the year 1902, the term 'collective memory' was first coined by Hofmannsthal. However, Halbwachs is generally considered the founder of collective memory research. Halbwachs contends that individuals cannot recall when they are outside their group contexts. He further asserts that individual and collective memories can be employed as tools to connect individuals' lives to their social groups.[2] Collective memory assists an individual in recounting past events and also helps in identity construction. According to Halbwachs, history is "a dead memory, a way of preserving pasts to which we no longer have an 'organic' experiential relation" and contested that "this understanding of the distinction negates the self-image of historiography as the more important or appropriate attitude towards the past: History's epistemological claim is devalued in favour of memory's meaningfulness."[3] In recent years historiography can broadly relate to the cultural and social fields. So, memory has become a pertinent aspect as it depends on history.

This paper examines the *Puyas* reminiscing the collective memory of the Meiteis in tracing and understanding the history of Manipur. The *Puyas* can be defined as the ancient written manuscripts of the Meitei community of Manipur in northeast India. As an invaluable literary piece, the *Puyas* deal with diverse fields such as medicine, astronomy, politics, religion, code of warriors, rites and rituals, manuals of administration, migration, history and natural phenomena. The *Puyas* were written in Meitei Mayek, an ancient script of the Meiteis. Materials like palm leaves, a local grass called *tengna*, copper plate, agarwood, bamboo pulp and jute fibre were used to write the *Puyas.* Their existence can be tentatively traced as early as the eighth century is of the view that the ancient script, Meitei Mayek, was developed between the twelvth and the fifteenth century A. D.[4] Consecutively, Laisram also affirms that Manipur's rich literary culture started to develop around the reign of King Khagemba (1597 A.D. -1652 A.D.).[5] To date, around 4000 *Puyas* are available. Many are transliterated into modern Manipuri script, and some are translated into English. They were undated and anonymously written until around the seventeenth century. The *Puyas* form a crucial canvas to reminiscence the cultural memory of the Meiteis. They have played a vital role in capturing how cultural identity, values, traditions and society were shaped, established and sustained. The Meitei community has contained the fundamental facets of their culture and civilization in the *Puyas*. As Halbwachs argues, individual and collective memories can be used as mechanisms to bind individuals' lives to their social groups, the *Puyas*, with their cultural knowledge, can be viewed to construct the identities of the Meiteis by tracing their history.

Review of literature

Cultural memory is shared among a group of people in the form of cultural objects, artefacts, books, ways of life, etc., and these memories encompassing their social identity and history become collective memories. Collective memories are memories experienced in groups and will chronicle the event's history, eventually influencing future generations.[6] Wang asserts, "Collective memory sustains a community's very identity and makes possible the continuity of its social life and cultural cohesion."[7] Relatedly, Sturken used the term cultural memory to mean a memory imbibed with cultural meaning. According to him, "Cultural memory as a term implies not only that memories are often produced and reproduced through cultural forms, but also the kind of circulation that exists between personal memories and cultural memories."[8]

Furthermore, memory and history are interconnected and form a pertinent aspect of an individual's social and cultural construct to society. The perception of collective memory became an important approach in pre-literate times as it assisted in accessing and reliving the past.[9] However, the development of education led to the transformation of these practices into the discipline of history.[10] It is believed that the claims of memory are not perfect, so it has to work in conjunction with the discipline of history. As history also has its own inadequacies, memory studies complement it. Thus, a study of collective memory in conjunction with history is an inevitable feature of constructing and revisiting the past. Poole asserts the importance of collective memory accounting for the interconnected relationship between individual memory and history.[11] Relatedly, Bosch[12] examined the diverse methods of memory studies from oral history and methods like discourse analysis used to recollect and reinvent the past in society through speech and language. Researches in contemporary memory studies, such as cultural memory and mnemohistory, have played a crucial role in interconnecting the past, present and future and also given new perspectives in history.[13]

As collective memory recounts an individual's past, the cultural and collective memories as perceived through the *Puyas* can act as a medium to reinvent, reconstruct and connect the past with the present. In this regard, Laisram details the critical study of the *Puyas* and asserts the importance of the *Puyas* in tracing the early Meitei history. As Naorem[14] states that an understanding of the rich Meitei civilization in the form of culture, literary heritage, and material culture could be seen through the *Puyas* or the manuscripts of the Meiteis, which are written in Meitei Mayek and further, these alphabets capture the story of civilization. Kabui[15] observed that the reconstruction of the early period of the history of Manipur was founded on the accounts of some of the *Puyas*.

Besides the memory studies perspective, the Puyas of Manipur can also be studied from the perspective of literature and history. The Rankenean model of history writing and the Marxian approach have been critiqued in recent decades. The publication of *Meta History* by Hayden White provided a new dimension in history writing. Raymond Williams also enriched the debate over literature and history. Important to mention that the Postmodernist scholars, too, provided a new dimension to the use of literary text as a source of history writing. The Puyas, hence, have to be analyzed as literary text and source of history. This paper of mine attempts to study the Puyas in a larger context of the history writing of pre-modern Manipur.[16]

Objectives and methodology

The study is analytical in the method. It aims to examine the collective memory of the Meiteis as manifested through the *Puya*s into telling and recounting the history of Manipur. As collective memories can be used as tools to bind individuals' lives to their social groups, the *Puya*s, with their invaluable knowledge, can be viewed to trace the history of Manipur. The study is based on primary and secondary sources, research journals and online sources.

Discussion

Collective memory assists an individual in reminiscing the bygone past. This innate consciousness enables an individual to remain rooted in their culture, traditions and identity. Consecutively, history also relates to an individual's culture, traditions and identity of the society they live in. Therefore, collective memory complements reading history and communicating past events. Time and again, the *Puya*s have consistently been able to bridge the gap in tracing the history of Manipur through the collective memory and consciousness of the Meiteis. As the *Puya*s cover diverse aspects of life such as religion, cultural festivals, rites and rituals, history, politics, etc., they delve into an individual's life to bring forth the collective memory, crucial in connecting the invaluable past with the present day. Some of the *Puya*s have chronicled the creation mythology of the Meiteis. The *Puyas*, such as *Khamlangba Erengba Puwari*, *Leithak Leikharon* and *Pudin*, detail the creation mythology, cosmology and history of the clan system of the Meitei community.[17] This assists in tracing the roots of the Meitei community.

The Meiteis believed in ancestor worship, forming their ancient religion's basis. In this regard, Laisram asserts, "The ancient religion passed through a long process of evolution of the Meitei society and survived even after Vaisnavism was declared the state religion of Manipur in the eighteenth century A.D."[18] Most of the Meiteis have been following a dual religion straddling Hinduism and Sanamahi. This ancient religion of the Meiteis, called the Sanamahi religion, can be comprehended by examining various *Puyas*. The *Puyas* such as *Erat Thounirol, Sanamahi, Pakhangba Laihui, Thalloi Nongkhailon* and *Sakok Lamlen Ahanba* recorded the rites and rituals, myths regarding the worshipping of Gods and Goddesses and philosophy of religion. The myth involving Lord Sanamahi is chronicled in the *Puya*, *Sanamahi Laihui*, so it is a relevant source for reviving the indigenous Sanamahi religion.[19] As collective memory records and revives a community's identity and culture, these *Puyas* have aided in sustaining social life by imbibing ancient religious narratives.

Collective and cultural memories are pertinent in relating an individual to their social groups, connecting them to their way of living, identity and history. The cultural memories perceived through *Lai Haraoba*, which is a social and cultural festival of Manipur, played a significant role in ascertaining an oral mnemonic structure of the Meitei community. The revered ancient deities called *Umang lais* during this festival are worshipped and venerated. *Puyas* like *Leithak Leikharon* and *Panthoipi Khongkhul* have chronicled the cultural practices, religious rites, and rituals associated with the *Lai Haraoba* festival. The myth of the origin of the festival can be observed through the *Puya*, *Panthoipi Khongkhul.* It details how the Khaba community built a temple and rejoiced to pay profound obeisance to Lord Nongpok Ningthou and Goddess Panthoipi. The *Puya*, *Leithak Leikharon*, narrates another myth of its origin associated with the theory of creation. As Singh observes, "In the ritual dance of *Lai Haraoba*, we see the performers demonstrating the cycle of life of a human being – from the foetus in the mother's womb to birth and to habitation with the erection of houses, cultivation and weaving of cloth for offering to the gods – by gestures of the hands and body" [20] To the present, *Lai Haraoba* festivals are celebrated through diverse songs, dances, rites, and rituals. The cultural memory unravelled through the *Puyas* still closely connects with the bygone past. Relatedly, the clan system of the Meiteis comprises of seven clans. They are *Ningthouja, Angom, Chengloi, Nganba or Khabanganba, Looang, Khooman* and *Moirang*. This clan system has been identified after a thorough study of the *Puyas* such as *Wakoklon Hilel Thilel Amailon Pukok, Khamoi Yangoi Sekning, Leithak Leikharon* and *Sakok Lamlen Ahanba.* [21] In this way, the *Puyas* have played an important role for the Meiteis to connect with past events socially, politically and culturally.

Concurrently, another important aspect of the cultural memory espoused through the *Puyas* is the revival of the ancient script of the Meiteis called the Meitei Mayek. The people of Manipur use two writing systems: Manipuri, written in Meitei Mayek before the nineteenth century, and Modern Manipuri, written in Bengali script in the later part of the eighteenth century. The spoken Manipuri is the same in both ancient and modern, but the written script differs. The ancient script, Meitei Mayek, nearly became extinct as a result of the infamous mass burning of *Puyas* related to the Sanamahi religion of the Meiteis called *Puya Mei Thaba* in the year 1732 in Kangla (the historic fort in Imphal and the seat of the kings of Manipur) at the order of King Pamheiba in the process of embracing Hinduism.[22] Furthermore, the Seven Years Devastation (1819-1826 A.D.) during which the Burmese empire occupied Manipur, was also attributed to the disappearance of the *Puyas*.[23]After that, the Manipuri language written in ancient Meitei Mayek came to be replaced by Bengali script. The *Puyas* gradually disappeared from the public domain. Subsequently, Manipur was merged into the Dominion of India in 1949 and slowly, Hindi and other Indian cultural influences can be seen in the life of the Meiteis.[24] The Meitei Mayek revival movement started around 1940 and was made possible through thorough research of the *Puyas* like *Wakoklon Thilel Salai Amailon Pukok* and *Wakoklon Thilel Salai Singkak.*

The present Meitei Mayek contains 27 basic letters as nine letters, derivatives of the previous 18 alphabets, were added. The Government of Manipur recognized the alphabet with 27 letters in 1980.[25] At present, Meitei Mayek is studied as a part of the academic curriculum in the schools, colleges and university of Manipur. The reinvention and reconstruction of Meitei Mayek exemplify how collective memory has been efficacious in reinstating the Meitei psyche with the almost lost ancient script. The success of the reconstruction of Meitei Mayek results from a thorough study of the *Puyas*. Unquestionably, the revival of the ancient script, Meitei Mayek, has assisted in bringing forth the cultural and collective memory of the Meiteis. The preceding discussions, therefore, detail the role of the *Puyas* in conserving and safeguarding the traditions, customs, language, religious and social practices of the Meitei existence. This has created a vital role in educating the cultural and collective memory of the Meiteis. As memory studies complement historiography, the cultural and collective memories envisaged by the *Puyas* have helped examine the history of Manipur. The claims of the *Puyas* to tell the history of Manipur through the collective memory of the Meiteis have assisted in reclaiming their past glories. However, in historiography, recording information without proper references and validations can often face challenges in the process of reconstruction. As the *Puyas* are written narratives without references and proper validations, the historical claims made by exploring the collective memories of the Meiteis became a challenging task for the historiographers. Nevertheless, the narratives of the *Puyas*, with their instrumental cultural implications, form a formidable force in tracing and comprehending the history of Manipur.

Conclusion

Memory studies have become an important aspect of remembering the past, and it has also played a vital role in connecting the past to the present. As collective memory recounts an individual's past, the cultural and collective memories as perceived through the *Puyas* have acted as a medium to reinvent, reconstruct and connect with the past. This, in turn, relates to the present culture and forms a deep connection to the past, which caters to strengthening its history. By comprehending culture through the lens of memory, a sense of revivalism pervades, and this helps in tracing, examining and understanding history. The preceding discussion contends that the *Puyas*, through its diverse subjects such as religion, festivals, clan system and language, have significantly contributed to the concept of identity construction of the Meiteis. As perceived through the *Puyas*, the collective memory complements recapturing the Meiteis' history. As the content of history includes various narratives connecting the past and the present, the collective experiences of the Meiteis defined in the *Puyas* assisted in strengthening the process of restructuring and reconstructing the history of Manipur. Therefore, the claims of the *Puyas* of tracing and examining the history of Manipur through the memory of the Meiteis delve into their psyche and significantly contribute to reclaiming their past.

Notes

1. E. Keightley & M. Pickering, (eds.). *Research Methods for Memory Studies*, U.K.: Edinburgh University Press, 2013, p. 2.
2. E. T. Bosch, "Memory Studies: A brief concept paper", available at https://eprints.whiterose.ac.uk/117289/1/Bosch%202016_Memory%20Studies.pdf. Accessed on 12-03-2023.
3. J. K. Olick & J. Robbins, "Social Memory Studies: From Collective Memory to the Historical Sociology of Mnemonic Practices," *Annual Review of Sociology*, 1998, pp.105-140.
4. A. D. Singh (2003, 12)
5. R. Laisram, *Early Meitei History: Religion, Society and the Manipur Puyas*, Akansha Publishing House, 2009, p.9.
6. J. Pennebaker, et al. *Collective Memory of Political Events: Social Psychological Perspectives*, Psychology Press, 2013.
7. Q. Wang, "On the cultural constitution of collective memory," *Memory*, 16 (3), 2008, pp. 305-317.
8. M. Sturken, *Tangled memories: The Vietnam War, The Aids Epidemic and the Politics of Remembering,* University of California Press, Berkeley, 1997.
9. R. Poole, "Memory, History and the Claims of the Past," *Memory Studies*, 1(149), 2008, p.150.
10. P. Nora, "Between Memory and History: Les Lieux de Mémoire", *Representations*, 26: Spring, 1989: pp.7–24; J. Le

Goff, *History and Memory*, trans. S. Rendall and E. Claman, Columbia University Press, New York, 1992.

11. R. Poole, *op.cit.*, p.150.
12. E.T. Bosch, *op.cit.*
13. M.Tamm, "Beyond History and Memory: New Perspectives in Memory Studies," *History Compass*, 11/6, 2013, pp. 458-473.
14. S. Naorem, *Manipur Past and Present Volume II*, Mittal Publications, 1991.
15. G. Kabui, *History of Manipur*, National Publishing House, 1991.
16. For details see R. Laisram, *Early Meitei History: Religion, Society and the Manipur Puyas, op.cit.*
17. R. Laishram, *op.cit.*, p.19.
18. *Ibid.*, p. 66.
19. *Ibid.*, pp. 19-20.
20. A. D. Singh, *op.cit.,* 13.
21. R. Laishram, *op.cit.*, pp. 36, 37.
22. *Ibid.*, p. 13.
23. *Ibid.*, p. 13.
24. A. Irengbam, (ed.) *Chainarol (Way of the Warrior)*, Human Rights Alert, 2012, p.12.
25. Manipur Gazette, No. 33, 1980.

2

The Social History of Koch Coins

Rima Sarkar

Introduction

'Social history can be defined as the history of the people with politics left out'.[1] However, when we talk about social history, material culture forms the basis to study the physical aspects of culture, objects and architecture surrounding society. Thus according to Nadine Pence Frantz, material culture can be used as an interdisciplinary field to designate the physical, material objects that cultures create and use in common life.[2] To reconstruct the past, every historian seeks to uncover information from the contemporary records left behind by the ancestors in the form of epigraphy, archaeology, coins and others. Among these records, coins play a distinct part as it throws light on the particular kingdom's political, cultural and economic development and its relationship with neighbouring and far of distant places. In India, coins have been significant in reconstructing history since ancient times. One of the remarkable features of Indian coins were the occurrence of numerous symbols such as a tree, animals, fish, insects, reptiles, the sun, the moon, constellation and stars, geographical, geometrical, temple, bow-arrow, trident, battle-axe, *svastika* etc.[3] Coins not only played as a fiscal unit in the ancient and medieval period but were also used in political and cultural elements such as issuing coins by the King during the time of accession to the throne and minting coins at the time of military victory etc. This extensive use of coins for various purposes can even be seen in terms of the northeastern region in general and the Koch Kingdom in particular, which was a gateway between the northeastern region and mainstream India in the medieval period.[4]

Coins are generally described as an object of utility, a medium of exchange, a means of payment or a unit of account etc. Historically coin provides a very complex picture than just a medium of exchange. Since ancient times, coins were used not only in the day to day transactions but also played a significant role in the socio-cultural and political lives of the people. Coins were issued in every important event by the kings, such as issuing coins at the time of accession, military victories, commemorative coins and others which throw important light on the socio-cultural background of a particular kingdom. Thus in every socio-political matter, coins became an integral part of the social life. These extensive uses of coins for various purposes in day-to-day life were also practised in the medieval Koch kingdom of northeast India.

The literature available on the Koch kingdom mainly deals with the socio-cultural and political aspects and is, thus, one-dimensional.[5] In most of the work, coins are 'partially' mentioned as a medium of exchange and occasional gifts, thus lacking a descriptive study. Therefore, this chapter attempts to study coins by examining the integration of texts, images and the existence of material objects. It will provide insights not only into the economic history of the Koch Kingdom but will also present an overall understanding of the social history of the Koches by examining their interactions with the material objects in the form of coins.

Discussion

Northeastern India in the medieval period witnessed the growth and development of many regional kingdoms, which, with time, expanded into a powerful states. One such kingdom was the kingdom of the Koches. The origin of the Koches is a matter of discourse among the scholars of the region.[6] The geographical boundary of the Koch kingdom frequently changed within the change of political relationships with its neighbouring areas. Therefore the geography of the kingdom roughly consisted of river Kushi or Tirhut in the west to Naranarayanpur in the north bank of the Brahmaputra valley in the east, and from Rangamati (Bhutan frontier) in the north to Goraghat in the south.[7] Prior to the establishment of the Koch kingdom, the Khen dynasty ruled the area. With the political advancement of Sultan Hussain Shah of Gauda, the kingdom of Khens was destroyed and overthrown, which led to political turmoil and anarchy in the region. In these circumstances, a new 'tribal' group rose to power under the leadership of Haria Mandal in this area. Haria Mandal, along with his son, namely, Biswa Sinha, fought against the existing rival group such as the Bhuiyans, the Turbak (Governor of Goalpara, recruited by the Sultan of Bengal) and other 'tribal' identities. Thus after overthrowing the rivals, the kingdom of Koch was finally established under the leadership of Biswa Singa in 1510 AD.[8] Even though the kingdom was founded by King Biswa Sinha, the process of state formation was carried out by his son and successor, King Naranarayan (Malla Deb), with the help of his brother and commander-in-chief of army Sulkadhvaja (Chilarai). Under King Naranarayan, the Koch kingdom reached its pinnacle of glory. However, the power and glory were short-lived. Soon after the death of Sukladhvaja (Chilarai), the army's Commander-in-Chief, the kingdom was divided into Koch Behar and Koch Hajo.[9] The division of the kingdom into two parts proved to be disastrous for both the kingdoms.[10] The constant war ushered in devastating consequences and hence resulted in further merging and acknowledging the suzerainty of the British by Koch Bihar in 1773, whereas Koch Hajo had to acknowledge the suzerainty of Ahoms.[11] Thus Koch Bihar and Koch Hajo remained under the suzerainty of the British and Ahoms, respectively, and finally merged with Indian Government in 1949.

The society of Koch kingdom was very complex and consisted of several racial elements such as Aryans, the Alphine-Iranians and Tibeto-Burmese. The society comprised both tribals and non-tribals or Hindus or non-Hindus, among which a small number of them were Brahmins who enjoyed a high position in the society. In terms of hierarchy, after Brahmins were the *Kayasthas* and *Daivajanas* or *Ganakas* (involved in bookkeeping and accountancy). There was a small number of Muslim populations in the society as well.[12] The overall characteristic of Koch society was feudal in character; the king was placed at the top of the hierarchy, and the nobility was totally under the influence of the king. At the bottom were the peasants who used to cultivate the lands. There was also a wide extent of slavery practised in the kingdom. Apart from this, there were various professional castes as well who were in charge of various businesses.[13] Koch kings were great patrons of education, music, dance, art and culture. The introduction of the neo-Vaisnavite movement launched by Sri Sankardeva and his disciple Madhavadeva gained popularity among the people and opened a new chapter of cultural progress. The ethnic communities of the kingdom worshipped the mother Goddess and were *Shatka* by faith. The people belonging to both Hindu and non-Hindu communities worshipped their own deities and performed their own rites. They also followed Viasnavism and Saivism.[14]

In the sixteenth century, with the state formation of the Koch kingdom under King Naranarayan, the economy played an important role in the growth and development of the kingdom. Due to its advantageous location, the Koch kingdom enjoyed a monopoly in trade by controlling the trans-Himalayan trade routes through Bhutan. It also controlled the trade between Bengal and Assam and Bihar and Assam, as the entry point to Assam by Brahmaputra river route was within this territory.[15] Thus, it can be presumed that to act as a buffer zone and carry on the voluminous trading activities between neighbouring areas and far-off distant countries, Koch King Naranarayan assured an adequate supply of metallic currency.[16]

However, apart from commercial use, the coins of Koches were also used to propagate the socio-cultural beliefs of the ruling monarch. King Nara Narayan was the first ruler to issue coins in the mid-1560s. The coins he issued came to be collectively called *Narayani Mudra* or *Narayani Tankas* and were full of artistic vigour. The coins were struck by using various symbols and art motifs, which depicted the artistic mastery of the kingdom. The art form inscribed in the coins portrayed a number of symbols which occupied a pre-eminent position from the time of King Naranarayan to the last ruler King Jagadipendra Narayan.[17] Generally considered 'primitive' in character due to their inscribed motifs and symbols, the Koch coins were undoubtedly a work of professional craftsmen. After a careful study of the legends inscribed in the coins, it can be seen that they invoke God and Goddesses of separate cults, namely Saivism and Vaisnavism. While studying the volume of coins available in the area, it can be said that coins with the invocation of Shiva are in plentiful than coins with the invocation of Vishnu. Thus, in the Koch coins, we do not find any pictorial representation of the king and the deity worshipped, but instead, we find in the obverse the name of the King and the date of accession and, on the reverse side, devoted to God. If we take the example of the first coins struck by King Naranarayan, we see that the basic design of those coins was an invocation of Shiva in the obverse and the name of the King with the date of accession in the reverse.[18] It is also seen that in most of the coins on the reverse side, the legends ' *Sri Sri Siva Charana Kamala-Madhuka Rasya*' and *'Sri Sri Hara Gouri Charana Kamala-Madhu Karasya'* was inscribed to show a strong affiliation towards Shiva while in some coins the epithet *'Sri Sri Krishna Charana Kamala-Madhuka Rashya'*, was engraved to show the affiliation of Ruler with Vaisnava.[19]

However, it was not only the religious factor that influenced King Naranarayan to strike coins of artistic ornamentation. Rather, King Naranarayan was also influenced by the contemporary coins available throughout the neighbouring and distant regions.[20] Thus, the Koch Kings' coins' structure remained unchanged. Koch rulers' coins were die-struck with either plain circles, dotted borders, or ornate borders and were inscribed in Sanskrit, Assamese, or Bengali. The coins were generally made of silver, but we also see coins made of gold in some cases.[21] Some coins of King Naranarayan have hexagonal diagrams in them, which can be said to have religious importance as the hexagonal shape is inscribed on the reverse side of the coin and looks like two triangles or six-pointed stars, the motive behind this diagram might be purely religious, as the star symbol is sacred in both Hinduism and Islam. Thus by striking such types of coins, King Naranarayan might have tried to imbed the Hindu and the Muslim belief system in the same platform. After the Death of King Naranarayan, his son Laxmi

Narayan ascended the throne and minted coins. However, his coins were somewhat different from his predecessor (King Naranarayan) in terms of design. The coins issued by him had a special character, such as his quarter *tanka* and half *tankas* were struck with special small dies and two extremely rare varieties of *tankas* were struck, one with the legend in a square and the other with an ornamental border of arches.[22] Biranarayan succeeded his father, Laxmi Narayan, and issued coins. The coins of Birnaraya were unique in the series, having an invocation of Lord Krishna instead of Lord Shiva and Goddess Parvati (Gara Gauri).[23] This was perhaps in the change of belief system in the later years of the Koch rule. King Prananarayan, son and successor of Birnarayan, issued a few remarkable coins, such as the use of a crescent symbol in the coins or specific dates of neighbouring kingdoms to commemorate special events. One such example of this was a gold coin where a particular date is written as 753, which must be the Nepal *Samvat* era that was used by the Malla dynasty of Nepal. Possibly this was the only time that such a date was used in Koch coins and had to do with the fact that one of Prananarayan's sisters, Rupamati Devi, married Pratap Malla of Kathmandu.[24] In the later years of Prananarayan's reign, the Mughals invaded the Koch kingdom and occupied the area for two years and coins were struck in the name of the Mughal Emperor. The newly struck Mughal coins were similar to the coins of King Prananarayan, with legends in *Urdu* but written in Bengali.[25] The successors of Prananarayan also used the crescent symbol in their coins but with little variations.[26] Koch King Nripendranarayan was regarded as the architect of modern Cooch Behar; thus, his coins had some unique features. In his coins, a crude version of the epithet on the reverse side was inscribed within a square of the box. The square box is placed in the centre of the coin, and the outer portion of the box is decorated with beautiful figures of flowers and arabesque[27] instead of any deity name or figure. Thus this coin can be termed as unique in its form as it shows some kind of secular orientation of Koch King, which might be the result of imperial influence.[28]

In the later years, after the Anglo-Koch Treaty of 1773, the British government withdrew the older Koch currency. Thus the Koch Kings issued a new type of currency where they used the symbol of the emblem of the state. This emblem was used in the government documents of the kingdom. The symbol was inscribed in the coins of later Kings, such as the coins of Raj Rajendra Narayan, Jitendra Narayan and Jagaddipendra Narayan. The royal symbol of the kingdom was engraved in the centre of the coins. On the obverse of the coin was written the name of the King who issued the coin, and on the reverse, the royal symbol was supported with a lion and elephant figures.[29] Perhaps the use of lion and elephant in the coins has more layers to it instead of being used only as a figurative symbol- as the lion is regarded as the king of all the animals and a symbol of bravery, and the elephant is seen as a symbol of mass power. Thus, it can be assumed that these two figurative symbols were used in the coins to signify the strength and power of the Koch Kings. Also, a Sanskrit sentence, "*Yato-dharma Stato Jayah*", was engraved under this royal symbol. The meaning of this sentence is "Where is virtue, there is victory". This writing shows the moral character of the Koch coins.[30] So the emblems inscribed on the coins by the later Koch rulers were well decorated and very significant, and they continued issuing 'ceremonial' coins until the kingdom merged with Independent India.

Conclusion

The changing political dimension of the Koches with their surrounding lands on the one hand (such as Ahoms and the neighbouring areas), and the Mughal, Bhutanese and British on the other, was shown while evaluating the changing structure of the Koch Kingdom. Koch coins revealed the shifting political landscapes. With the reorganization of the kingdom's power structure, the art and motifs imprinted on the coins also changed over time. In any case, the Koch rulers made certain that their coinage retained their unique individuality. The Kings' intentions are shown in the employment of Sanskrit and Assamese or Bengali languages, with Sanskrit serving as the court language and Bengali and Assamese serving as the common people's language. The use of Bengali script in the coins by the Koch rulers signifies that the coins struck were not only meant for large transactions in trade or as commemorative coins but also for the use of the common masses. The coins also reflected the nature of the transition from a 'tribal' Koch kingdom into a Hindu kingdom. As mentioned above, the origin of the Koches has an obscure history (relating them to the Dravidian or Mongoloid group); with time, to trace themselves with the divine theory, they adopted and worshipped Hindu Gods like Shiva, Vishnu and Goddess Parvati. This belief system was also replicated in their coins as almost all the rulers used the invocation of either Shiva or Vishnu in their coins. Not only the Hindu symbols or motifs but in later years, it is also seen that due to the Muslim influence, few sacred symbols like hexagonal coins, use of crescents and arcs were inscribed in the Koch coins. Hence it can be concluded that the Koch coins not only reflected the state's economic status, but it provided a vivid description of the socio-cultural and political dimension of the kingdom as well as the culture of medieval northeast India. By the art motifs and diagrams inscribed in the coins, it can be said that although there was a lack of technological advancement for minting coins, the craftsmanship was the same as professional. Thus, it contributed to the numismatics heritage of India.

Evaluating the changing structure of the Koch kingdom, it revealed the changing political dimension of the Koches with its surrounding areas on the one hand (such as Ahoms and the neighbouring regions) and with the Mughals, Bhutanese and the British on the other. The changing political relations were reflected in the Koch coins. With the change of power within the kingdom, the art and motifs inscribed in the coins were also changed from time to time. But in any circumstances, the Koch rulers also made sure to keep their unique identity in the coins. The use of Sanskrit and Assamese or Bengali language in the coins reflects the very purpose of the rulers as Sanskrit was used as the court language, and Bengali or Assamese was the language of common people. The use of Bengali script in the coins by the Koch rulers signifies that the coins struck were not only meant for large transactions in trade or as commemorative coins but also for the use of the common masses. The coins also reflected the nature of the transition from a 'tribal' Koch kingdom into a Hindu kingdom. As mentioned above, the origin of the Koches has an obscure history (relating them to the Dravidian or Mongoloid group); with time, to trace themselves with the divine theory, they adopted and worshipped Hindu Gods like Shiva, Vishnu and Goddess Parvati. This belief system was also replicated in their coins as almost all the rulers used the invocation of either Shiva or Vishnu in their coins. Not only the Hindu symbols or motifs but in later years, it is also seen that due to the Muslim influence, few sacred symbols like hexagonal coins, use of crescents and arcs were inscribed in the Koch coins. Hence it can be concluded that the Koch coins not only reflected the economic status of the state but it provided a vivid description of the socio-cultural and political dimension of the kingdom as well as the culture of medieval northeast India. By the art motifs and diagrams inscribed in the coins, it can be said that although there was a lack of technological advancement for minting coins, the craftsmanship was the same as professional. Thus, it contributed to the numismatic heritage of India.

Notes

1. See, G. M. Trevelyan, *English Social History: A Survey of Six Centuries, Chaucer to Queen Victoria*, Books way publication, 2014. However, different scholars have given their views regarding social history. Charles Tilly has defined social history in two ways, such as, 'retrospective': which consists of asking how the world we live in came into being and how it's coming into being affected the everyday lives of ordinary people, and 'prospective': which consists of asking what could have happened to everyday experience at major historical choice points, and then inquiring how and why outcomes which occurred won out over other possibilities, in his article, *"Two Callings of History"* in https://deepblue.lib.umich.edu/bitstream/handle/2027.42/43664/11186_2004_Article_BF00208777.pdf;sequence=1.
2. Nadine Pence Frantz, "Material Culture, Understanding and Meanings: Writing and Picturing", *Journal of the American Academy of Religion* Vol. 66, No. 4 (Winter, 1998), pp.791-815.
3 Jash Pranabananda, *Coin and Cultural of Early North India*, Pratibha Prakashan, New Delhi, 2008.
4. S. K. Bose describes that the medieval Koch kingdom, which covered some parts of the modern northern division of West Bengal and the lower region of Assam, occupied an enviable position in the trade map of the northeastern division of the Indian Sub-continent, as it did, between the Mughal province of Bengal, on one end, and the northeastern kingdoms and

tribal territories, including the Ahom state (Assam) and the Himalayan kingdom of Bhutan, Sikkim and Nepal, on the other, and commanding the traditional trade routes if the subcontinent to Tibet and China, in his, *The Commercial Coinage of Koch Kingdom*, Mira Bose, Kolkata, 2013, p.5.

5. Khan Choudhuri Amanatulla, *Cooch Behar Itihas*, State Press, Cooch Behar, 1936; Nirmal Kumar Basu, *Assam in the Ahom Age*, Arunima Printing works, Calcutta, 1970; S.N. Bhattacharya, *A History of Mughal North-East Frontier Policy*, Spectrum publication, Guwahati, 1998; Edward Gait, *A History of Assam*, EBH Publishers, Guwahati, 2012 (reprint); Ajit Kuman Borauh, *The Koch Kingdom: Polity, Society and Economy*, DVS Publishers, Guwahati, 2011; D. Nath, *History of Koch Kingdom (c.1515-1615)*, Mittal Publication, New Delhi, 1989.

6. D. Nath, *op. cit*, p.2. He suggested Koches be non-Aryan and non-Hindu, were a 'Dravidian' tribe of the Northeastern region among whom there are grounds for suspecting some admixture of Mongolian blood; According to Dr. Buchannon Hamilton, all tribes having the name 'Koch' sprung up from the same stock and that most of the Rajvamshis are Koches, in H. N. Chowdhury, *The Cooch Behar State and its Land Revenue Settlement*, Nripendra Nath Pak (ed.), N. L. Publisher, Siliguri, pp. 123-124; W. W. Hunter, in his account, described that the three tribes of Koch, Rajvamshi and Pali are of the same origin, and their features clearly mark them as of different race than other Hindus, in *A Statistical Account of Bengal and Koch Behar*, N. L. Publisher, Siliguri, 2012 (reprint), p.24.

7. Md. Shah Noor Rahman, "The Emergence of the Koch State in the 16th Century" in J. B. Bhattacharya and David R. Syiemlieh (eds.), *Early States in North East India*, Regency Publication, New Delhi, 2013, p.50.

8. Rup Kumar Barman, *op. cit.*, pp.72-75.

9 According to *Darang Rajvamshabali*, the circumstances that led to the division of the kingdom, although King Naranarayan married, he was childless for long years, resulting in Raghdev Narayan, son of Chilarai being chosen as the apparent heir after King Naranarayan. However, after the birth of Laxmi Narayan, the son of Naranarayan, the son of the ruling king, had a greater claim over the throne. This situation led Raghudev Narayan to discontentment, and he suspected that he could be overthrown by Laxmi Narayan at any time. This mutual hostility by two apparent heirs led to the division of the kingdom, which further destroyed the growth and development of the kingdom. For more details, see D. Nath, Quoted *Darang Rajvamshabali*, *op. cit.*, 83-84.

10. The division of the kingdom led to mutual hostility and constant war between the two kingdoms. To prove their superiority and extend their kingdom, the kings from both sides continued to rage wars against each other, further weakening the kingdoms. At times Koch Hajo had to surrender and accept the suzerainty of Ahoms and the Mughals. At the same time, the hostility between Koch Bihar and the Mughals compelled the king of Koch Bihar to conclude an agreement with the Bhutanese, which allowed the Bhutiyas to interfere in the internal matters of the kingdom. See Sarat Chandra Ghosal, *A History of Cooch Behar: From the earliest times to the end of the 18th century* AD, Printed at the State Press, Cooch Behar, 1942, pp. 193-200; Rup Kumar Barman, *op. cit.*, pp. 92-100; Moonshi Jadhunath Ghose, *Rajpokhayan or History of Cooch Behar*, Rev. R. Robinson (tr.), Baptist Mission Press, Calcutta, 1874, pp.39-45; S.N. Bhattacharya, *op. cit.*, pp.144-145.

11. H. N. Chowdhury, *op. cit.*, p.250; Rup Kumar Barman, *op. cit.*, pp.103-104.

12. D. Nath, *op. cit.*, p.133; Amalendu Guha, *Medieval and Early Colonial Assam: Society, Polity, Economy*, K. P. Bagchi & Company, Calcutta, 1991, p.19.

13. *Ibid.*, pp.135-138.
14. *Ibid.*, pp.141-143.
15. S. K. Bose, Qouted from, N. G. Rhodes, *The Coinage of North-East India*, Hyte, 1994, p. 60; A. Deb, "Cooch Behar and Bhutan in the context of Tibetan Trade", *Kailas*, Vol. 1, No. 1. 1973, pp. 80-88, in his, *The Commercial Coinage of Koch Kingdom*, *op. cit.*, p.4.
16. From the various materials available, it can be concluded that King Biswa Sinha (predecessor of King Naranarayan) did not mint any coins, as not a single coin was found under his name. Thus it can be assumed that during the early years of the Koch kingdom, transactions were done either by barter system or special types of items such as *kris* and gold *mohurs*. In some cases, even 'Almond' fruit was also accepted as money in D. Nath, *Ibid.*, pp.157-158.
17. Nicholas Rhodes & S. K. Bose, *The Coinage of Cooch Behar*, Dhubri, 1999, pp.1-29.
18. S. K. Bose, *op. cit.*, p.19.
19. Khan Chowdhuri Amanatulla Ahmed, *op. cit.*, pp.293-296.
20. The currency, both from Bengal and Delhi, was available in Koch Kingdom even before the minting of *Narayani tanka* by the King. Hence, King Naranarayan was influenced by the artistic beauty of those coins and planned to mint coins with artistic symbols and motifs. The *Narayani tanka* of King Nara Narayan was the same as the coins of Hussain Shah's *Sultani tanka* in weight and standard. Apart from Muslim coins, the contemporary coins of the Hindu kingdom also might have influenced King Naranarayan profoundly, as in his childhood, King Naranarayan stayed in Varanasi (Hindu-dominated kings since ancient times) for a few years to pursue *Sanskrit* education. For details, see, *Ibid.*, pp.290-293
21. There were no silver mines in the Koch Kingdom during the reign of King Naranarayan, so gold and silver that were

plundered from the neighbouring areas or those which were reccived as booty or tribute were transformed into coins in Kanai Lal Chattopadhyay & Rajarshi Roy, *Northeast Researches: Special Issue on Northeast Indian Numismatics*, Institute of Northeast Studies, Kolkata, 2018, p.40.

22. S. K. Bose, *op. cit.*, pp.24-24; This square shape was inscribed in the coins because, most probably, Laxmi Narayan was influenced by the Manikya coins of Tripura, where this type of coin was available. Also, this was the time when Laxmi Narayan was having mutual hostility with Raghudev Narayan. Raghdev Narayan, who was the king of the eastern Koch Kingdom (Koch Hajo), issued coins in a similar design to King Naranarayan. So, maybe Laxmi Narayan intentionally used a different style in minting his own coins to differentiate them from the coins of Raghudev Narayan, S. K. Bose, "Raghudev's coins in Naranarayan's Name", *Proceedings of NEIHA*, 1990, pp.20-22.
23. S. K. Bose, *op. cit.*, p.28
24. *Ibid.*, p.29.
25. *Ibid.*, p.31.
26. Crescent symbols were used in Muslim coins in the medieval period. Thus the use of such symbols in the Koch coins shows some kind of Muslim domination over the Koch kingdom even after the Mughals left the Koch kingdom (From AD 1661-1663), in A. K. M. Yakub Ali, *Muslim Mudra O Hastalikhan Silpa*, (Bengali), Dhaka, 1989. p.96.
27. *Ibid.*, p.42.
28. In 1772, the dispute between the Koch King and the neighbouring Bhutanese state over the new King Dhrendranarayan's accession led to a clash between the two kingdoms. Thus this compelled the Koch King to appeal for help from the British. The British government helped the Koch King to overthrow the Bhutiyas from their kingdom, and in return, the Koch Kingdom accepted the imperial suzerainty and concluded with a treaty called the

'Anglo-Koch' treaty in 1773. Koch Kings, after accepting the feudatory status under the British government, had to make many new changes introduced by the British government, including its name from 'Koch Behar' (Koch kingdom) to 'Cooch Behar'. The British government also compelled and withdrew the older Koch coins. Thus the new coins issued by Nripendranarayan with the design of flower and arabesque were the influence of British currency. For details, see H. N. Chowdhury, *op. cit.*, p.294: Rup Kumar Barman, *op. cit.*, pp.103-105.

29. S. K. Bose., *op.cit.*, pp.43-44.

30. Debajit Dutta, "A Royal Seal of Cooch Behar", *Proceedings of NEIHA*, 2010, pp.256-259.

3

Representation of the Mizo in Colonial Ethnography: A Critique

Lallianzuali Chhangte

In discussions of the Orient, the Orient is all absence, whereas one feels the Orientalist and what he says as presence; yet we must not forget that the Orient's effective absence enables the Orientalist's presence.[1]

Etymologically, the term 'representation' can be understood as a presentation drawn up not by depicting the object as it is but by representing it in a new form and/or environment.[2] Cultural representations help form the images people have of others; thereby, they get embodied in institutions and inform policies and practices. According to Stuart Hall, two processes and two systems of representation are involved. First, there is the 'system' by which all sorts of objects, people and events correlate with a set of concepts or mental representations we carry around in our heads.Language is the second representation system involved in the overall process of constructing meaning.[3] Thus, according to Hall, representation involves understanding how language and systems of knowledge production work together to produce and circulate meanings. Historically, all human societies have had particular representational practices for perceiving themselves and those they considered 'Other'.

But it was only with modern European imperialism that systematic representation revolving around issues of power and control on a massive scale emerged. Representation of the 'non-Western Other' lies at the core of all colonial discourses. Colonial representations of colonised people have been perpetuated through the ways in which knowledge about them was collected, classified and then represented in various ways back to the West, and then through the eyes of the West, back to those who have been colonised.[4] Colonial discourse usually employs various representation techniques such as stereotyping, labelling, objectification, erasure and metonymic representation.

With the end of colonialism, a new range of studies devoted to re-examining the history, politics, psychology, and language of colonisation have come up. Hence, the post-colonial scholarships have contributed immensely to understanding the once colonised people. The enterprise of post-colonial theory has highlighted how Western knowledge and representations of the non-Western world are implicated in the West's will to power and its imperial adventures. The politics of representation, its divisive nature and ensuing impacts in shaping power narratives have been primarily investigated, debated, analysed, (re)presented and theorised by Edward Said in *Orientalism.* Homi Bhabha, in his paper 'The Other Question', has offered a challenging and innovative engagement with issues of racial/ cultural otherness and that of the colonial stereotype.[5] Gayatri C. Spivak has underlined how representations, especially of marginalised groups from developing countries, are intimately linked to positioning: socio-economic, gendered, cultural, geographic, historical, and institutional.[6] Within the field of Indian history, scholars such as Bernard S. Cohn, Nicholas Dirks, and others have drawn attention to how colonially instituted practices and knowledge systems affect the formation of new subjectivities and cast a lasting shadow over the emerging politic of identity. A few scholars from the northeast have worked on critical examinations of ethnographic accounts related to their particular tribe. For instance, A. K. Thakur[7] re-examines the role and significance of ethnographic traditions from the viewpoint of a historian working on northeast India and Hoineilhing Sitlhou[8] has attempted to critically analyse the writings of protestant Christian Missionaries in North East India during the nineteenth-twentieth centuries, while Arkotong Longkumer[9], through studies of rituals and festivals, signs and symbols, shows how the representation of Nagas as exotic has a long lineage.

The Mizo of northeast India, too, are not left out of the representation as described above, which started from the colonial period. The reconstruction of Mizo history is based largely on accounts either by the missionaries or the colonial officers who represent the Mizo in various ways. However, a critique of the available colonial accounts is lacking. This paper aims to fill up the gap in history writing or reconstruction of the history of the Mizo by analysing colonial ethnography focusing on the representation of the Mizo. Hence, this paper is a descriptive analytical research that primarily depicts the colonial notions of representation and binaries to define, label and represent 'the others' with respect to the Mizo tribe. The first part of the paper focuses on a configuration of ideas in the nineteenth century that formed the anthropological, legal and moral framework, with which the British categorised non-European peoples, conceded them sovereignty and recognised their title to their lands concerning India. The second part of the paper elaborates upon the representation of the Mizo in colonial ethnography and their critique. The third part deals briefly with the Mizo way representing the 'others' and the conclusion.

I

When the British started extending their rule across India during the late eighteenth and nineteenth centuries, they had to confront the problem of how to govern this far-flung dependency and, more importantly, how to justify this governance to themselves. How could the British, as a member of a society who adopted the ideals of nationalism, in good conscience extend their authority over this distant and densely peopled land?[10] Therefore, the British thus, drew upon a range of ideas that had, for a long time, shaped their views of themselves and, more generally, of the world outside their home. Among the intellectual foundations on which the British sought to comprehend their rule in India was the notion of 'orientalism'. Under the influence of the ideals of the Enlightenment, the British, as did the Europeans, announced their pre-eminence as a 'modern' and 'civilised' people. The distinction was made between 'the East' and 'the West', 'the Orient' and 'the Occident'. The 'Orientals' arc therefore shown to be gullible, devoid of energy and initiative, much given to fulsome flattery, intrigue, cunning, and unkindness to animals; inveterate liars, lazy, suspicious and in everything oppose the clarity, directness and nobility of the Anglo Saxon race. [11] In the Western eyes, the 'oriental' is irrational, depraved (fallen), childlike, and 'different'; thus, the European is rational, virtuous, mature, and normal. [12] According to Said, all accounts of 'the Orient' were prone to generalisations attributing collective significance to acts of individuals. Since the Oriental, to the Western eyes, was "a member of a subject race, he had to be subjected".[13] This discourse justified the West's hegemony and dominance over 'the Orient'. As Bhabha stated, "The objective of colonial discourse is to construct the colonised as a population of degenerate types based on racial origin, to justify conquest and to establish systems of administration and instruction."[14]

By the latter half of the eighteenth century, the British endeavoured to secure an understanding of India's unchartered civilisation and a sense of mastery over it. This knowledge enabled the British to classify, categorise and bind the vast social world that was India so that it could be controlled. According to Bernard S. Cohn, these imperatives, elements in the larger colonial project, shaped the "investigative modalities" devised by the British to collect the facts. Knowledge of local languages was considered the first necessary step for colonial knowledge production. Therefore, the British began the program of appropriating Indian languages to serve as a crucial component in their construction of the system of rule. Cohn considered the years 1770 to 1775 as the period when the British began to produce an apparatus: grammars, dictionaries, treatises, class books and translations about and from the language of India. The production of these texts and others that followed them began the establishment of discursive formation that defined an epistemological space, created a discourse (orientalism), and converted Indian forms of knowledge into European objects.[15] Most of them were imbued with the dual purpose of investigating the sciences and the arts of Asia and of advancing knowledge and improving the arts at home. William Jones, who founded the Asiatic Society of Bengal on 15 January 1784, insisted, "Asian learning could supply many 'valuable hints for our improvement and advantage. Nevertheless, Europe's superior advancement in all kinds of useful knowledge remained unquestioned."[16] Jones' goals were to rule, learn, and compare 'Orient' with 'Occident'. The interpretations such studies yielded, and the self-assured mastery over it became lasting foundations for the British claims to rule India.[17] These methods were systematically applied in every newly acquired and annexed Indian Territory to the British Raj.

The British came into contact with the hill tribes of Northeast India with the annexation of Assam because of their frequent raids on the plains. Very little was known about them before this. In 1865, a leading article in the Pioneer of the day declared, 'the only idea which most men had, with reference to the hills and forests [of Assam], was that they were the habitat of savage tribes, whose bloody raids and thieving forays threatened danger to the cause of tea'.[18] This idea is also clearly expressed by T. H. Lewin, who writes:

It is unfortunate too often the custom among the English people, as a body, to condemn and despise all races speaking an alien tongue, while as for people like these hill races, whose skin is dark and breech bare, out and alack, they are savage and barbarians forsooth, very little better, indeed, than the apes among whom they reside.[19]

Early in the year 1866, Dr. J. Fayrer, C. S. I., submitted to the Asiatic Society of Bengal an extraordinary ethnological congress in Calcutta, which was to bring together in one exhibition typical examples of the races of the Old World to be made the subject of scientific study when so collected. The wild tribes of India were to be fully represented. However, there were some difficulties with this scheme. It would not be an easy matter to induce the hill tribes to proceed to an unknown region for a cause they would not be able to comprehend. The Commissioner of Assam stated his conviction that twenty typical specimens of the hill tribes of his province could not be conveyed to Calcutta. For these and other reasons, the scheme was dropped.[20] Serious attempts to prepare an official ethnography were made for the first time in 1903, when Sir Bampfylde Fuller, then Chief Commissioner of Assam, proposed, and the Government of India sanctioned, the preparation of a series of monographs on the more important tribes and castes of the province of Assam.[21] This project was to be undertaken by writers who had special and intimate experience of the races to be described, the accounts of earlier observers being at the same time studied and incorporated; a uniform scheme of treatment was laid down, which was to be adhered to in each monograph, and certain limits of size were prescribed.[22] But in the meantime, the Government of Bengal and the supreme Government had, in compliance with the request of the society, called on all local authorities to furnish complete and accurate lists of various races found within their jurisdictions. But as Edward Said writes, "Who writes? For whom is the writing being done? In what circumstances? These, it seems, are the questions whose answers provide us with the ingredients making a politics of interpretation."[23]

II

The British decided to contact the Mizo as their frequent raids into the plains where the British had recently established tea estates were becoming an increasing annoyance. Colonial officers first acquired some knowledge of the Mizo from those who visited the frontier bazaar like Kassalong, Rangamati and Tlabung in the Chittagong Hill Tracts, Paletwa in Arakan Hills, Sylhet, Tipperah and Cachar. Brojo Nath Shaha, an agent of the British in the Chittagong Hill Tracts who compiled *Grammar of the Lushai Language* in 1844, stated that dialect and popular songs of the Lushais were gathered by himself from the 'Zau' people who visited the *bazaar* at Kassalong.[24] T. H. Lewin, who was appointed Deputy Commissioner of Chittagong Hill Tract to confront the problem of how to come to terms with the hostile Lusei and Mara chiefs, stated in his record expressed that he was able to speak some Lushai himself and the chief's *karbaris* were acquainted with bazaar Bengali.[25] The British also gathered some information on the Mizo from their neighbours who inhabited the regions adjacent to the Lushai Hills, particularly the Bengalis and their cognate tribes, and also from the escaped captive slaves. Therefore, the data collected from these people and the help of interpreters employed by the Colonial officers formed the basis of knowledge production in the period before the British came into actual contact with the Mizo. As such, the information that they got from these sources was usually perplexing and sometimes misleading. However, in the absence of any other written documentation on the tribe, either by the tribesmen themselves or by other Indian writers, these accounts were considered to be an authoritative description of the tribe that formed the basis of the colonial representation of the Mizo.

Various expeditions were sent into the Lushai hills, and the reports documented by the British officers who participated in the expeditions provided descriptions of the early interactions with the Mizo. The early narratives on the Mizo were replete with references to a "savage and warlike tribe'. The savagery of the Mizo was represented in contradistinction to that of the enlightened West. The Mizo were thereby represented as uncivilised, wild, barbaric, war-like and savages, and this perspective about them compelled the intervention of the colonial power to bring enlightenment and civilisation. T. H. Lewinconsidered the Mizo a wild, a 'horde of simple savages' and a 'band of very dangerous marauders'.[26] These characterisations were exemplified by their accounts of the head-hunting practices. Mackenzie narrated about the Lushai Raid of 1844:

> Now no Kookie Chief could go on his last long journey unaccompanied by attendants to do his bidding in the unseen world. However, the affection of his clansmen was not put under too great a strain. They had not themselves to go away before their time, so long as they could supply Bengali slaves, whose heads piled around the corpse of the Chief were earnest that their ghosts were keeping company with him. But slaves were scarce in the hills since the British Government had discouraged this trade, so LalChokla and his cousin... hung their great relative's body in the smoke, and set forth on the warpath to slay the prescribed number of victims. Spies sent before marked out as the doomed village, the Manipuri colony of Kachabari, in Pertabgar. On the night of the 16 April, 200 savages surrounded it, and amidst the horror of the darkness, the bloody work went on till twenty heads were secured and six live captives taken.[27]

Lewin also asserted that "it is customary for a young warrior to eat a piece of the liver of the first man he kills; this, it is said, strengthens the heart and gives courage."[28] Robert Reid, in his work *The Lushai Hills*, repeatedly referred to the Lushai as a band of savages and stated, "We cannot permit the continuance in our midst of groups of head taking savages without responsible chiefs, without organisation, and not amenable to political control."[29]

It is a misconception that the Mizo hunted for heads. Mizo conducted raids not to take heads but to procure their material needs. J. Shakespeare, writing in the early 1900s, refuted that the Lushais were head-hunters. While he did not deny the fact that the Lushais cut off heads, he maintained that Lushai parties did not go out simply to get heads, but when a man did kill a person, he brought the head home to show that he was speaking the truth.[30] Shakespeare argued that this did not make them head hunters since their motive was loot and slaves, objects recognisably different from head trophies. He also remarked:

> I have also made careful enquiries in all parts of the Hills as to whether there is any truth in the commonly accepted theory that on the death of a chief, a party was at once sent off to kill people in order that their heads might adorn his memorial and their ghosts wait on his spirit in the other world, but I never heard anything which lent any colour to the idea, and, as regards Lushais, I believe it to be a pure invention.[31]

The confirmation of the notions of savagery was vital not only to show that it was the actions of these people which compelled and prompted the British domination but also to establish systems of administration and instruction. This colonial ideology did not escape even among the Christian missionaries. The missionaries were compelled to note their observations in the awareness of a particular audience: their fellow countrymen in general, colleagues, and their patron or monarch. Awareness of this audience affected their perception and influenced them to select certain kinds of information or to stress particular aspects that would find resonance in their nation. Addressing the 'anticipated' readers, R.A. Lorrain, in his book For God and Empire, stated, "Cannot you, my reader, consecrate your money, your time and your talents, your all, that one stream of light may pierce that terrible darkness, the true light of the Son of God."[32] Accounts of the missionaries were intended mainly for the Western readers who would be sympathetic to their cause, i.e. taming and converting the wild savage head-hunters and 'devil appeasers' and rendering financial help. Rev. D.E. Jones, the Welsh missionary in the Lushai Hills from 1897 to 1927, while reporting on the Lushai raid at the Alexandrapur tea garden in Assam on 23 January 1871, wrote that the Lushais rushed forward to cut off Mr. Winchester's head as their custom was.[33] Grace R. Lewis also remarked that the

Mizo "love fighting. To practice on their tame spirited lowland neighbours was an irresistible temptation".[34]

The body of the primitive becomes as much the object of examination, commentary, and valorisation as the land of the primitive in colonial discourse.[35] The natives' bodies were examined as an object, and their Euro-centric notion of beauty commented upon their physical appearance. Most colonial ethnographers gave detailed accounts of the appearance and physical characteristics of the Mizo in their writings. Lewin, in the context of the Lushai, recorded:

> In physique both, men and women are well-made and wonderfully muscular. The average height of the males is about 5 feet 8 inches, and of the women, 5 feet 4 inches. They are never corpulent. Their physiognomy is not pleasing, being generally sulky and forbidding appearance.[36]

N. E. Parry wrote that the Lakher are not remarkable for their beauty. He wrote: "Good looks are less common. Looks vary somewhat in the different villages, the inhabitants of Chap and Chakang having rather repellent and surly faces. Even the few who have any pretence to good looks are spoilt by their unwashed condition."[37] Suakpuilala, the Western Lushai chief who negotiated a *sanad* with Edgar, Deputy Commissioner of Assam in 1871, was described as 'a shrewd, hard-faced old barbarian with a gimlet eyes'.[38] Most of the missionary accounts recounted the disgust with the smell of the unredeemed Mizo. The Mizo were repeatedly referred to as "abominably filthy". The manufacture and continuous repetition of such a sensory stereotype was an important part of the missionaries' civilising mission and of the construction of a Mizo "race", seeking to protect the senses against affront as defined by a missionary-normative nose.[39]

Stereotype representation of the character of the Mizo as quintessentially lazy, ignorant, cruel, imprudent etc., and represented as fixed by nature, also strengthened imperial designs. John Shakespear described the Lushai as lazy fellows 'who preferred ease and idleness to toiling' and who 'instead of earning money by work or trade, prefer to lie smoking in the sun'.[40] Thereby, thecolonial creation of an image of the lazy native legitimised the implementation of *corvee (*forced labour) to teach the Lushais, who were too lazy to do anything except under compulsion.

> You forced us to occupy your hills, we had no wish to come up here, but you would raid our villages, so we had to come, and so now you have got to bear as much of the cost of the occupation as possible, you cannot expect us to spend the money of the people of the plains on importing coolies to do the work, that you are too lazy to do except under compulsion.[41]

Grace Lewis described the Lushais as very improvident, just like other primitive people, and used so much rice in making beer that their food supply ran out before harvest.[42] Carey and Tuck wrote:

> The slow speech, the serious manner, the respect for birth and the knowledge of pedigrees, the uty of revenge, the taste for and the treacherous method of warfare, the curse of drink, the virtue of hospitality, the clannish feeling, the vice of avarice, the filthy state of the body, mutual distrust, impatience under control, the want of power of combination and continued effort, arrogance in victory, speedy, discouragement and panic in defeat are common traits throughout the hills.[43]

A. G. McCall described the Lushai as follows:

> He is crafty, clever, and determined, to the point of obstinacy. Resourceful and brave in battle, he is capable of frenzied cruelty in victory. The means justify the ends at the cost of any duplicity, such ability affording greater power over others. The quest for power is rarely absent, in some form or degree, from any enterprise, big or small. The Lushai is a master in jungle craft capable of the greatest physical endurance and achievement. He will engage in a venture with far-reaching implications on any whim. The tendency to excess pervades every phase of Lushai life.[44]

Thus, it is through the imperial gaze that the Mizo were defined. Colonial representation of the Mizo manifests a cultural hegemony where the Western perspective has been seen as the norm. The Mizo were projected as fundamentally different from 'the self' (coloniser). There are no individual aspects taken into consideration when describing them. They are portrayed as if they are a homogenous mass, driven by instinctive emotions which are determined by race rather than by conscious choices and decisions. The Mizo way of living differed much from the standardised description of savagery given by Mill and his contemporaries and was widely accepted by the end of the eighteenth century in Britain. According to John Stuart Mill,

> ...a savage tribe consists of a handful of individuals, wandering or thinly scattered over a vast tract of country....In savage life there is no commerce, no manufactures, no agriculture, or next to none....each person shifts for himself: except in war (and even then very imperfectly...thereis little or no law or administration of justice: no systematic employment of the collective strength of society to protect individuals against injury from one another: every one trusts to his own strength or cunning, and where that fails, he is generally without resource...they incapable of acting in concert,...[45]

The Mizo had their own system of laws and customs. A vital element of group survival prevailed within the village, manifested by close cooperation and help rendered to each other in the labour process, with sharing, selflessness and sacrifice (*tlawmngaihna*) as a guiding principle of human conduct. Their physical endurance and aggressive or war-like nature might have stemmed from living in an environment where survival from their enemies and wild animals was of utmost importance. The simple material culture of traditional Mizo society was responsible for their so-called improvidence and laziness. They were self-sufficient and did not desire much. After coming in contact with the Lushai, Lewin remarked:

> What struck me most among them was the contentment and well-being of their lives, as compared with the feverish anxieties of civilised life.... They cultivate the earth sufficiently for their wants and ... they can raise enough food for a year. They have none which they fear to lose, nor do they desire more. They require no knowledge other than what they have; they know how to sow and when to reap; they have their pharmacopoeia of simples, herbs and roots; their women weave warm cloth; and cunning are the snares by which they entangle all sorts of animals, few there be that escape the pot. In a word, they know what is necessary for their happiness and well-being; to know more than this would make them unhappy.[46]

The Mizo greatly resented *corvee* (forced labour) imposed by the British, not because of the labour but because it was found to be 'degrading. Though drinking rice beer was part and parcel of the most important social and cultural functions, the unofficial rules and the self-imposed protocols of drinking rituals regulate both levels of consumption and drinking behaviour far more effectively than 'external' or legal controls in the traditional Mizo society.[47]

III

Though the impact differs due to the power relations, the Mizo have also been caricaturing and labelling 'the others'. Since contact was mainly limited to the Burmese and the plain people before the colonial era, the term *kawl*was employed to refer to the Burmese and *vai* was used to denote the plain people. These terms did not seem to carry any derogatory meaning at first. Moreover, the feeling of 'self' and 'other' did not seem strongly ingrained in the pre-colonial period, even though ethnic and linguistic differentiation certainly existed. Some Mizo young men married young women captured by them while raiding the plains. Vanlalchhuanawma tracing the genealogy of one of the first converts to Christianity named Tlira, wrote, "Tleithanga, Tlira's father, belonged to AirawnPawi and he joined Bengkhuaia offensive against the British in Cachar when Mary Winchester was captured in 1871. He married a girl named Nokiri, whom he brought as a captive. Their fourth child, Tlira, was born at Vawmkalkhang (Burma)in 1878 ...".[48] The *vai* encountered by the Mizo during the colonial era consisted mainly of armed sepoys, unscrupulous Bengali merchants or clerks. Thus an unfavourable impression of the idea of *vai* took shape. *Vai*s are perceived to be crafty, sly and acquisitive.These negative stereotypes associated with the *vai* continued even in the postcolonial period.

There is little that can be gleaned from British official reports on the Mizo perception of the *sap* (white men) who undertook a series of military expeditions to chastise these 'savages'. At first, the Mizo had no idea of who the British were and even called the British expedition in the Lushai

Hills '*Vailen*' (plain people's raid). But soon, they were able to differentiate between the *vai* (people from the plains) and the white Europeans whom they called *sap* (corruption of the word *sahib).* Travel accounts of early colonial encounters suggest that the Whiteman was perceived as a pale-faced freak, carrier of diseases, or bearer of gifts. Then an oral society, only some of the plaintive notes of lament have been noted and recorded for posterity by which an idea of the local perspective could be drawn. The Mizo perception of the *sap* (white men), established based on violent encounters, was denoted by fear and distrust. They were perceived as intruders who wrecked their homes and defiled women, as could be seen from one of Mizo's songs composed at the time of the British expedition:

> Thlangah Sappuidanruallohvin a lian e,
> *Darngotlanrawhlentuhnuaiah,*
> *Tang a chul Sappuilianin.*
> (the indomitable white men are coming.
> Damsels, run to the woods, lest they violate you).

This disdainful attitude of the Mizo towards the *sap* was slowly replaced with respect and warm approval by the end of the 19th century due to the complete subjugation of the Mizo, efforts of the British in famine relief and the coming of Christianity. Until today, a *sap* is shown much respect and admiration since it was the *sap*, as most Mizo would say, who brought Christianity among the Mizoand transformed them from ignorant, naked, savage head hunters to well-clothed, educated and peace-loving Christians. These views held by many Mizo reflect how the colonial desires of the West got invested and have been continuously upheld among the Mizo.

Colonial ethnographers' ways of representing the Mizo have contributed to the general impressions and milieu of ideas that have informed Western knowledge and the Western construction of the Mizo. The experience the writers had and their encounters with 'real life savages' continually fed the imaginations of people 'back home'. In the case of religious missionaries, the viewpoints expressed were designed as much to justify further financial support from their central base as to justify any ideological motivations. The more primitive and savage the people, the stronger the imperative was to carry out God's work. This is not to say that all Europeans writing on the Mizo misrepresented it, but that the dominant misrepresentations were, unfortunately enough, the ones that captured the public imagination in the West. Even when the Mizo started writing about themselves, they continued with this perspective or a sense of reality seen through the lens of the colonisers. They have internalised the colonial ruler's description of their tribe so much so that they saw the jaundiced descriptions as truth, and hence embracing, or at least assenting, to errors and falsehoods about themselves. As Frantz Fanon asserts: "Colonialism is not satisfied merely with holding a people in its grip and emptying the native's brain of all form and content. By a kind of perverted logic, it turns to the past of the oppressed people and distorts, disfigures and destroys it. This work of devaluing pre-colonial history takes on a dialectical significance today."[49] Thus, the colonial construct of the Mizo tribe was continued by early Mizo writers in their attempt to eulogise what they claimed were the blessings of British rule and the enlightened works done by the Christian missionaries.

Colonial ethnography did no doubt lead to an expansion in knowledge of the world, but it was a tainted knowledge that served the colonial vision, and hence the native's voices were silenced. But one cannot do away with colonial ethnography to reconstruct the history of the Mizo as they produced first-hand information on the tribe. Therefore, to ultimately arrive at a less prejudiced narrative, colonial ethnography should be re-read and critically examined, considering the politico-cultural background in which the ethnographic accounts were prepared and complimented with indigenous sources. To redress the issue related to colonial representation, the Mizo have to reclaim their past and erode the colonial ideology by which the past has been devalued. As Salazar rightly observes: "A way to bypass the dilemma of representation of and for others is to acknowledge and articulate how power enters into the process of cultural translation. In the end, the crisis of cross-cultural representation can be resolved only through cross-cultural communications that are actually, rather than virtually, decentered and multi vocal, that is, through the empowerment of others to participate as equal partners in the conversation of humankind."[50]

Notes and References

I presented this paper at the International Seminar on "Writing History on Highlanders of North East India", organised by the Department of History and Ethnography, Mizoram University, held on the 5th& 6th of March 2019. Since the Seminar's Organizers have no plan to publish the Seminar's proceedings, I am sharing the revised paper here with the consent.

1. Edward W. Said, *Orientalism*, Penguin Books, London, 1978: reprint, 2003.
2. N. B. Salazar, "Representation in Postcolonial Analysis" in William A. Darity Jr. (ed.), *International Encyclopedia of the Social Sciences,* McMillan Reference, New York, 2008 (2nd Edition), p.172.

3. Stuart Hall, "The Work of Representation" in Stuart Hall *(ed.), Representation: Cultural Representations and Signifying Practices*, Sage Publishing, London, 1997, p. 17.
4. Linda Tuhiwai Smith, *Decolonizing Methodologies: Research and Indigenous Peoples*, Zed Books Ltd., London, 1999, pp1-2.
5. H. K. Bhabha, *The Location of Culture,* Routledge, London, 1994.
6. Gayatri C. Spivak, "Can the Subaltern Speak?" in Cary Nelson and Larry Grossberg (eds.), *Marxism and the Interpretation of Culture,* Macmillan Education, Basingstoke, U. K. 1988, pp. 271–313.
7. Amrendra Kumar Thakur, "Ethnographic Accounts and the Reconstruction of the Historical Past of Northeast India" in *Proceedings of North East India History Association*, 36th Session, Aizawl, 2015, pp. 36-43 and *idem*, "Colonial Ethnography in North-East India: A Critique" in H. Sudhir (ed.), *Ethnography, Historiography and North-East India*, The Asiatic Society, Kolkata, 2019, pp.57-75.
8. Hoineilhing Sithlou, *Deconstructing Colonial Ethnography: An Analysis of Missionary Writings on North East India,* Ruby Press, New Delhi, 2017.
9. Arkotong Longkumer, "Representing Thenagas: Negotiating National Culture and Consumption" in Neeladri Bhattacharya & Joy L. K. Pachuau (eds.), *Landscape, Culture, and Belonging: Writing the History of Northeast India*, Cambridge University Press, U.K., 2019, pp. 131-150.
10. Thomas R. Metcalf, *Ideologies of the Raj*, Cambridge University Press, Delhi, 1995: reprint, 2017, p.1.
11. Edward Said, *Orientalism*, *op. cit.*, pp.38-39.
12. *Ibid.*, p.40.
13. *Ibid.*, p.207.

14. Homi K. Bhabha, *The Location of Culture*, Routledge, London, 1994, p.70.
15. Bernard S. Cohn, *Colonialism and Its Forms of Knowledge*, Princeton University Press, New Jersey, 1996, p. 21.
16. Quoted in Thomas Metcalf, *op. cit.*, p.15.
17. *Ibid.*, p.9.
18. Quoted in Verrier Elwin, *India'sNorth-East Frontier in the Nineteenth Century*, Oxford University Press, 1959, pp. xv & xvi.
19. T.H., Lewin, *Wild Races of South Eastern India*, WH. Allen & Co, London, 1870, p.3.
20. Edward Tuite Dalton C.S.I, *Descriptive Ethnology of Bengal,* Office of the Superintendant of Government Printing, Calcutta, 1872, p.i.
21. C. J. Lyall, "Introduction" in P. R. T. Gurdon, *The Khasis*, Akansha Publishing House, New Delhi, 1906: reprint, 2010, p.xiii.
22. *Ibid.*
23. Edward Said, 'Opponents, Audiences, Constituencies and Community', in Mitchell, W. J. T. (ed.), *The Politics of Interpretation,* University of Chicago Press, Chicago,1983, p. 7.
24. Brojo Nath Shaha, *Grammar of the Lushai Language,* Bengal Secretariat Press, Calcutta, 1844, p. iii.
25. T. H. Lewin, *A Fly on the Wheel or How I Helped to Govern India,* T.R.I., Aizawl, 1912: reprint, 2005, p.284.
26. *Ibid.*, p.265.
27. Alexander Mackenzie, *The North-East Frontier of India*, Mittal Publications, Delhi, 1884: reprint, 1979, pp.288&289
28. T. H. Lewin, *Wild Races of South Eastern India, op.cit.*, p.269.s
29. Robert Reid, *The Lushai Hills*, Firma KLM Pvt. Ltd, Calcutta, 1942: reprint,1978, p.9.

30. J. Shakespear, *The Lushei Kuki Clans*, Spectrum Publications, Guwahati, 1912: reprint, 2004, p. 60.
31. *Ibid.*
32. R.A. Lorrain, *Five Years in Unknown Jungles: For God and Empire,* Lakher Pioneer Mission, London, 1912, p.108.
33. D. E. Jones, *A Missionary's Autobiography*, Liansailova Publication, Aizawl: 1998, p. 6
34. Grace R. Lewis, *op. cit.*, p.18.
35. David Spurr, *The Rhetoric of Empire*: *Colonial Discourse in Journalism, Travel Writing, and Imperial Administration,* Duke University Press, London, 1993, p.22
36. T. H. Lewin, *Wild Races of South Eastern India, op.cit.*, p.257.
37. N. E. Parry, *The Lakhers,* Firma K. L. M. Pvt. Ltd., Calcutta,1932: reprint, 1976, pp. 25-27.
38. *Pioneer*, 19 July 1870, reproduced in Alexander Mackenzie, *op.cit.*, p. 566.
39. Kyle Jackson, "Hearing images, tasting pictures: making sense of Christian mission photography in the Lushai Hills district, Northeast India (1870-1920)" in Maja Kominko (ed.), *From Dust to Digital: Ten Years of the Endangered Archives Programme,* Open Book Publishers, Cambridge, 2015, p. 471.
40. J. Shakespear, *op. cit.,* pp. 23-24.
41. C. B. 1, G-9, *Administration Report of the South Lushai Hills for 1898-1899*, Mizoram State Archive.
42. Grace R. Lewis, *op. cit.*, p.26.
43. Bertram S. Carey, & H. N. Tuck, *The Chin Hills,* Vol I., Tribal Research Institute, Aizawl, 1896: reprint, 1976, p. 165.
44. A. G. McCall, *Lushai Chrysalis,* Tribal Research Institute, Aizawl, 1949: reprint, 2003, p. 66.
45. John Stuart Mill, "Essays on Politics and Society" in J. M. Robson (ed), *Collected Works Of John Stuart Mill Volume Xviii*, Routledge&KeganPaul, London, 1977, p.120.

46. T. H. Lewin, *A Fly on the Wheel or How I Helped to Govern India, op.cit.*, pp.286-287.
47. For details, see Lallianzuali Chhangte, "Drinking Culture in the Traditional Mizo Society: Some Aspects" in *Proceedings of North East India History Association* 38th Session, Mirza, Kamrup, Assam, 2017.
48. Vanlalchhuanawma, *Christianity and Subaltern Culture*, ISPCK, Delhi, 2006: reprint, 2007. p. 207.
49. Frantz Fanon, *The Wretched of the Earth*, Translated by Constance Farrington, Grove Press, New York, 1963, p. 201.
50. N. B. Salazar, *op.cit.*, p. 173.

4

Khasi Films as Texts of Social History: Position of a Man

Marhunlang Kharwanlang

Introduction

The understanding and scope of history have undergone changes in the present day; new areas of history are opening up with new sources.[1] History is slowly moving away from its traditional moorings and no longer putting its focus only on the conventional study like that of politics, wars, battles, treaties; history is now moving to the study of society, culture, identity issues and also on themes that would provide an image on the way that life would unfold for the masses. For many years, the idea that films "might be worthy of attention as a medium for seriously representing the past was unthinkable."[2] Of late, historians are increasingly drawn to the study of films and social history. Now major journals like the American Historical Review and the Journal of American History devote sections to films.[3] Moreover, through the popularity of the films, "history, as seen on the screen, has reached a far wider audience than the writing of professional historians"[4] In his article, Hayden White discussed the close relationship between history and films. He termed the use of films for the study of history as "Historiophoty."[5] He says historiophoty is "the representation of history and our thought about it in visual images and filmic discourses."[6]

The study of social history has been an attraction among historians for the past several years. Of late, however, it is observed that the study of social history through films has become the latest trend. However, the use of films in the study of social history must be studied with caution. This is so because films, especially feature films, are made not with the purpose of being used as a study for academicians but rather as a source of entertainment for the public. Since it is a source of entertainment, fiction and imagination play a great role in their making. S. Barber wrote, "... however, despite their importance as social and cultural texts, all films must be interpreted cautiously."[7] Barber further adds that "all films offer insight into the period in which they were made, yet they must be considered as crafted and sculpted artefacts rather than as uncritical mirrors of contemporary culture."[8] However, it is also observed that films are indeed being used to study social history, and they also act as mediums of social change and spreading social awareness.[9]

Films as a medium of study for social history can also be applied to the study of North-East India in general and Meghalaya in particular since the region has a limited number of films dealing with various genres. Undoubtedly, northeast India is quite different from the rest of the country, even more, so the societies of the Khasi, and Garo of Meghalaya. This difference is because, unlike their neighbours in the rest of northeast India, their societies are matrilineal, and they have many customs and beliefs peculiar to them. Being a matrilineal society, the study of the position of women has been an attraction among many scholars. This article, however, attempts to study the position of a man in Khasi society as depicted in Khasi films.

Position of Woman

The position of the man in Khasi society is interlinked and woven side by side with the position of a woman. Therefore, one can only appreciate the man's position only after understanding the woman's position. The Khasi society is matrilineal, the descent is traced through the female line, and the property is passed from the mother to the youngest daughter, known as *Ka that duh*. The *Khatduh* is the inheritor and custodian of the ancestral property. However, the *Khatduh* is not a priestess, and hence she is in no position to perform the religious rituals and ceremonies. The duty of the *Khatduh* with regard to religious ceremonies and rituals is confined to the preparation of the things needed for the rituals.[10]

Being a matrilineal society, the position of a Khasi woman is 'better' than that of her counterparts in the patriarchal society. With regards to the position of Khasi women, Emmanuel Paul Philemon[11] wrote that the Khasi women enjoy a position of unusual dignity and importance.

Ostensibly, a Khasi woman enjoys certain liberties and is held in high regard in society. Maybe in certain areas, this might be so. Still, an in-depth study of the position of women in the Khasi Hills shows that they are not so different from their counterparts in the patriarchal society, either in the patriarchal society or in the modern-day Khasi society. Traditionally, it was seen that women were subjected to the rules and norms of the men in the society, be it her maternal uncles, brothers, husband and others. It is also observed that in any major decision-making in the household, the mother is consulted. However, the maternal uncles always make the final decision in traditional Khasi society, and in many households, the father takes the final decision in modern-day Khasi society.

Traditionally, in Khasi society, the mother holds an important position and is held in high regard by her children. However, authority and control are in the hands of the *Kni* or the maternal uncles. Though the *Khatduh* inherits the family property, she is only the custodian and the keeper of the house and the ancestral property, but she does not have the right to dispose of the property at will without the consent and counsel of the *Kni* and her brothers.

Further studies on the role of the *Khatduh* in Khasi society reveal that her responsibilities do not only stop with her parents but also extend to all her unmarried siblings, orphan of her sister/s, divorced/separated brothers or sister, as well as any family member who had fallen onto dire straits.

Position of the man

In the traditional Khasi society, a man has double roles in that he plays a father in his children's house and a maternal uncle in his sister's house. However, he is more inclined towards his sister's house. As a maternal uncle (*Kni*), he is responsible for his sister's children. Traditionally, the role of the maternal uncle is to protect and maintain the well-being of the members of a matrilineal group,

According to I. M. Syiem

The *Kni,* among other things, is the spiritual and moral guide for the sisters' children and, at times, even provides them should the need arise. His concern extends to adulthood when they are ready for marriage and even until death. He is the main spokesman in marriage negotiations between the two families concerned. He is also the major decision maker[12] The traditional roles of the *Kni* are very well reflected in the film by Kitbor W. Nongrum, 'Ka Ri Mon'.(1987) In this film, the maternal uncle of *Ka* Rimon, who is the main protagonist in the film, took major decisions and is involved in the affairs of his sister's house, even when the husband of the sister is there. This shows that the maternal uncle is highly respected in Khasi society, especially in the past. Later in the film, *Ka* Rimon was adopted by her maternal uncle following the death of her parents. It is observed that the film reflects the roles and duties of the maternal uncles in traditional Khasi society.

Adding to the above films, the film 'Manik Raitong', set in the traditional Khasi society, gives us an idea of what Khasi society was like in the past. The film portrays the Khasi society as a matrilineal one which was, however, dominated by men. Important decisions were always the sole preserve of men. For example, in the film, it was shown that the marriage of Lieng Makaw to *U Syiem* was decided by Lieng Makaw's maternal uncle, her father and *U Syiem*. The film shows the patriarchal values in Khasi society.

There is a change in the role of the maternal uncle in the present Khasi society. We see a shift from the maternal uncle to the father. A Khasi man in the present day is more involved in the affairs of his children rather than that of his nieces and nephews. Though the maternal uncle is still consulted in the major affairs of his sister's children, the final decision in any of these matters in many modern Khasi households is seen to be taken by the father and not the maternal uncle.

This changing role of the maternal uncle is reflected in another Khasi film, 'Onaatah- Of the Earth'; the role of the *Kni*, as reflected in this film, is very minimal. This film shows the changing position of the maternal uncle in present-day Khasi society. In the film, though the maternal uncle is shown comforting and caring for his sister's daughter, who is a rape survivor, major decision-making regarding Onaatah is taken by the father and not the maternal uncle. The father plays a significant role in the daughter's life throughout the film. Here we see the reflection of the changing position of the father and the maternal uncle in modern-day Khasi society.

What is interesting about the film 'Onaatah: Of the Earth' is that, besides Onaatah, there are no other main female characters. In her journey to rediscover life and to revive herself, the support that she got was mostly from male figures. In this film, it was quite apparent that the role of the father was given more importance.[13]

According to I. M. Syiem[14] the change in the position of the *Kni* in the Khasi society is due to the introduction of Christianity. She wrote,

> Where family values and authority are concerned, nowhere does the maternal uncle figure prominently in Christian teachings. Through marriage, a sacred institution, the husband becomes his family's social protector and authority figure. There have been mutual adjustments in culture and religion for first and even third-generation Christian converts.

Barnes L. Mawrie[15] gave many reasons for the decline in the position of the maternal uncle in his sister's house, which he termed as "Reasons for the decline of Kni-ship."[16] Mawrie divided the reasons into Exogenous factors, under which he included urbanisation, Christianity, the Influence of British rule, changing economy, the influence of Western individualism and liberalism and the impact of Western education and Endogenous factors, which he included dispersion of clan members, change in the institution of *khatduh* (youngest daughter who is also the heir and custodian of the ancestral property), cross-cultural marriages, educational disparity, economic disparity, diversity in religious creed and laxity in assuming their roles.[17]

Like any society in the world, the Khasi society is changing with time. These changes could be positive or negative; they are sometimes taken by filmmakers and used as themes in their films. It is a welcome sign that more and more films are being produced to ostensibly reflect the ethos of any given society at any given time. However, care must be exercised to ensure that depictions and reflections of such societies are as true as far as possible to a particular society at any particular time or context.

With the declining role of the maternal uncle in the modern period, there arose the importance of the father, which Barnes L Mawrie has stated in his book[18] as the rise of the "Kpa-ship'. This rise of kpa-ship in modern times is reflected in the film, 'Onaatah: of the Earth'. In this film, one can see the close relationship between the father and his daughters, especially his eldest daughter, Onaatah, who is also the main protagonist in the film. Furthermore, it can be seen in this film that major decisions regarding the daughters are not taken by the maternal uncle, who in the film is shown to play a lesser important role in his nieces' lives. This reflects the important shift from the maternal uncle to the father. The importance of the maternal uncles in the traditional Khasi society is not to say that the father has no role or no responsibility towards his children; in fact, the father is upheld in a respectable position as he is usually called "*U Kpa uba lah uba iai*" (the father who upholds everything)[19] In the present day, with the shift of power from the maternal uncle to the father, this does not mean that the maternal uncle or the *Kni* has completely lost all rights and respect in his sister's house, but it simply means that he is more involved with his children rather than his nieces and nephews. Furthermore, the *Kni* is almost always consulted when there is any major decision to be made in the modern day, but the father takes the final decision in modern-day Khasi society.

Wind of change is seen in many aspects of the Khasi society. As such, it is observed that there is a change in the modern Khasi society, even in terms of inheriting property, especially in the well-off society. Traditionally, the youngest daughter or the Khatduh, inherited all the ancestral property. Of late, however, in families where the parents can afford and are well-off, the property is distributed to all the children, both sons and daughters. However, the lion's share of the property is still given to the *Khatduh*.

Concerning the distribution of property among the Khasi, few Khasi films have been made with this theme as the centre of the storyline. The Doordarshan Kendra Shillong has produced several films aired on their channel. These films are usually made in a series of dramas and shown on the Doordarshan Kendra Shillong channel once a week. 'Balei Tang ia I Thei' is one such film directed by K. Kharlukhi. In a subtle manner, the film challenged the matrilineal system and the distribution of property among the Khasi. The film depicts the importance given to the daughters in the Khasi society and questions why the same importance is not given to the sons.

The film is about a family with two children, a son and a daughter. The two were treated differently by their parents from childhood to adulthood. In all matters, preferences were always given to the daughter. For example, the daughter was sent to school and later to a college; on the other hand, the son was made to drop out of school to take care of the chores in the house. The film questions the Khasi system of inheritance. Another feature Khasi film, 'Iaishah; The Fruit of Perseverance' (2008), directed by Lucky D. Kharsati, has a similar storyline to the one mentioned above. Like the commissioned film, 'Balei Tang ia I Thei?' (1988), this film also, in a very subtle manner, shows and questions the partial treatment given by parents to their children (daughters were more favoured by the parents). Again, just like in the film 'Balei Tang ia I Thei?' in this film, the youngest son, Kyrshan, was not given the same kind of treatment that was given to his sister from childhood to adulthood. His decisions regarding his own life were not favoured and supported by his parents. However, the parents supported the daughter in whatever decision she made. These two films bring out the frustration among Khasi men regarding the rules of inheritance and the favourable treatment of parents towards their daughters.

This frustration among the men in the Khasi society with regards to the distribution of family property which in most cases is only to the daughters, and the special treatment that daughters received from their parents is not only something that has been portrayed in films, but it is something that these films have taken from the reality of the society. The Maitshaphrang Movement started a movement on this, where they strongly opposed the distribution of properties only to the daughters. In their banners from the movement, which they have hung around the city of Shillong and its outskirts, they have put up this saying, "*Ngi mih na kaiju ka kph bale ba don tang iwei I nongioh? Ai byte ia ki khun baron lang, Cynthia bad syncing.*" ("We come from the same womb, why is there only one inheritor? Pass down your properties to all your children, male and female.") While some Khasi men have shown their frustration with the age-old tradition among the Khasi by objecting to the inheritance of property, others have altogether challenged the whole matrilineal system of the Khasi.

A challenge to the Khasi matrilineal system can be traced back to the 1960s when the organisation known as Ka Seng Iktiar Longbriew Manbriew was formed with its main objective as the dissemination of patrilineal descent, inheritance and succession. The leaders of this movement tried to persuade the people of their objectives by publishing articles in the local newspaper and distributing booklets; they also organised seminars and discussions to propagate the objectives of their organisation and to persuade the masses that matriliny is no longer functional in the modern age.[20] This movement, however, proved to be futile.

Matriliny in the Khasi hills was again challenged by the foundation of another movement in 1990 called Ka Syngkhong Rympei Thymmai, meaning New Family System. This challenge can be seen in the objectives of the movement, which are laid down as under

1. To empower the father of the family to be the head of his own wife and children and that his wife should be his strong support.
2. The family's lineage should henceforth be from the father's side and no longer from the mother.
3. That the family property be equally divided among the sons and daughters, however, the daughter will lose her share of the property if she marries a non-Khasi.
4. That the family's eldest son will assume the responsibility of looking after the parents.
5. If the wife is harassed and persecuted by her husband, the woman's parents or brothers and sisters have the right to recall her. She has the right to be protected by her relatives. Any man who leaves his wife has an obligation to look after her well-being until she is married to another person and has her own family.[21]

Interestingly, in another documentary film titled 'Khasi Women Wisdom', which is in the form of interviews, whereby some Khasi men and women were interviewed. These interviewees, when asked by the interviewer about the position held by Khasi men and women in the society, they were of the same view that the status of the men and women in the Khasi society is equal. Adding to this, one of the interviewees (a female) commented that though she is an only daughter, all her brothers were also given some share of the family property and that times are changing, and there is no longer any distinction between sons and daughters. She further added that though the youngest daughter still gets the lion's share of the property, especially the ancestral property, her siblings do get some smaller shares. However, as mentioned earlier, this is the case only in well-off families who can afford to do so. In other cases where the parents have little property, only the youngest daughter gets a share of the family property.

In the short documentary film titled 'The Mei and Khuns of Meghalaya: Matriliny and Gender Relations in the Khasi Society' (2018), one of the interviewees in the film commented that with the wind of change that has swept the Khasi society, one of the changes is the inheritance of the family property which is no longer rigid, to her, in modern times it is not necessary for the youngest daughter or *Ka Khatduh* to inherit the property, but the property can be inherited by any of the children male or female, whoever is willing to look and care for the parents in their old age. Again, such cases are exceptional only to some. Though some Khasi families practise this, it is not accepted and adopted by the majority. Especially in families that still hold on to the age-old practices and traditions, the youngest daughter always inherits the ancestral property.

The position of men in Khasi society is changing with time. With such changes, frustration among men, especially with regard to the unequal distribution of property, has started surfacing. What is interesting is that films are used as one of the ways to channel this frustration. What is even more interesting is the fact that some of the films which highlight such issues are directed by female directors.

Notes

1. For further details, see Peter Miskell, "Historians and Films", in Peter Lambert and Phillip Schofields (eds.), *Making History,* Routledge, Oxon, 2006, pp.245- 256.
2. Robert A. Rosenstone, *Visions of the Past,* Harvard University Press, London, 1995, p.2
3. *Ibid.*
4. Peter Miskell, *op. cit.*, p.245.
5. Hayden White, "Historiography and Historiophoty" in *The American Historical Review*, Vol.93, No.5(Dec. 1988), pp. 1193-1199, http://www.jstore.org/stable/1873534, accessed 03-10-2019.
6. *Ibid.*
7. S. Barber, "Films and Cultural History", in *The British Film Industries in the 1970s*, Palgrave Macmillan, London. Accessed on http://doi.org/10.1057/9781137365923.2
8. *Ibid.*
9. See Chaitali Wadhwa, "Cinema as a Medium of Social Change", in *QRIUS,* April 6, 2014. Also see Archana Sharma, "Role of Cinema in Creating Social Awareness" presented at a conference: Mass Media: Current Scenario and Future Trends at Chandigarh University, Punjab, India, Volume 1.
10. Hiyo Sutnga, *The Role of the Mother in the Khasi Family,* M. Phil Dissertation (unpublished), North-Eastern Hill University, Department of Khasi, 2001, p. 55.
11. Emanuel Paul Philemon, *Meghalaya: Land of Matrilineal Lineage,* ISPCK Publication, Delhi, 2011.

12. I. M. Syiem, "Khasi Matriliny in Transition", in Margaret B. Challam (ed.), *Dynamics of Family System in a Matriliny of Meghalaya,* printed at Directorate of Printing and Stationery, Meghalaya,1999, p.31.
13. Marhunlang Kharwanlang, "Representation of Women in Khasi Films: The Case of 'Onaatah- of the Earth", *Proceedings of NEIHA*, 38th session, D. K. Girls' College, Mirza, 2017, pp.380-381.
14. *Ibid.*
15. Barnes L. Mawrie, *From Maternal Uncle to Father: An Anthropological Study on Changing patriarchy among the Khasis,* Vendrame Institute Publication, Shillong, 2015.
16. *Ibid.*
17. *Ibid.,* pp. 138-160. Also see A. N. Passah, "Matriliny in Meghalaya: At the Crossroads? – Some Insights", *op. cit.,* pp.182-190.
18. *Ibid.*
19. *Ibid*, p.182.
20. V. Pakyntein, "Dynamics of Gender Roles in Khasi-Pnar Matrilineality", in R. Khongsdier and Sarthak Sengupta (eds.), *People of North-East India: Bio-Cultural Dimension,* Kalpaz Publication, Delhi, 2017, p.57.
21. *Ibid.*

5

Women's Wings of Christian Missions in Khasi-Jaiñtia Society

Rishababiang L. Nonglait

The subject understudy focuses on *Ka Jingiaseng Kynthei* or the 'Women's Wings of the Church' in Khasi-Jaiñtia Society. These women's wings are part and parcel of church organisation and exist in many Protestant and Catholic churches in Khasi and Jaintia Hills. We must keep in mind that the nineteenth-century. Khasi-Jaintia society witnessed tremendous change in the socio-cultural dimension. It was a period where foreign Christian missions made their way into the Khasi society by asserting their influence; and the impact of the denominations continued in the subsequent centuries. The period was also accompanied by the growing consciousness of the people through education and external exposures that changed their worldviews. Interestingly, these women's wings were inclusive of women by propagating their support for women welfare and well-being and also by permitting women to form organisations within their fold. This course of action prevented an internal schism and was eventually endorsed by the women. For instance, *Ka Jingiaseng Kynthei* within the Welsh Khasi-Jaiñtia Presbyterian Church carried out their activities in the late 1840's but gained popularity only from 1899 onwards.

Several works that have been done on Presbyterian and Catholic Christian missions which however have failed to encompass the roles of women's wings in the church.[1] Hence, this paper aims to highlight the origin of the women's wings, to ascertain the purpose of their formation and to examine their roles and activities. On paper and in principles, it seems this women organisation was formed for empowering women in spiritualty and religious activities, however, a close examination of church papers (published) indicates otherwise. This wing gradually from sewing to knitting training for women for their empowerment through independent earning gradually became a tool in the evangelical mission. Hence the paper debates this dichotomy especially about the role of the women's wings of the church.

Ka Jingiaseng Kynthei of the Presbyterian Church in Khasi and Jaintia Hills

In 1843, Rev. William Lewis and Mrs. Mary Lewis joined the mission and were entrusted to supervise schools. Mr. Lewis was in charge with education of the boys and Mrs. Lewis in educating and training young girls and women. In February 1849, the first women prayer fellowship was held at Nongsawlia.[2] Initially it started as a women's fellowship with just a handful of the newly converted Christian women who often gathered together for Bible studies, prayer meetings and group counselling. The first unit of *Ka Jingiaseng Kynthei* was started in the Church of Nongsawlia under the leadership of Mrs. Sidney Margret Roberts (1871-1896), a missionary wife of Dr. John Roberts.[3] From 1849-1888, *Ka Jingiaseng Kynthei* functioned only within the jurisdiction of individual churches and were under the supervision of the women missionaries and missionary wives with the aim 'to involve the women of the church in their mission.[4] Miss Annie Wozencraft Thomas (1897-1965), a woman missionary, became a trail blazer in the formation of women's wings in Mawkhar, Laban, Ri Bhoi, Ri War sub-districts and other Presbyterian churches.[5]

In 1899, *Ka Jingiaseng Kynthei* held its first meeting at Umsaitjain Mawlai Presbytery Shillong and about 300 women attended the meeting and it was chaired by selected women.[6] In 1927, women delegates selected from *Ka Jingiaseng Kynthei* were made members of the Khasi-Jaiñtia Presbyterian Assembly.[7] Once a year, the Church Assembly was usually held for three days in pre-arranged churches. In addition, church leaders and the office bearers of *Ka Jingiaseng Kynthei* Khasi-Jaiñtia Assembly organised separate meetings and sessions. In the Women's Assembly, the meeting was presided by the chairman in the presence of the secretary, treasurer and women delegates of the presbyteries. They discussed various matters relating to different programmes carried out by *Ka Jingiaseng Kynthei*, such as report of *Khawkham*[8] sub-committee from different presbyteries, report of temperance (fight against alcohol abuse), etc. There was also a discussion on the appeal to the secretary of the General Assembly and the male members to allow the women delegates to participate in the Holy Sacrament of Communion and other matters relating to women and church affairs.[9]

Eventually, from 1953 onwards, the *Jingiaseng Kynthei* was expanded into other local Churches in sub-districts and in Presbyteries under the supervision of the Assembly. The highest Church Court known as the 'Synod' was renamed 'Assembly' and the Constituent Assemblies were called Synod in 1953. Therefore, the 'Khasi-Jaiñtia Presbyterian Assembly' was renamed as Khasi-Jaiñtia Presbyterian Synod and from 1954-2001, Ki Jingiaseng Kynthei were unified under the

'Khasi-Jaiñtia Presbyterian Synod.' The first Jingiaseng Kynthei Synod meeting was in 1954, at Laitkynsew and since then it was organised annually at a selected church. Ka Jingiaseng Kynthei Synod carried out similar activities as the Assembly i.e., to conduct prayer meetings, counselling and the like. It undertook new resolutions to set up sub-committees and funds for *Ka Seng Sang-Kiad* (anti-alcohol unit) and funds for the poor.[10]

In March 1965, at a meeting held in Mairang, the members of *Ka Jingiaseng Kynthei* of the Khasi-Jaiñtia Presbyterian Synod realised the need to form a new constitution and they unanimously agreed to form a sub-committee to do so. The new constitution was adopted in 1973 with the fundamental objectives as follows to: (i) build and strengthen the spiritual life of women in the church (ii) create a feeling of solidarity amongst women and "unity in God and the Saviour Jesus Christ" (iii) propagate the Gospel of Christ through evangelism and contributions according to one's capacity (iv) eliminate evils from the church and society such as the abuse of Alcohol and so on.[11] *Ka Jingiaseng Kynthei* agreed to revise the constitution in 1994 yet kept the 'fundamental objectives' untouched, and it was drafted by the Executive Committee. In 1995, it was approved by the Synod.[12] Gradually in 2002, the Khasi Jaiñtia Presbyterian Synod was then bifurcated into the Khasi Jaiñtia Presbyterian Synod Mihngi (East) and the Khasi Jaiñtia Presbyterian Synod Sepngi (West). This resulted in creation of two Jingiaseng Kynthei Synods, one in eastern and the other in the western regions. The two constituent synods came under the supervision of the Khasi-Jaiñtia Assembly.[13]

Activities

In 1908 an initiative to collect *U Khawkham* was started by the Presbyterian Church Laitumkhrah in which a handful of uncooked rice is stored daily as a donation to the church. It is then collected from each household by persons appointed by the *Jingiaseng Kynthei* of the local Church after few months. The collected rice is then sold and the funds received are collected by the *Jingiaseng Kynthei Synod.* Nonetheless, the total fund is submitted to and managed by the Synod Rangbah (the main body of the Khasi-Jaiñtia Presbyterian Synod) till 1985. Originally, the funds were utilised for setting up and maintaining of primary schools. Eventually, five percent of the collected funds were allocated to the *Ka Jingiaseng Kynthei* for the purpose of strengthening its evangelical mission and also to support teachers, Bible men/women and missionaries in their different fields and in allocating grants to mission schools.[14]

Furthermore, from the collected sources we found evidence about the role of the *Jingiaseng Kynthei* in social services among the Khasi-Jaintia people. Effosrt were made to initiate social work activities such as the eradication of alcoholism, drug and opium addiction too and this came in the form of a Temperance movement which started towards the end of 1909 at Nongsawlia church. It was initiated by Miss. Hughes and other Khasi women including T. Shullai, Lariam Khongwir, Hilda Bhajur and K. Kharsati. In 1965, *Ka Seng Sang Kyiad* was formed with resolutions to educate people to stop voting members to the State legislative Assembly and members to the District Councils who indulge in alcohol and to organise a protest in front of the Meghalaya Chief Minister's office, to oppose the government's issuance of Liquor licences. However, the Khasi-Jaiñtia Presbyterian Synod disapproved of the resolutions undertaken and it had to be withdrawn.[15] A committee for the abolition of alcohol consumption and production was held on 8th March 1966 and the *Ka Jingiaseng Kynthei* wrote a memorandum to the Chief Minister to close down the production of alcohol in Khasi-Jaiñtia

Hills.[16] This was also carried out for the Government to pressure the Supreme Court to implement the Excise Act in the Khasi-Jaiñtia Hills.[17] The *Seng Sang Kyiad* collaborated with the *Ka Seng Pynduh Kyiad U Khasi Jaiñtia Hills*, a social organisation formed to encourage Christians of other denominations, non-Christians, along with a few Khasi Chiefs to unite in the fight against the alcohol nuisance. In 1984, the Synod permitted the *Ka Jingiaseng Kynthei Jowai Ri War Presbytery* to write to the excise minister through the Members of the State legislative Assembly, to reduce the licensing of illicit alcohol sellers.[18] As a result, in this battle against alcohol, counselling Centres were opened in 1995. The Temperance organiser, Paila Pariat of the *Ka Jingiaseng Kynthei*, called on the need for counselling centres to counsel, teach and to cater proper and necessary aid to the addicts that will help them to quit alcohol abuse. Two centres were opened, one in Shillong with Pariat as the counsellor and one in Jowai with Q. Giri as the counsellor. People belonging to different churches, groups and non-Christians as well who needed help visited these centres.

In 1968, the Welsh missionaries handed over the administration of the two Mission hospitals to the Synod. As, reported in 1967, that the *Jingiaseng Kynthei*, contributed monetary help from donations, fetes etc., to the building of the nurses' hostel of the 'Khasi Jaiñtia Presbyterian Hospital' and also to buy an ultrasonogram.[19] Hence, in 1970, it embarked on creation of funds for the two mission hospitals, one in Shillong and the other in Jowai. A hospital committee was formed in the Synod and Presbyteries, also a representative from the *Jingiaseng Kynthei Synod* was selected to be a member of the managing Committee of the Mission hospital in Shillong. The different presbyteries often scheduled for annual hospitals visits. Fetes were frequently organised to raise funds to help the hospitals. Due to lack of nurses at the hospitals, the *Jingiaseng Kynthei* appealed to the Synod to create opportunities for young women who have cleared their High School Exams (H.S.LC) and even under matriculation students to be trained in the nursing schools of the hospitals and certificates to be issued by the Synod after the programme, so that they could be of service to the hospitals.[20]

There were also other projects undertook by the *Jingiaseng Kynthei* including the Project Thaiñjaiñ (Weaving and Knitting Project) at Lalmati, Assam which began with the appointment of a bible-man to one of the church districts at 'Tynhor' (Rambrai Presbytery) to work amongst the Rabha community in Lalmati, Athiabari, Assam, in 1984. From 1990 onwards, the Jingiaseng Kynthei supplied the materials and machines for the start-up of the weaving project and appeal was sent to all Jingiaseng Kynthei districts and presbyteries, to contribute to this initiative. Harking to the calls, many women donated sizeable amounts of monetary donation to the project. The objective was to help the Rabha women and families who had been ostracised and abandoned by their families. In 1994, the cloths were woven according to the instructions of *Ka Jingiaseng Kynthei Synod* and were brought to Shillong for sale during the Synod gathering. The profit gained was invested to expand the project. In 1998, a church was constructed for the Rabha Community. It must be mentioned that in 1997, the *Jingiaseng Kynthei* also formed the Children's Ministry which played a major role in teaching and instructing the children in the Church.[21]

Ka Jingiasyllok Seng Kynthei of the Catholic Church in Khasi Hills

It is one of the Church units that are concerned with the well-being of women members within the Parish. All women communicants undertake a pledge at the altar through the 'holy communion', in the presence of the '*Lyngdoh*' or priest and the Church congregation as witnesses. Thus, it is the duty of the members to fulfil their duties as bestowed by the Seng Kynthei. It was founded on 1st April 1934 with Father Vendrame as its founding father. There were 20 women who readily and enthusiastically responded to Father Vendrame's counsel.[22] The foundation of the *Jingiasyllok Seng Kynthei* was encouraged by the then Archbishop Louis Mathais, Archbishop Stephan Fernando, Father Joseph Foglia and Father Peter Tonello.[23]

On the 1st April 1934, a committee was held and the following women were selected as the first committee members: (i) President- Laurentia Kormai Nongkhlaw (ii) Secretary-Maria Dingmon Dynpep (iii) Assistant Secretary-Rosa Synnah (iv) Counsellors- Paulina Bisha Suting and Regina Desi Rani. Along with thirteen other council members. Madame Pieroz[24] was the Spiritual Adviser of the Council. Since its inception she had been a motherly figure in helping the *Seng Kynthei* Council. The women had to pay a membership fee of Rs. 2/- anna per month, for the purpose of conducting the Holy Communion usually on the last week or fourth week of every month and also in remembrance of the 5 departed communicants. This *Ka Jingiasyllok Seng Kynthei* soon expanded, and was set up in other parishes and villages.[25]

When they first started the women were initially inexperienced, and were few in number, but their efforts and dedication and the guidance and supervision of *Ki Kpa Mynsiem* (Spiritual Father) and Father Vendrame, led to the *Seng Kynthei* sreading roots in local village Churches in the outskirts of Shillong. The motive of the Church to establish the *Seng Kynthei Katholik* was to teach Catholic women to love God and their neighbours, by living a good Christian life and being an example to others, to teach and guide their own children and lead them through the Christian Teachings. They were encouraged to be helpful to their neighbours or other people in times of peace and especially in difficult and trying times in their lives.

The *Seng Kynthei Katholik*, Cathedral Parish, Shillong is responsible in unifying all the members of the Seng. It is under the supervision and regulation of the priests; hence it is not independent. The first role is to organise '*ritrit*' or retreats which were frequently held every year during '*por len* 'or fasting period before the crucifixion of Christ and the themes were selected in relation to it. It also organises seminars generally before the yearly celebration of the *Ka Jingiasyllok Seng Kynthei Katholik* and well-known speakers were often invited to give their talks usually on themes in the societal context, such as its welfare and well-being, '*ka Hok Longbriew Manbriew*' or rights as humans, the relationship between the Seng Kynthei and the Church. *The Seng Kynthei* on Christmas Eve would visit orphanages and children's homes bearing donations, gifts of food and clothing. It often helps and supports fellow Church members in times of need, such as financial strains or ill health. The *Jingiasyllok Seng Kynthei Katholik* Laitumkhrah Cathedral Parish lends help to a night school, for underprivileged students and domestic helpers which is administered and managed by the *Synjuk Ki Seng Kynthei Katholik* (Council of Catholic Women, Shillong Archdiocese). It organised fundraising programmes, house visits to fellow members' homes taking along with them food items and snacks to partake with the family after a prayer meeting, visits the Shillong District Jail to counsel the inmates.[26]

The *Jingiasyllok Seng Kynthei Katholik* meetings are usually held once a month, to set goals and resolutions to (i) organise special prayers for all communicants and Church members and other deceased members (ii) collect donations and membership fees in the process of becoming communicants of the Catholic Church.[27] Its members not only volunteer for Church work or in counselling and helping fellow members, some of the members donated their land and property to the Church. When a fire broke out in 1936 and reduced the Laitumkhrah Catholic Church to ashes, the *Seng Kynthei Katholik* were at the forefront donating money, in whatever way they could. There used to be an old age home for the elderly known was 'St Vincent' earlier located at the present-day Nazareth Hospital and the women of the *Seng Kynthei* frequently visited the aged. The *Seng Kynthei* also helped in administering and teaching the Bible, counselling and praying for the spiritually weaker members, visiting the sick either at home or the hospitals.[28]

Thus from the above presentations we can understand that *Ka Jingiaseng Kynthei* of the Presbyterian Church was founded either because of the positive intervention, support and encouragement of men or because of the women's consciousness on the need of forming a women's wings. It emerged because obligated duty to help the converted Christians. However, through the years the women's wings have become more involved in other activities such as opening of schools, raising funds for the different missions and for the welfare of their congregation members. Some women's wings have evolved from performing religious activities to providing social services to their community and society in general. Two examples of the women's wings that transcended beyond the walls of the church include the Presbyterian Women's Social Welfare Organisation (PWSWO) of the Jingiaseng Presbyterian Church Mission Compound Jowai and the Thadlaboh Presbyterian Women Social Welfare Organisation of the Jingiaseng Kynthei Ladthadlaboh Presbyterian Church, Jowai. They extended their services to the local community particularly women and children and registered themselves under the local Registrar of Societies so that they could avail governmental aids and assistances for the people and communities in need. Additionally, both these organisations run and administer their respective crèches to lessen the burdens of working women and night schools for the under privilege.

The Presbyterian has permitted and encouraged women to participate in the Church, but with some exceptions, they are yet to recognise or acknowledge women's rights, to be ordained as pastors, priests and deacons of the Church. Moreover, the authority to decide on important matters lies in the hands of the advisers and elders who are generally pastors or deacons of the church and without the approval of the male religious hierarchy, e.g., the *Jingiaseng Kynthei* is not an independent unit, for at every level, local church, District, Presbytery, or Synod, advisers are usually appointed to assist the group on any matter. Hence, it cannot take independent decisions, even if it does, the decision has to be scrutinised and undertaken on the advice and approval of male elders. Examining the disposition of the women's wings one can clearly see that the Presbyterian church is a male dominated organisation. Women members on the other hand, play a more subservient role.

Ka Jingiasyllok Seng Kynthei Katholik too cannot proceed ahead with their meetings without the Spiritual Adviser present in their midst. Here, one notices the paradox, women are allowed to freely participate in Church activities but when it comes to important matters, women are not permitted to act alone and take independent decisions. Apparently, one must bear in mind that the Church is a patriarchal institution, However, this misconception cannot be entirely blamed on the males, Christian women themselves, as a matter of fact, feel that men are better equipped and suited for the role of administering religious and Church duties and most women are more than happy with the arrangements. The younger generation Christians and feminist theologians are questioning such views and practices.

In conclusion we may say that the cultural milieu of the early nineteenth century Khasi-Jaiñtia society played a determinant role in the emergence, role and growth of Women Wings in the churches of both Presbyterians and Catholics. Initially, the *Jingiaseng Kynthei* and the *Jingiasyllok Seng Kynthei Katholik* were only concerned with organising prayer meetings and counselling women. Today, their women's wings can be found in every Khasi-Jaiñtia Presbyterian Church and Catholic Church and coordinate their activities as per directed instructions. Ultimately, these women's wing, their only desire is to ensure that the upcoming generation of women in particular and the society in general should be more inclusive of women i.e., in the Church and other organisations.

Notes

1. For more readings on this see, John Hughes Morris, *The History of the Welsh Calvinistic Methodists Foreign Mission to the end of the year 1904*, C.M. Book Room, Wales, 1910; Nalini Nataranjan, *The Missionary among the Khasis*, Sterling Publishers Pvt. Ltd., New Delhi, 1977; Frederick Downs, *History of Christianity in India, Volume V, Part 5, North East India in the Nineteenth and Twentieth centuries*, The Church History Association of India, Bangalore, 1992; O. L. Snaitang, *Christianity and Social Change in North East India: A Study of the role of Christianity in Social Change among the Khasi-Jaiñtia Hill Tribes of Meghalaya*, Firma KLM Private Limited Calcutta, Vendrame Institute Shillong, 1993; Frederick Downs, *The Christian impact on the Status of women in North-east India. Professor H.K.*

Barpujari Endowment Lectures, North-Eastern Hill University Publications, Shillong, 1996; Sebastian Karotemprel, *The Catholic Church in Northeast India: 1890 – 1990*, Vendrame Institute, Shillong, 1993; C. Becker, *History of the Catholic missions in northeast India 1890-1915*, translated & edited by G. Stadler and S. Karotemprel, Firma KLM, Calcutta, 1980; T. B. Subba, Joseph Puthenpurakal and Shaji Joseph Puykunnel (eds.) *Christianity and Change in Northeast India*, Concept Publishing Company, New Delhi, 2009; George Maleikal, *History of the Catholic Church Among the Khasis*, Don Bosco, Shillong, 2005.

2. Maurice G. Lyngdoh, *Ka History Ka Balang Presbyterian Ri Khasi-Jaiñtia*, Bluebell Warjri, Shillong, 2000, p.69.
3. T. Nongsiej, *Ka Kam U Blei ha ka Mawphlang-Khadsawphra Presbytery (1896-1949) Shillong*, 1984, pp. 96-97.
4. Emeralda Rynjah, "The Activities of the Women's Wing of the Khasi Jaiñtia Presbyterian Synod and the Role of women in the Church and Society," in *Centenary Celebration ka Jingiaseng Kynthei K.J.P. Synod 1899-1999*, Souvenir, Mawkhar Presbyterian Church, Shillong, 1999 December 16-19, p.15.
5. J. Meirion Lloyd, (ed.) *Nine Missionary Pioneers: The Story of Nine pioneering missionaries in North-east India*, Mission Board, Wales, 1989, pp.31-37.
6. Information gathered from an interaction with (L) Ivory Knight, the former Secretary of the *Jingiaseng Kynthei Synod* (1986) at her residence in Saitsohpen Sohra on 22.08. 2019 12: 30 pm IST.
7. "Ka Jingiaseng Kynthei 1927 L'ber 10-13," in *Ka Report Shaphang ki Kam bad ki Rai jong ka Assembli kaba Lai, jong ka Balang Presbiterian ha Ri Khasi-Synteng kaba la long ha Shillong*, Ri-Khasi Press, Shillong, p.12.
8. a donation program in which a handful of rice was collected from all households of the church.

9. "Ka Report jong ka Jingiaseng Kynthei Ka Assembly 1929-1953," in *Ka Balang Presbyterian ha Ri Khasi- Jaiñtia, Ki report Ka Assembly from the year 1929-1953*, published by the Assembly, Ri Khasi Press, Shillong, n.p.
10. "Ka Report na ka Jingiaseng Kynthei (1954-1964) Khasi bad Jaiñtia Synod," in *Ka Balang Presbyterian ha Ri Khasi-Jaiñtia ka report jong ka Synod 1954-1964*. K.J.P. Synod, Ri Khasi Press, Shillong, n. p.
11. "Ka Report ka Jingiaseng Kynthei K.J.P. Synod kaba la long ha Nongsawlia ha ki Tarik 7th-11th March 1973," in *Ka Balang Presbyterian ha Ri Khasi Jaintia, Ka Report jong Ka Synod kaba Arphew ha Ha ka Rukom Synshar bad Pyniaid kaba Thymmai kaba long ha ka Balang Nongsawlia March 7-11 1973*, the Presbyterian Church in North East India, Khasi Jaintia Presbyterian Press, Shillong, 1973, p.66.
12. "Ka Jingiaseng Kynthei K.J.P Synod 1995 March 8-12," in *Ka Balang Presbyterian ha Ri Khasi Jaiñtia, Ka Report jong Ka Synod kaba Arphew Ar ha Ha ka Rukom Synshar bad Pyniaid kaba Thymmai kaba long ha ka Balang Mylliem*, Shillong Ri War Presbytery, Khasi Jaiñtia Synod, Ri Khasi Jaiñtia Press, Shillong, p. 83.
13. "Ka Jingiaseng Kynthei K.J.P Synod 1995 March 8-12," in *Ka Balang Presbyterian ha Ri Khasi Jaiñtia, Ka Report jong Ka Synod kaba Arphew Ar ha Ha ka Rukom Synshar bad Pyniaid kaba Thymmai kaba long ha ka Balang Mylliem*, Shillong Ri War Presbytery, Khasi Jaiñtia Synod, Ri Khasi Jaiñtia Press, Shillong, p. 83.
14. Budon, "Ka History Lyngkot bad ki Kam Jong Ka Jingiaseng Kynthei lyngba kine ki Snem," in *Dosquicentennial Jubilee Souvenir of the Presbyterian Church in Khasi-Jaiñtia Hills, Meghalaya 1841-2016,* Vanrica Printing Press, Mawkhar Shillong, 2016, p.47.
15. "Ka Report ka jingiaseng Kynthei (1972 March 15-19) K.J.P. Synod kaba la long ha Mawphlang 16-19 March 1972," in *Ka*

Balang Presbyterian ha Ri Khasi-Jaiñtia Ka Report Jong Ka Synod kaba Khad Khyndai ha ka Rukom Synshar bad pyniaid kaba Thymmai kaba la long ha Mawphlang, Ri Khasi-Jaiñtia Press, Shillong, p.79.

16. Copies of the letter were also sent to the Bishop of the Catholic Church, Secretary of the 'Seng Khasi', Chief Executive Member of the District Council and to a few Members of the State Legislative Assembly.
17. "Ka Report Committee kaba Pyrkhat Shaphang kaba Pynduh Kiad (1966 March 8-11)," in *Ka Balang Presbyterian ha Ri Khasi-Jaiñtia, Ka Report Jong Ka Synod kaba Khadlai ha ka Rukom Synshar bad pyniaid kaba Thymmai kaba la long ha Mawkhar*, Ri Khasi-Jaiñtia Press, Shillong, p.13.
18. A recommendation was also sent to the Synod general body to; (i) appeal to the government to implement a law prohibiting youths below 20 years of age to consume alcohol (ii) ban the black marketing, selling of liquor at restaurants, markets, in localities and villages (iii) install sign boards on the roadside emphasising the evil consequences of alcohol. See, "Ka Report Lyngkot Ka Jingiaseng Kynthei K.J.P. Synod Kaba La Long ha Balang Nongpyndeng ha ki Tarik 7th-11th March 1984," in *Ka Balang Presbyterian ha Ri Khasi Jaintia Ka Report Jong Ka Synod Kaba Laiphew Wei ha ka Rukom Synshar bad Pyniaid Thymmai kaba la long ha Nongpyndeng (Sub-District Nongstoin) Nongstoin Presbytery March 7-11 1984*, The Presbyterian Church of North-East India, Khasi Jaintia Presbyterian Press, Shillong, 1984, p.70.
19. P. Lamare, "A Review of the 75 years in the life of the Khasi-Jaiñtia Presbyterian Synod Hospital" in *Platinum Jubilee Souvenir of the Khasi-Jaintia Presbyterian Synod Hospital*, Ri Khasi Press, Shillong, 1997, pp.26-27.
20. "Ka Jingiaseng Kynthei Synod Report 1988 March 9-13," in *Ka Balang Presbyterian ha Ri Khasi-Jaiñtia Ka Report Jong Ka Synod kaba Laiphew san ha ka Rukom Synshar bad pyniaid kaba*

Thymmai kaba la long ha ka Balang Nongsawlia Sohra Presbytery, Khasi-Jaiñtia Press, Shillong, p. 96.

21. Q. Giri, "Ka Jingtrei ka Jingiaseng kynthei haka kam Temperance and counselling," in the *Centenary Celebration Jingiaseng Kynthei K.J.P. Synod 1899-1999 Souvenir, December 16-19*, Mawkhar Presbyterian Church Shillong, 1999 p.35.
22. H. A. Mihsuk Nongrum, "Editorial," in *Ka Synjat Sah Kynmaw Seng Kynthei Katholik Cathedral Parish, Laitumkhrah Shillong, Motto: Shakri ia ka Balang bad ka Jaitbynriew 1934-2009*, Platinum Jubilee Souvenir, Shillong, 2009, n.p, p.1.
23. Ophilia Dkhar, "Ka Report Jong Ka Seng Kynthei Katholik Cathedral Parish," in *Ka Synjat Sah Kynmaw Seng Kynthei Katholik Cathedral Parish, Laitumkhrah, Shillong, Platinum Jubilee Souvenir*, Shillong 2009, n.p, p.12.
24. She was fondly known as 'Mem Pero' wife of Mr. Pieroz. They were both devout Catholics who came to Shillong from Switzerland in the 1920s and they were the founders of the Pinewood Hotel Shillong that was opened in 1928. They were not just religious followers but were strong pillars and supporters of the Catholic Church. They were also close friends of Archbishop Mathais the first bishop and Archbishop Ferrando the second bishop of Shillong till 1956, when Mr. Pieroz returned to Switzerland after selling off the hotel to the government of Assam.
25. *Ibid.*, Fr. C. Vendrame, SC, "Ka Report na u Parish Priest Laitumkhrah Parish, December 1938," (sent to the bishop) p.4.
26. Ophilia Dkhar, *op. cit.*, pp. 13-15.
27. *Constitution Ka Jingiaseng Kynthei Katholik, Cathedral Parish Laitumkhrah*, Shillong, n.p.
28. Martina Bon Marbaniang, (Senior member of the *Seng Kynthei*) and Flora Ranee (5th President, Seng Kynthei Cathedral Parish, 1962-1968, "Ki Longkmie Nongmait Phang ka Seng Kynthei Balang Katholik,"

6

Traditional Medicine Men and Their Methods of Healing: A Study on the Lotha Naga

Adeno N Kithan

Introduction

Even before humans appeared on the earth, diseases already existed among beasts. Fossils, bones, and teeth tell the tragic tale of a pre-historic human succumbing to various diseases. Forrest E. Clements[1] in his pioneering paper on "Primitive Concepts on Disease" in 1932 drew out the theories of illness where he stated that the explanations of illnesses in the context were rooted in primitive religion. Relatively, we have Edward B. Tylor[2] with his convictions in his "Primitive Culture", who opines that religion itself was derived from the concepts of diseases. This understanding of religion and its close association with disease, illness and treatment provides a deeper understanding of the behaviour and reaction of the people living in a particular society. The theories on illness were based on criteria developed in part from modern medical science and in part from anthropological theory. One would come across the basic dichotomy in these theories: the theories of natural causation and supernatural causation. However, over the years, a germ, toxin or gene is held to account for most ailments, while the importance of predisposition, bodily constitution, and social or environmental circumstances has diminished.[3]

The first physicians, therefore, were humans; over time, a traditional healing system developed; this includes the first medicine they used and their instinctive attempts at self-healing by licking, sucking and blowing on their lesions. When these individual reactions became stereotyped, the ritual became as important as the treatment. Tools formerly used as weapons began to make incisions and trepanations. Licking and sucking were replaced by bloodletting, scarification, amputation, and surgery with stone tools.[4] Hence we may say that "Traditional Healing is the oldest form of structured medicine, that is, a medicine with an underlying philosophy and set of principles by which it is practised. It is the medicine from which all later forms of medicine developed, including Chinese medicine, Graeco-Arabic medicine and modern Western medicine. Traditional Healing was originally an integral part of semi-nomadic and agricultural tribal societies, and although archaeological evidence for its existence dates back to only around 6000 B. C., its origins probably date back from well before the end of the last Iceage."[5] It is important to note that the role played by medicine men is essential in keeping the tradition and developing the whole process. "The traditional medical practitioner or traditional healer can be defined as someone who is recognised by the community in which he lives as competent to provide health care by using vegetable, animal and mineral substances and certain other methods based on the social, cultural and religious backgrounds as well as the prevailing knowledge, attitudes and beliefs regarding physical, mental and social well-being and the causation of disease and disability in the community."[6] Thus, "traditional healing treatments are always integrated and involve a combination of approaches such as psychotherapeutics, herbal medicine, nutritional therapy and physical therapeutics."[7]

Tribes have always relied on their environment and its products for food and medicine. Tribal medicines are usually herbal and animal-derived products. The knowledge and their belief in plants and herbs are worth mentioning. It strikes one's mind to think about the people pioneering to discover medicinal herbs, plants and fruits in which their life might have ended. The trial and error method was adopted, and foragers of such herbs have been killed in the process, much like the plight of modern-day guinea pigs as they first used it on themselves or their families. Nevertheless, it became a natural process of learning and adapting to meet the needs of the people. Indigenous knowledge and practices have been learned over centuries and diligently passed down throughout generations.

Whenever the Naga society is discussed, the essence of life itself is often left out; sickness and illness, which affected the people and later shaped their whole belief system and culture and dictated their entire life, were not given due importance. There is a call for the need to take up this facet of society, the need for one to study and highlight the indigenous medicines, healers and methods of treatment and to bring forth the fact that they knew medicine too, not in the modern allopathic way but medicines they used and relied on their own in their ecological surrounding and were proven effective and would interest one to realise how they are still in practice today with all the modernity surrounding them. The study is done to break away from the treatment of tribal indigenous knowledge as less or insubstantial to Western medicines and treatment practices as represented by the missionaries. And although the Lotha traditional healer was empirical, religion played a significant role in the execution of their work. Life was dear to all, then and now; therefore, the institution which worked in this area of social organisation needs to be studied in depth to draw a holistic picture of the past and the society which thrived during those times. In this context, the paper aims to explore the traditional method of healing among the Lotha tribe of Nagaland and the role played by the local medicine men in the process.

Review of Literature

Although many have written on the Naga tribes extensively, those on the medicine men or the healing practices and practitioners have largely been neglected. Particularly, the writings on the Lotha traditional healers and medicine have not gained much attention. Nevertheless, there remains C. Browner's edited book[8] which incorporated various scholars and their takes and explanations on disease, illness and their human relation/explanation, and multiple theories of illness provided in the book became useful in understanding the subject of illness in humans. Another prominent figure to have exponentially discussed health and sickness from a sociological perspective was Talcott Parsons, one of the first sociologists to have health as part of the social system. Oscar Lewis (1958) and Pedersen and Baruffati (1989) too have advocated the advantages of learning about the indigenous beliefs and practices of the community holistically since it provides an insight into their worldview linked to agriculture, politics and interpersonal relations.

A. K. Thakur has discussed medicinal plants and the method of their use in his book *Technology of the Tribes of Northeast*

India. He gives examples from various tribes of northeast India, but not from the studied tribe in this paper.[9] J. J. Roy Burman's book focuses on Sikkim in his book *Tribal Medicine: Traditional Practices and Change in Sikkim* among the Bhutias and the Lepchas.[10] Inferences are drawn from this book where tribes of this state share similarities with the Naga tribes, therefore, with the Lotha Naga traditional healers and medicines. Burman concluded that knowledge of medicine and its relation to other fields of social life like the economy, religion, magic and law was necessary for a complete understanding of any society. Vibha Joshi[11] is one to write extensively on the subject under study with the Angami in focus, who happens to have a close association with the Lotha given their geographical location and also the fact that they (the Lotha and the Angami) are said to be from the *Tengima*[12] group; hence much insight and information was gathered from this book. Specifically, on the Lotha Naga, we have N. S. Jamir, Takatemjen and Limasemba's paper[13] dealing with Lotha usage of medicinal plants found in the Wokha district in Nagaland; however, the paper was purely a work of botany and was found wanting of social discussions.

The Lotha Naga medicine men and their methods of healing

The Lotha Naga, who also calls themselves *'Kyong'* meaning man simply, made the district of Wokha their home and is one of the major tribes inhabiting the state of Nagaland. Their settlement area was known as 'the land of plenty' in Nagaland due to its high yield of rich fruits and vegetables that are popular among the Nagas.

Since the earliest times, human attempts to combat diseases developed in two lines: magic and empiric, moving either parallel or divergently toward one another. In the world of the Lotha Nagas, healing and treatment of illness and diseases were done by empirical healers who employed physiotherapeutic methods and traditional medicines made out of plant and animal extracts. Besides the empirical healers, we have the institution of the Shaman or *Ratssen*, as it is called among the Lotha, which was a sacred one, usually considered a psychopath or schizophrenic whose technique was based on magic or supernatural powers. Both the offices are not appointed by the fellow villagers, for they are believed to be inherited/gifted and are private practitioners. The focus of the paper is on the empirical healer.

The Lotha manner of treatment was not just faith in the supernaturals but had a scientific bend to it in that they knew the properties of the herbs in the forests and their use in the treatment of various illnesses, diseases and wounds. "Their association and dependence on forest forced them to depend on nature, which has been reflected in their traditional culture, local beliefs, folklores and the interesting valuable knowledge of ethnological importance. It is known that the tribal people are familiar with the knowledge of ethnologically important species in their ecosystems and understand the ecological interactions of the various components of their resources."[14] Not just remedies and concocting potions, but the Lotha medicine men performed treatment of fractures and minor surgeries as well.

The disease is a phenomenon encountered by all societies, but if the population is small, even the loss of an individual affects the functioning of the social organisation.[15] Living closely in clumped villages, the Lotha populations, with their less hygienic conditions, became seeded with pathogens and were victims to many diseases which impacted the area's demography. Villages became scarce in the human population due to their warring activities, but poor health and living conditions were major factors behind the declining population. Also given the location of their villages at the summit of the hills brought water scarcity causing 'skin and intestinal diseases and goitre. Diseases and sicknesses such as malaria, pneumonia, dysentery and smallpox were also common.'[16] Diseases were also contracted due to human movements, especially by traders who went down to the plains of Assam to trade with the Miris and the abutting tribes of Ao, Angami and Rengma. Diseases were also brought by the colonialists and the Christian missionaries who were foreign to the Nagas at that time, like cholera. Snakebite, frostbite, common cold, cough, cuts and wounds, high blood pressure, epilepsy, dysentery, diarrhoea and fever were common. Diseases such as tuberculosis, chicken pox, diabetes and rheumatism are not known for sure whether they were prevalent before colonial rule or were introduced by Europeans and Missionaries alike. "However, epidemic diseases such as typhoid, measles, diphtheria, smallpox, yellow fever, and cholera were unknown to the primitives before the arrival of the white man."[17]

"Every society patronises a theory of disease and provides an efficacious, given the state of knowledge, treatment for the disorders. It is carried out by a medical system, an inseparable part of every society. The set of medicines consists of these cultural practices, methods, techniques and substances embedded in a matrix of values, traditions, beliefs, and patterns of ecological adaptation that provide the means for maintaining health and preventing or ameliorating disease and injury in its members."[18] The medicines were usually not disclosed to the people and were guarded by the explanations given that they lose their efficacy when known by others. This would be to do with the medicine man trying to keep the information to himself so that he has his job obviously, for when the knowledge is accessible, he would have no patients and hence no income. But this is the general belief among the Lotha Naga medicine men to not disclose their medicines to keep the properties of the medicines effective and hence their potency to cure.

The traditional medicines made up of fruits, leaves, barks and roots of trees, and tubers collected and preserved during the seasons of each plant: everything was naturally derived and was preserved in powdered, dried, smoked above kitchen hearths, in paste form and in the concoction to be taken orally or applied on a surface. Raw materials would be collected during the season and were stored away carefully in leaves and jars for later use. The manner and time in which they were to be used were prescribed by the medicine men. Usually, the medications included where one could apply for the medicines directly on the wounds, powder the wounds or turn them into a paste by mixing some water into it. Sometimes the pastes made by the medicine men have to be applied on the spot/wound secured by some bandages, and at times the barks and stems and leaves in dried form were to be boiled simply in water and taken in concentrated form, tasting mostly bitter.

Vibha Joshi impressively brings out the importance of diet, stating that where disease and illness are under consideration, the role of diet cannot be out of place. "Diet is a reflection of ecology, culture and biology. Ecology has an important role as the climate has a direct effect on the diet and also on the disease environment that must be endured. Cultural factors are reflected in the food-producing technologies, food preparation, food habits and its differential distribution to the people. Biology conditions the degree of acclimatisation and adaptations to stress conditions."[19] Therefore, the kinds of diet prescribed to the patients must be brought to light. Food was to be kept simple and light while undergoing medication and treatment, such as abstinence from strong or fermented food such as dried fish which is popularly enjoyed by the Lotha Naga and fermented soybean. Some other food item to abstain from is the fermented bamboo shoot liquid which is used as a vinegar substitute in the Lotha cuisines. And some other times, certain meat and fish varieties were prohibited. Contrarily, game meat was prescribed, such as squirrel meat for cough, asthma, pneumonia and fever; roasted bats were prescribed for tonsils; roasted cockroach for bladder problems; frog for healing operation wounds faster; fox meat for recurrent stomach pain, porcupine stomach for malaria typhoid, bear's gall bladder for fever, python's fat for cuts and burns known to have a speedy recovery and so on. Likewise, sugarcane and crabs were believed to cure jaundice, rhododendron for throat infection and for incidents when fish bones get stuck in the throat, Roselle leaf and fruit extracts for indigestion and gas forms, etc.

Medicine men were more common than the shaman in the Lotha society. They knew their ecology well and explored the vastness of their village and even beyond on peaceful days. The medicine men, too, were not very different from the shaman, in the sense that they too possessed some form of supernatural powers in that they too could locate the pain, knew how to cure it and what medicines to prescribe and this trait too was considered hereditary and ran in the family. Sometimes the inheritance of the gift could be passed on to the next generation and, at times, could jump to the next, the grandchildren or the great-grandchildren and so on. It would only be appropriate to add here that not all were willing to accept the gift, some chose to reject them as it took a toll on the person given the physical work, but also the interaction with the spirits was draining; they say since. But their way of healing was not magic per se but included empirical work. Both men and women could inherit the gifts, and it was not prohibited or tabooed towards any gender. They were practical and practised medicine in the form of herbs mostly in dried form. This form of treatment is very common not only among the Lotha but goes to include the entire Naga tribes. They were proficient in bone setting, massaging and curing poisoning from animals, insects or plants. People mostly came to them for sprains and bone settings. Massage was a popular form of treatment. The masseur or the masseuse, after examining the patient's body, would locate the exact affected area and tell them what went wrong and would then treat the patient. They would make use of animal horns and teeth, and bird beaks to assist them for this purpose if needed. Cupping therapy was applied using the horns of animals to suck out the bad blood accumulated, which could be hampering the system from functioning properly. The Lotha medicine men would, at times, operate by slicing off a bit of skin from the wounded or infected area and would use insects such as bees to extract the poison and the illness from the body of the patient; the bee, after having removed the substance, dies. There were other forms, too, like biting directly into the wound, sucking out from the wound of the patient and sealing the wound with burning coal; at lesser aggressive times, the wound would be bandaged. In cases of fracture and dislocation of bones, massage was given to bring the bone to its proper position, after which it was bandaged with clothes within which a stick, usually a straight bamboo stick, was inserted to keep the area uptight. For fractures, certain meat for food was prescribed for a quick recovery. The principal way of treatment was, however, medicines to be taken orally. And for this, the medicine men would work hard, exploring, testing it on themselves or their families, and researching for a lifetime. The medicine men are also known to take on the illness of their patients many times, it is a supernatural belief, however, but the belief is strong and well accepted among the Lotha Naga, and this is why medicine men would take rests to recover one and their special powers. Interestingly, they are known to have a certain day or days in a week where their ability and powers are at their best and can perform better and cure. It would be interesting to note in this context that some were gifted in bone settings, some in massage and some in herbal medicines, but some possess all the above abilities. Some medicine men possessed supernatural powers that they could assist in the illness or problems without even touching or treating the patient. A rare case is of medicine women having the ability to induce childbirth by just walking around the house where the woman was in labour.

The missionaries had always been suspicious and apprehensive about traditional medicines and their practitioners. Kyle Jackson writing on the Mizos, explains how "the missionaries were suspicious of the Mizo view of their past including the medical system, as a result, they unconsciously attempted to reconstruct from the perspective of western linear world view. There is a possibility of deviating from the true cultural essence with ambiguity in such reconstruction. One needs to look at the logic of socio-cultural practices. The cultural practices in most of the 'tribal societies' are a combination of real life, myth, legends or metaphor. If any part of the socio-cultural practices is separated and translated into little terms, it makes little sense. This is what makes the non-literate society difficult to understand. And the colonisers and missionaries were frequently trapped in this dilemma."[20]

Conclusion

The westernisation/modernisation period in the Lotha Naga community began with the Christian missionaries who came in the nineteenth century in the form of American Baptist Missionaries. They brought Christianity into the land, which changed the lives of the Lotha, but modern medicine too came along with religion, and credit can, without doubt, be attributed to them for eradicating many diseases like cholera, diarrhoea, goitre, etc., which improved the mortality rate and the general health of the people up to a great extend. But it should not put one in a position to assume that treatment and curing of diseases and illnesses were completely unknown to the people under discussion. It may not have been in the form of tablets and capsules, but the tribal men did know medicinal plants and animal by-products to cure many of the illnesses common to the people and the land. The missionaries and the British rule also brought sickness hitherto unknown to the natives and introduced to the natives some deadly diseases as well, so not everything British or colonial rather should be embraced as all good and mighty, for there are instances, many for that matter which the Colonial rule brought upon the people that were destructive and hampering to the natural growth and well being of the natives. There was also the added cultural prejudice that the Colonialists very much inserted in their descriptions of the tribes, having everyone believe what they projected through their many writings on the Naga tribes. Despite all these diseases and illness effected on the Lotha, 'the Nagas, in general, tend to be healthy most of the time, and epidemics were almost absent.'[21] Besides, the role of disease plays a major role in describing and shaping society. It acts like a thorn in society's functioning as war is detrimental to a society's progress so does diseases and illnesses. A village, a tribe or a state immersed in disease directly impacts its political powers; with the decline in population due to deaths, there is a direct decline in warrior or soldier numbers, and the economy is burdened with an ultimate decline in surplus production, thereby affecting trade.

The role of ecology in the human experience of varied forms of disease is irrefutable. People undergo different kinds of diseases as dictated by the terrain and their ecology. These experiences go on to shape their ideologies, institutions and roles in society and shape and define them. The importance of disease in the social organisation and people's way of life is much deeper than it seems to appear. Policies, rules, taboos and gennas are fashioned out of these diseases and imposed on every member of society.

The study on diseases in the Naga society is still very scanty. It is imperative to undertake this aspect of society as it is very much a part of the social life of the people and plays its due part in religion and in the making up of the ideological structure of the society itself. Diseases and illness play a role in framing the society's structure to some extent, and it later explains the diseases in the society's understanding. A broader picture of history can be construed when it is studied in totality. 'We need to know more about the individual experience of disease in time and place, the influence of culture on definitions of disease and of disease in the creation of culture, and the role of the state in defining and responding to disease. We need to understand the organisation of the medical profession and institutional medical care as in part a response to particular patterns of disease incidence.'[22]

Notes

1. Forest E. Clements, *Primitive Concepts on Disease*, University of California, Berkeley, 1932.

2. Edward B. Tylor, *Primitive Culture*, Cambridge University Press, London, 1871.

3. Warwick Anderson, "Disease and Its Meanings", *Health and History*, Vol.1, No.4, December 1999, pp.246-247.

4. Felix Marti-Ibanez (ed.), *A Pictorial History of Medicine*, Spring Books, London, 1965, p. 17.

5. Ramashankar, Sourabh Deb & Bipin Kumar Sharma (eds.), *Traditional Healing Practices in North East India*, North-Eastern Institute of Folk Medicine, Department of AYUSH, Ministry of Health and Family Welfare, Government of India, July 2009, Pasighat, Arunachal Pradesh, p.26

6. Ibid, p. 26

7. Ibid, p. 27

8. C. Browner (ed.), *Medical Anthropology: Health, Healers and Culture*, Cosmo Publications, June 2000,

9. For details, see Amrendra Kumar Thakur, *Technology of the Tribes of Northeast India*, DVS Publishers, Guwahati, 2017, pp.97-125.

10. J. J. Roy Burman, *Tribal Medicine*, Mittal Publications, New Delhi, 2003.

11. Vibha Joshi, "Health, Disease and Social Structure: Their Relationship in a Naga Village", *Indian Anthropologist*, Vol. 16, No. 2, Dec. 1986,

12. The Angami, Ao, Lotha and Sema are said to belong to the Tengima group at one point of time in history when they were still in their migratory phase. They are said to have been brothers and hence descendants of one stock.

13. N. S. Jamir, Takatemjen and Limasemba, "Traditional Knowledge of Lotha-Naga Tribes in Wokha District, Nagaland", *Indian Journal of Traditional Knowledge*, Vol.9, No.1, January 2010, pp.45-48.

14. Ramashankar, Sourabh Deb & Bipin Kumar Sharma (eds.), *Traditional Healing Practices in North East India*, North-Eastern Institute of Folk Medicine, Department of AYUSH, Ministry of Health and Family Welfare, Govt. Of India, July 2009, Pasighat, Arunachal Pradesh, p.12
15. Vibha Joshi, Health, "Disease and Social Structure: Their Relationship in a Nagaland Village", *Indian Anthropologist*, Vol. 16, No. 2, Dec 1986, p.125.
16. Inato Yekheto Shikhu, *A Rediscovery and Rebuilding of Naga Cultural Values: An Analytical Approach with Special Reference to Maori as a Colonised and Minority Group of People in New Zealand*, Regency Publications, A Division of Astral International Pvt. Ltd., New Delhi, 2016, p.33
17. Erwin Heinz Ackerknecht, *A Short History of Medicine*, Baltimore, Johns Hopkins University Press, 1982, p.21 as cited in Andrew Lalruatkima, "Social History of Epidemics in Lushai Hills", Unpublished M. Phil Thesis, 2019, p.27.
18. Vibha Joshi, *op.cit.*, p. 126.
19. Ibid., p. 134.
20. Kyle Jackson, Mizos, *Missionaries and Medicine: Religious and Medical Contact in Lushai Hills*, M.A. Dissertation, School of Oriental and African Studies, University of London, 2009, p. 120 (as cited in Andrew Lalruatkima, "Social History of Epidemics in Lushai Hills", Unpublished M. Phil Thesis, 2019), pp. 9-10.
21. Report on the Administration of the District of the Naga Hills for the Year 1878-79, 1879, p.9, Writer's Building, Kolkata.
22. Charles E. Rosenberg, "Disease in History: Frames and Framers", *The Milbank Quarterly*, Vol.67, Supplement 1, Framing Disease: The Creation and Development of Negotiation of Explanatory Schemes, 1989, p. 14.

7

Health Care Practices of Sikkim: A Historical Study

Jigme Wangchuk Bhutia

The working parameters of healers worldwide and cultures are diverse, with a principalintention to healthe sick and help the community maintain good health. Death and diseases at first were not observed as natural phenomena. Whereas common maladies such as cold, fever, etc., were accepted as a part of existence, serious and disabling diseases were believed to be originated from supernatural forces. Herbs were the first medicines used by prehistoric people. They are, therefore, part of every cultural tradition and have helped the development and growth of the medicinal culture. The story of human well-being evolved along with the stages of reasoning and a tedious process of trial and error. Indigenous health practices or folk medicine evolved on the use of plants, herbs and different food sources, which were sourced colloquially from the nearby regions. At extremities, it also involved counterspells, incantations, potions and other means as a part of treatment upon patients suffering from more serious diseases suspected to have been driven by spells, wizardry, visitation of a malevolent demon, offence taken by Gods, etc.

The World Health Organization (WHO) estimates that 4 billion people, i.e., 80 per cent of the world population, presently use herbal medicine for some aspect of primary health care. The northeast part of the Himalayas exhibits a broad diversity of plant life. It is sometimes calledthe "Cradle of Flowering Plants", which offers a considerable amount of medicinal plants for traditional healers who have used them to cure and prevent diseases.[1] In Sikkim, herbal medicine is a significant component of the indigenous traditional healing system.[2] Joseph Dalton Hooker (1871-97), the first European who did an extensive floristic study in Sikkim which was later followed by Biswas(1956), identified up to 400 species of plants with medicinal properties, being used by the ethnic communities as traditional medicines.[3]

The Sikkim Himalaya is floristically one of the country's richest and most interesting areas. About one-third of species of the Indian flora are found in the state's tropical, temperate and alpine areas. Sikkim, a melting pot of assorted cultures, is well represented by its lively people, religion, language, art and craft, and medicinal practices. Folk medicine, as an effort to cope with an environment, undoubtedly came through trial and error, using various plants and other methods derived from observation of how animals reacted to and treated illnesses and injuries. Over time, individuals within family and travel groups became more skilled at helping the sick and injured. Some of these became responsible for carrying out healing ceremonies, religious rituals, and other rites designated to ensure the safety and health of their communities.[4]

The vernacular health traditions varied in accordance with the diverse communities inhabiting different parts of Sikkim. In north Sikkim, it is more traditional in specific areas like Lachung, Lachen and Dzongu, in and around the Kanchenjunga

Biosphere Reserve. Here, the locals are well-informed on the medicinal properties of plants and their utilisation in curing diseases. The people of Sikkim, by tradition, have adapted themselves to their natural surroundings by living intricately with their environment and developing their social and cultural mechanisms accordingly. Hence, their medicinal practices, too, were dovetailed within these norms.

The ethnic communities of Sikkim have their traditional health practices. Among them, we shall take up the case of the *Lepchas*, *Bhutias* and *Limboos* and their respective folk medicines and traditional healers. Apart from this customary practice, Sikkim's ancient medicinal system of *Amchi* also exists, which continued and was popularised by Buddhist groups for their traditional Tibetan Pharmacopoeia[5].

I

The use of indigenous health practicesin Sikkim has traditionally existed for many years and is learned informally by word of mouth. In Sikkim, people have tremendous faith in traditional medicine, but the topography of the region inhibited close contact with other developed systems of medicine, which somewhat inhibited its growth. However, this isolation also helped them to develop a unique healthcare culture. [6]

Several religious priests or Shamans/ herbalists/ community healers of different communities are known by different names; the Lepcha healers are called *Bongthing;* the *Bhutia* call them *Pau* and *Neyjum,* and the Limboo call them *Phedemgma.* The materials used or treatment include herbs, plants, animal products, and religious chants or *mantras*. Even to date, these traditional community healers exist alongside modern medicinal practices, especially in rural areas.[7]

Lepcha Therapeutic Tradition

The Lepcha are primarily animists and follow the Mahayana Buddhism sect. They have their script and distinct costumes, languages, and culture. Since the Lepchas are deeply connected with nature, their knowledge of medicinal plants is very wide and recorded in the Lepcha epics called *Namthar*.[8] Diseases of greater severity were also correlated with the supernatural. They believed certain semi-divine beings or guardian spirits known as *Lungzee,* residing in giant trees, a cluster of trees, grass, a tarn, a cave or a special hillock, and other natural objects were responsible. It is often believed among the Lepchas that if they are uncared for or any disrespect is shown to them, it will invoke wrath upon the village or the particular individual; they may suffer from serious sickness or even death.[9]

Since the Lepcha are animists, traditionally, only the *Bongthing* (male Lepcha priests) and *Mun* (the female Lepcha priestess) were called during sickness and for cultural and funeral ceremonies. Such is the influence of the *Mun / Bongthing* that even after their conversion to Buddhism, the *lamas* (Buddhist monks) performed their rituals in close association with them. The *Mun*, however, perform rituals connected with supernatural forces in which the *lama* have no role.

The Lepcha are natural botanists, and their knowledge of plants and usages has helped them overpower health-related difficulties. Some of the plants used by them are *Rungkyen (Swertiachiratahair)* for high fever, *Selek (Curcuma aromatic Salish)* for curing stomach pain and evil eye, *Nam nongmuk (Eupatorium cannabinum Linn)* used for healing wounds, nose bleed, *Syambem (Heracleumwallichii)* for stomach pain, *Tiknyel (Artemisia vulgaris Linn)* to stop bleeding, nose bleed and skin related diseases, *Heng (Zingiberofficinale Rose)* for a stomach disorder, *Peju Kung* for body ache, *Ruklop (Acourscalamus*

Linn) for fever and infection, *Sugarsabanjara and Ribum* for poisoning etc.[10]

A particular medicinal plantthat plays a vital role in the Lepcha culture is the*Pougorip/Totola* (Oroxylumindicum). It is essentially a medicinal plant and is often used even in Ayurveda as an ingredient for *Dashamula*[11]. For the Lepchas, it was very sacred, and they believed it was not even touched by the bees, signifying purity. It is primarily used as a liver tonic and as an anti-diabetic medicine. The plant's fruit is shaped like a big sword; the seeds from inside the fruit are flagellated like paper silk and used in any auspicious ceremony, similar to the use of turmeric in Hindu culture.

Apart from the plants and herbs, the Lepchas also use animal parts for health-related matters. For instance, *suku-kombu(*deer skin) is consumed in case someone has mushroom poisoning, *suhu-maon* (monkey meat) for curing high fever, *home-maon* (beef) for asthma, *Sinha-kep*t (bear meat) for curing tuberculosis and swelling, *charming –fo* for regulating diabetics, lard/ pork fat for measles, honey from stingless bees *(Aithu)* for diphtheria, etc.[12]

A health drink called *Chi* (millet beer) plays a very important role in Lepcha culture and is frequently used. It is believed that Chi, due to its high-calorie properties, is useful to protect oneself from cold and also provides strength to women after giving birth to gain strength back. *Chi* has multiple uses, is prepared differently for different uses, and is sometimes also used as an offering to the Gods. However, overconsumption is generally discouraged.[13]

Bhutia Therapeutic Tradition

The Bhutia follow the tradition of Tibetan Mahayana Buddhism. However, elements of pre-Buddhist religion called

Bon,[14] is also amply seen in this religious fusion. Geoffrey Samuel explicates; Bon is the 'Original' religion of Tibet as projected by Western scholars, 'Nameless religion' by Rolf Stein or 'Folk religion' by Giuseppe Tucciare not appropriate. The reason for this contestation is; a fluid and organic continuity of Bon faith and not just an abrupt transformation to Buddhism.[15]

The Bhutia also have their spiritual healers called *Bon ban Bongthing*, *Pau* (male healer) and *Ney-jum* (female healer). These personalities are said to have special abilities to connect with the supernatural and often act as a bridge between the human and the spiritual world. In a Bhutia community, when a person is afflicted with any illness, these healers first ascertain the cause of the illness through different practices such as bead counting, throwing dice etc. It helps them to understand the cause of illness, whether emanating from local harmful spirits (*nop*e) or not and tries to find a solution. Offerings of banana leaves for local deities are placed before the patient's house to pacify the spirits.[16] The *Bon ban bongthing also* performs ancestral worship *(Pho lha Mo lha).* If the patient does not recover, they approach the *Pau* and *Ney jum.*

When an afflicted person is being cured, a *Pau* enters a trance state to communicate with the spirits and discover why they have afflicted the patient with an illness. Another way of diagnosis is by divination with the help of a plate full of rice or sometimes with payer beads. The *Pau* shakes the plate until the symbol of the evil spirit appears in the rice or may count the beads, which have signification meanings in the numbers. The *Pau* performs *Phupti*, which are rites, by offering money, eggs, and clothes to the malignant spirit. These things are thrown out, and only the clothes are brought back. Patients are believed to be cured within three days of the ritual. [17]

Folk healing practices among the Bhutias are also closely knitted with their usage of medicinal plants. Vernacular herbs and plants used by the Bhutias are *Dumsing (Abiesdensa Griffith)*, used for toothache. *Peyogokhum (Bergeniapurpurascens)* for body ache, wound and throat pain, *Dambrumchoem (Elatostemaplatphylla Wedd)* used for de-worming, *Sudag (Acoruscalamus Araceae)* for asthma, pneumonia, bronchitis and diarrhoea, *Khempo (Artemisia indica Asteraceae*) for skin diseases, weak stomach, *Hong –Lem (Bergenia ciliate Saxifragaceae)* for vomiting cough, fever and pulmonary infection etc.[18]

LimbooTherapeutic Tradition:

The community of the Limboos belong to the Mongoloid stock and has been residing along the districts lying on the eastern or left bank of the Arun River, extending up to Sikkim since ancient times. [19] The Limboos are primarily animists and follow their religion called *Yumaism* and derive their *spiritual* guidance from *Mundhum*, an oral spiritual instruction of the Limboo society.[20] Among the Limboos, there are *Phedangmas* (shamans) who perform special rituals, particularly for the Limboo community, for physical and mental diseases. Since Yuma religion is primarily confined to animism, shamanism and ancestral worshipping, many diagnoses related to health matters are subscribed to the supernatural. The Limboo believe that these *phedangmas* are intermediaries between humans and the Mother Creator (*Tagera Ningwaphuma*), who can perform rituals to appease the deities as per the instructions laid down in *Mundhum*.[21]

The Limboo are well aware of the benefits of plants and herbs and have a specialist who is thoroughly versed in medicinal knowledge. A *Sidapangdang*, also a *Phedangma, is* generally ascribed to curing different illnesses. Badola and Pradhan, in their study related to Limboo response to sickness and their usage of medicinal herbs in the Himalayas, have stated that Limboo women kept a wide knowledge of diseases associated with children, especially stomach ache, diarrhoea, dysentery, intestinal worms, cough, cold, fever etc., and possible herbs and its usages associated will the diseases.[22]

The Limboo use different types of wild plants and herbs to cure different ailments, such as *Wana/Ana*, used for fever and green dysentery among children; *Gobre Salla (Abiesdensa Griff)*, used for curing asthma, bronchitis and stomach pain; *Lalgeri (Abrusprecatorius Linn)* used sore throat, *Setisiris (Albezzizprocera)* to contain fever, *Kadam (Anthocephaluschinensis)* for stomach ache, *Saur (Betulautilise)* for cleansing would for its antiseptic properties, *Bhangreysisnu (Girardiana palmate)* roots are taken in skin diseases and kidney problem, *Sayapatri (Tagetes patella linn)* for sorethroat, cough and mouth ulcers, *Bhaleytimmer (Zanthoxyllumalatum Roxb)* used for treating diarrhoea and stomach ache.[23]

As in any tribal society, the parameters of illness in Sikkim Himalaya can be categorised as per the theories of illness. Healers worldwide adopt different methods but follow a common working pattern. They identify the name of the illness and its probable causes. This wins over the patient's trust and confidence, believing he/she can be cured. A suitable healing method is selected, keeping the subject's background and symptoms in mind. The healing practices in Sikkim are a response to a mixture of Personalistic and Naturalistic theories of illness. Personalistic ideas of illness may be linked to a moral or spiritual transgression. They may also involve inappropriate behaviour, violation of social norms, or breaches of religious taboos on the part of the patient. On the other hand, naturalistic theories view illness as disharmony between the person and the environment. Thus, the perception of illness is highly culture oriented.[24]

Apart from these, there are many plants and herbs that are generally used as medicine for different diseases, such as; *Bikhma (Aconitum bisma)*, which is used in food poisoning, asthma, cough and bronchitis. *Titepati* (Artemisia ciliate) is used on cuts and bruises to stop bleeding, mostly on nose bleeding. *Kainjal (Bischofiajavanica)* fruits of *Kainjal* are used in making wine; stems and barks are used for irregular mensuration and pain—*Kagatey (Daphne bhava)* for fever and intestine worms. *Banmara (Eupatorium connubium)* leaf and stem are applied on cuts and bruises to stop bleeding and infections. *Chimphing (Haracleum Wallachia)* fruits of *chimping* are used during influenza, and their roots as an aphrodisiac. *Timbur (Linderanessiama)* flowers of *Timbur* are used for excessive seminal discharge in dreams; fruits are used to induce vomiting. *Papari (podophyllum)* is used for septic and diarrhoea. *Taubarkey (Stephinaglabra)* is crushed intopowder and used for regulating diabetes, tuberculosis, asthma and fever.[25]

II

Sowa -Rigpa /Amchi (Tibetan Herbal Medicine)

The *Sowa-Rigpa /Amchi*, or the Tibetan medicinal system, is a holistic approach towards well-being and has a rich cultural heritage. Tibetan medicine originated with the local folk tradition that dates back to about 300 B.C. and was formally recorded by Xiepu Chixi, the physician to the Tibetan King Niechi Zanpu, in 126 B. C.[26] *Amchi* is derived from the Mongolian word *Am-Ojai*, which means 'superior to all': the practitioners of medicine are also known as *Amchi*, and the Tibetan system of medicine is also named after the same, explains Padma Gourmet. He further cites that *Amchi* is one of the world's oldest surviving well-documented medical traditions. It has been popular throughout the central Asian regions of Tibet, Mongolia, Bhutan, some parts of China, Nepal, the Himalayan regions of India including Ladakh, Arunachal and Sikkim, and a few parts of the former Soviet Union,[27] where communities of Buddhist people have long been established, many non-Buddhists also seek out the treatment of this traditional system because of its good reputation.

In Sikkim, the *Amchi* medicine came with the migration of Bhutias and their Tibetan influence. The people of Sikkim were acquainted with *Amchi* Medicine Plants throughout the Namgyal dynasty.[28]

The Amchi system and it is deeply rooted in the Buddhist culture. *Amchi* practitioners are highly respected, both socially and spiritually, for they are believed to be the representatives of *SangayMenla* (Medicine Buddha). Besides, the *Amchi* were the village's most learned and resourceful people. The physiology, pathology and pharmacology sciences of the *Amchi/ Sowa – Rigpa* is based on the principles of *Jumg-wa-lna* (five elements) and *NespaGsum* (three bad causes). A physician of *Sowa-Rigpa* employs three main tools for diagnosing patients; visual diagnosis, diagnosis by touching and diagnosis by questioning. The treatment follows sections- diet, behaviour, medicine and external therapies.[29]

III

After 1765, the disastrous Dual System of governance in Bengal was exacting a heavy toll on the Company, and to add to it, the Bengal famine of 1770 precipitated the crisis. The Company soon realised that Bengal had become a desolate province and its treasury on the verge of bankruptcy.[30] The Charter of the

East India Company authorised an act of war against any regional authorities to meet its ends, which changed the nature of this trading corporation. After 1765, the Company was no longer an international trading firm dealing with silks and spices; it had transformed into an aggressive colonial power. In less than forty years, it managed to garner 200,000 men, twice the size of the British army. This helped to establish the East India Company's paramountcy over the entire subcontinent.[31]

The Great Bengal Famine of 1770 necessitated a search for a new commercial venture in the hitherto unexplored region of the Eastern Himalayas. The famine had caused massive fiscal loss, mainly the export of grain and cotton industry, which was the plinth of Bengal's economy.[32] Thus, the Court of Directors ordered an investigation into the possibility of northern trade for which explorers were dispatched to the Himalayan kingdom.[33] The rising Gurkha power in the eighteenth century blocked all the trading routes of Nepal with the adjoining kingdoms, especially Tibet. Seeing this, the East India Company sought an alternative course of action to establish commercial relations in the Eastern Himalayas, sometimes through a policy of conciliation and sometimes through belligerence.

With regards to Sikkim, the British policies began as early as 1815 with the rise of Gurkha expansionism followed by Captain Llyod Mission in 1835, Archibald Campbell and Dr JD Hookers Expedition in 1854, Gawler and Eden Mission in 1861, JW Edgar Mission in 1873. By 1890, British Resident was firmly established in Sikkim with John Claude White as its First Political Officer. The establishment of the administrative centre of the Political Officer in Sikkim after 1890 saw the beginning of the Western health care system in Sikkim. Such health institutions were entirely the result of British preoccupation with health issues. It began with a dispensary for the British Agency at Gangtok in 1890.[34]

The beginning of the Western health care system in Sikkim was entirely the result of British preoccupation with health issues. It began with a dispensary for the British Agency at Gangtok in 1890. From the beginning, the Gangtok dispensary grew as a health centre for the public. Evidence gave us details about how the dispensary meant for the British Agency at Gangtok also grew as a health centre for the public. In 1891, Army Medical Officer Surgeon D. G. Marshall, at the Gangtok Agency dispensary, felt it necessary to extend medical facilities to the public also.For this concern, he wrote many letters to Political Officers to make the civil dispensary at Gangtok not only for the British Officers but also for the local people as well under the control of a Medical Officer, who could look after

Table 1: Attendance at the Gangtok dispensary between January 1891 and February 1892

Period	*No. of patients*
25 January - 25 February 1891	39
25 February - 25 March 1891	64
25 March - 25 April 1891	62
25 April - 25 May 1891	37
25 May - 25 June 1891	47
25 June - 25 July 1891	30
25 July - 25 August 1891	33
25 August - 25 September 1891	66
25 September- 25 October 1891	128
25 October - 25 November 1891	54
25 November - 25 December 1891	81
25 December - 25 January 1892	85
25 January 1892- 25 February 1892	78

Source: Foreign Department Proceedings, Government of Sikkim. External B, January 1891-1892

the patients, also can perform minor operations and also act as a Civil Surgeon of Gangtok as well as of Sikkim. [35] The average attendance of this dispensary in each month during the year 1891 was 60.

The table records the maximum number of outdoor patients from 25 September – 25 October 1891, numbering 128, and the minimum numbers between 25 June- 25 July 1891, numbering 30. However, the average number of patients seeking modern medicine shows a constant increase in attendance, showcasing its rising popularity.[36]

Dispensaries now became a medium through which organised public health care systems came to be monitored in Sikkim from the late nineteenth century onwards. With the reorganisation of administrative patterns in Sikkim, a modern health system was also developed along this pattern, first through Dispensaries and later through full-fledged Hospitals.

Gangtok Dispensary was the first Dispensary to be opened in Sikkim after the approval by the Government of India; First Civil Dispensary was finally placed at Gangtok in the year 1891 under the charge of a Medical Officer attached to the regiment at the station. The dispensary building was also extended, and the allowance to the Medical Officer of 50 rupees per month was also granted, which has to be paid from Sikkim revenue for attending the dispensary to give medical aid. In 1900, the dispensary at Gangtok was fully established as a small hospital where indoor patients were received. This small hospital proved to be the first hospital in Sikkim with provision for accommodating eight male patients, five female patients and two special patients. Minor operations were also conducted in the hospital. Other than the Medical Officer, two civil hospital assistants were appointed for the Gangtok hospital and the Chidam dispensary, respectively. [37]

Next, the Chidam Dispensary (present-day Sadam, in south Sikkim) was established in 1897 by Scottish Christian missionaries. The *Darbar*, the British Residency and newly established business house at Gangtok, *financed the hospital.* In 1904, MessersJetmull and Bhojraj contributed Rs. 24 monthly, financed for the upkeep of 3 beds.[38]

In 1906, the Political Officer submitted his proposal for the reorganisation of the medical arrangements in the Sikkim Agency and urged the appointment of an Agency surgeon; the reasons he adduced for the change were that the European population of the Station had increased considerably and necessitated the employment of a whole time medical officer. His proposal was immediately looked after, and soon rearrangement was done in 1908, where J.N Turner was appointed civil surgeon or assistant surgeon at the Gangtok hospital. Sikkim Darbar and British Residence contributed to the payment of civil surgeon and establishing of an office for Surgeons. Under the new arrangement, the hospital assistant had to look not only at hospitals and dispensaries but also at jails, police lines and schools. For carrying out such additional duties, the hospital assistant was granted an additional allowance of Rs.8 per month. A similar facility was prevailing in Bengal at that time, and the entitlement was Rs.15 per month.[39] Following this,a dispensary in addition to Gangtok and Chidam was opened at Rangpo in the year 1908.

The year 1912 saw the construction of a new hospital building at Gangtok. The building was ready for use in 1917. Maharaja TashiNamgyal inaugurated it on 24 September 1917. A sum of Rs 1,444 was spent on the purchase of equipment required for the hospital. The newly constructed administrative block accommodated rooms for the civil surgeons, medical officers, stores, dispensaries, medical examination units and two main wards. Dr J.N Turner continued to be the Assistant civil surgeon of the hospital.

The new hospital was named after the late Maharaja Sir ThutopNamgyal and came to be called Sir ThutopNamgyal Memorial Hospital. After this, the Namchi District Hospital was established with six beds in the year 1925, and then the Gyalshing District Hospital in the 1960s for the West District.[40]

The popularity of Western medicine was also due to the contribution of the Christian Missionaries towards building Public Health in Sikkim. However, The Sikkimese Durbar was reluctant towards the support of Christian missionaries in the development process. The Durbar was apprehensive as they suspected the Missionaries would upset the indigenous societies and create political instability. With the establishment of a Political Officer in Gangtok, it was of considerable interest to the missionaries, for whom expansion into Sikkim was a logical consequence of their existing work in Kalimpong-Darjeeling. By the 1880s, missionary strategists were confronting the problem of how best to encourage 'native' conversion. Their initiatives towards Sikkim developed at a time when medical services were increasingly seen as the most effective tool for conversions to Christianity. As a result, both the missionaries and the Government of India contributed to the early development of Western medicine in Sikkim.[41]

While eventually overtaken by state initiatives, the missionaries continued to be important agents for the spread of medicine, particularly in remote areas, down to the 1930s and 1940s. As in Kalimpong and elsewhere, their influence on professional standards and the moral and ethical boundaries of the medical profession was also significant. Demonstrating a strong work ethic and dedication to service, they set high standards of professional care that their Sikkimese trainees were required to emulate, no doubt aided by the fact that the Christian construct of the 'compassionate doctor' and ideals

Table 2: Number of people vaccinated from 1904 to 1932

Year	*Number of people vaccinated*		
	Male	*Female*	*Total*
1904	NA	NA	1,524
1905	NA	NA	3,220
1906	NA	NA	3,578
1907	NA	NA	4,712
1908	NA	NA	5,735
1909	NA	NA	5,652
1910	3,326	2,777	6,105
1911	3,282	2,393	5,675
1912	NA	NA	9,580
1913	5,279	4,301	11,195
1914	6,213	4,982	8,043
1915	4,462	3,581	11,503
1916	NA	NA	5,928
1917	NA	NA	6,163
1918	3,039	3,124	6,614
1919	3,250	3,391	4,489
1920	2,331	2,158	5,939
1921	NA	NA	3,870
1922	1,901	1,969	3,339
1923	NA	NA	6,676
1924	NA	NA	5,085
1925	NA	NA	7,010
1926	3,782	3,228	7,137
1927	NA	NA	9,477
1928	NA	NA	7,884
1929	NA	NA	5,915
1930	3,303	2,612	8,379
1931	5,027	3,352	2,451
1932	NA	NA	NA

Source: Administration Report of the State of Sikkim, Government of Sikkim from 1904 to 1932

of service to the poor translated without difficulty into similar Buddhist ideals.

Regarding diseases and vaccination programs, Sikkim was divided into four circles, with headquarters at Gangtok, Namchi, Seriyong (Soreng) and Mainbong (Maneybong). Each centre had its licensed vaccinator for the vaccination of the people and charged a fee of two annas for each vaccination. These circles were sometimes inspected by a Civil surgeon and the Sub-Inspector of vaccination.[42]

The table set above indicates an increasing trend in the number of people acquainted with Modern Western Medicine and, thus, opting for vaccination. The twentieth century ushered in modernity in Sikkim but also exposed diseases hitherto unknown to the indigenous people. Moreover, the establishment of new health centres and Hospitals gradually decreased the validity of vernacular medicine, rendering it obsolete.

The Colonial administration's intent was to develop health centres primarily for their own benefit, but this led to the de-recognition of the Vernacular knowledge system in Sikkim. This continued up to 1974, till the last reigning monarchs of Sikkim.

Alex Mc Kay writes:

> In the wider sense, the introduction of bio-medicine is part of the history of the encounter between non-Western culture and Western modernity. Medicine was one of several modern systems, sciences and technologies introduced into the Himalayan during this period. Its history provides a specific example of how that encounter produced stress and fractures in the existing socio-cultural, political and economic structures and processes and how it resulted in far-reaching transformations in indigenous worldviews...[43]

In the Sikkim Himalaya, the concluding decades of the nineteenth century increasingly witnessed great impetus for promoting Western medicine. Deepak Kumar mentions that Western medical discourse held a crucial position in colonisation.[44] It was a tool the British utilised for multifaceted psycho-cultural domination leading to the marginalisation of the indigenous health practices in Sikkim. Colonial literature addressed these traditions on the negative side and perceived them as superstitious, barbaric and irrational. This perception was carried by the administrators and missionaries alike, who eventually formulated policies and religious campaigns leading to the de-recognition of indigenous medicinal knowledge, substituting it. With the lack of people's faith and state patronage, folk healers and their knowledge gradually disappeared.

However, indigenous health practices are seeing their resurgence. The unremitting reliance upon folk medicine in rural areas compelled the authorities to encourage the study of the indigenous knowledge system. Currently, the institute of *Sowa-Rigpa* established at the Namgyal Institute of Tibetlogy (NIT) in 2015 as mandated by the State Government of Sikkim offers a bachelor's Degree in *Sowa-Rigpa* Medicinal Science (BSRMS).

Notes

1. Armen Takhtajan, *Flowering Plants; Origin and Dispersal.* Edinburg, Oliver and Boyd, 1969.
2. J. R. Subba, *History, Culture and Customs of Sikkim.* Gyan Publishing House: New Delhi, 2011, p. 23.
3. H. Bhirkumar Singh, R. Prasad and L. Rai, "Folk Medicinal Plant in the Sikkim Himalaya of India", *Asian Folk Studies*, Vol. 61, 2002, pp. 295-310,
4. *Ibid.*, p. 235.

5. T. K. and Sharma S. Sharma, *Medicinal Plants of Sikkim,* Sharma and Sharma Publications, Gangtok, 2010, pp. 1-6
6. Ashok Kumar Panda and Sangam Misra, "Health Traditions of Sikkim Himalaya", *Journal of Ayurveda and Integrative Medicine,* Vol 1, Issue 3, July 2010, p. 183.
7. J. R. Subba, *op. cit.*, p. 235
8. A *Namthar* is a spiritual biography or hagiography of Guru Padmasambhava of Tibetan Buddhism.
9. Ashok Kumar Panda and Sangam Misra, *op. cit.,* p.184.
10. Tenzing Zangmu Lepcha, "Health care practices in rural Sikkim: A Case Study Among Lepchas of Bakcha and Chojo Villages", Unpublished M. Phil Dissertation, Department of Anthropology, Sikkim University, 2018, pp. 73-90
11. Dashamula is a name given collectively to the Ten roots of certain plants, which is widely used in Ayurveda for many health conditions related to nerves, muscles, bones and joints.
12. Tenzing Zangmu Lepcha, *op. cit.*, p.90.
13. Heleen Plaisier, "Tales of LepchaCi, The Traditional Medicine for Lightheartedness", *Buddhist Himalaya: Studies in Religion, History, and Culture*, Volume II, 2011, p. 283.
14. *Bon*is an ancient religion of Tibet, and despite its assimilation with Buddhism, it is still practised today. For more readings on this, see Sudash Lama, "From Bon to Buddhism-Social and Cultural Changes of the Tamangs", Unpublished Ph. D Thesis, Department of History, University of North Bengal, 2013, p. 135,
15. Geoffrey Samuel, *Tantric Revisionings: New Understanding of Tibetan Buddhism and Indian Religion*, Motilal Banarsidass Publishers Pvt. Ltd., Delhi, 2005, pp. 123-24.
16. Yishey Doma, *Faith Healers of Sikkim: Traditions, Legends, and Rituals, Trysts & Traces* (For Information & Public Relations Department), Government of Sikkim, Haryana, 2018, p. 99.

17. J. J. Roy Burman, *Tribal Medicine*, Mittal Publication, Calcutta, 2003, p. 64.
18. D. Mandal, A. K. Panda and M. Rana, "Medicinal Plants Used in Folk Medicinal Practices Available in Rich Biodiversity in Sikkim", *Environment & Ecology* 31 (3A), July-September 2013, pp. 1445-1449.
19. H. H. Risley, *The Gazetteer of Sikkim*, Bengal Secretariat Press, Calcutta, 1894, p.2
20. J. R. Subba, *op. cit.*
21. Purna Hang Subba and Rangalal Mohapatra, *Society and Economy: The Limboos of Sikkim*, Blue Rose Publishers, Gangtok, 2018, p. 73.
22. Hemant K. Badola and Bharat K. Pradhan, "Indigenous Knowledge of Limboo Tribe in Khangchendzonga Biosphere Reserve", *Indian Journal of Traditional Knowledge*, Vol. 12, (1-4), 2013. pp. 355-369.
23. *Ibid.*
24. C. Helman, *Cultural, Health and Illness*, Butterworth Heineman, Oxford, 1990, pp.143-54.
25. A. K. Panda and S. Mishra, *op. cit.*, p. 185.
26. J. R. Subba, *op. cit.*, p 240.
27. Padma Gourmet, "Sowa Rigpa: Himalayan art of Healing", *Indian Journal of Traditional Knowledge*, Vol(3) 2, April 2004, pp.212-218
28. House of Namgyals was the Dynastic ruler of the erstwhile Kingdom of Sikkim who ruled over Sikkim from 1642 to 1974.
29. Padma Gourmet, *op. cit.*, pp.214-216
30. Shantiswarup Gupta, *British Relations with Bhutan*, Panchsheel, Prakashan, Jaipur, 1974. pp. 39-40.
31. William Dalrymple, *The Anarchy: The East India Company Corporate Violence and the Pillage of an Empire*, Bloomsbury Publishing, London, 2019.

32. Arbinda Deb, *India and Bhutan: A Study in Frontier Political Relations (1772-1865),* Firma KLM, Pvt., Ltd., Calcutta, 1976, p. 56.
33. S. C. Sarkar, "Some Notes on the Intercourse of Bengal with the Northern Countries in the Second Half of the Eighteenth Century", *Bengal Past and Present.*Vol.XLI, 1931, p. 121.
34. Sunita Kharel and Jigme Wangchuk Bhutia, *Gazetteer of Sikkim*, Government of Sikkim, Gangtok, 2013, p. 476.
35. *Ibid.*, p. 476.
36. *Report of Foreign Department Proceedings*, Government of Sikkim, August 1892, pp. 140-157.
37. Sunita Kharel and Jigme Wangchuk Bhutia, *op. cit.,* p. 447.
38. *Ibid.*, p. 478.
39. *Ibid.*, p. 479.
40. *Ibid.*
41. Mckay. *op. cit.* p. 29.
42. Kharel, Sunita & Bhutia, Jigme Wangchuk. *op. cit.,* pp. 480-481.
43. Alex Mc Kay, *op. cit.,* p 29.
44. Kumar Deepak, *Medical Encounters in British India, 1820-1920,* Vol. 32, No.04 Journal of Economic and Political Weekly, 1997, pp. 166-170.

8

Epidemic and Community Resilience amongst the Khasi-Jaintia of Meghalaya: A Social History

Sashi Teibor Laloo and Andrew G Marwein

The outbreak of the Covid-19 endemic worldwide, health issues and the reaction and response of societies have given historians a new lease of life to turn their attention and look back to the epidemics and the community resilience that had occurred in the past. The community, which suffers at the one hand and prepare to survive and fight the epidemic, is important. In the past, in Khasi-Jaintia society of Meghalaya has witnessed an epidemic in the form of plague, and the society has shown its resilience. Though there were many types of research on modern political, economic, cultural and social histories, church histories, and the colonial impact on Khasi-Jaintia society, the aspects of epidemic and social resilience have not caught the attention of earlier writers exclusively. This aspect had also yet to find focus in the studies on the development of health missions of the Christian and other missionaries in the Khasi-Jaintia Hills. It is in this background that this paper explores the outbreak of plague and the social resilience of the Khasi-Jaintia society. The article is divided into three parts.

The first part deals with the importance of oral history as a methodology for obtaining information from oral sources. The second part briefly deals with the concept of social history and its implication in the hills, and the third part consists of discussion and analysis.

I

According to a famous belief, the indigenous Khasi-Jaintia community trace their origins from a sacred hill called *Lum* Sohpetbneng and, over time, settled in the central, eastern hills and foothills of Meghalaya. This sacred hill was believed that the earth (man) and heaven (God) were once connected by a Golden Ladder, also revered as the navel of the earth. However, a tragic event led to a decree that forever disconnected the ladder and social bond. In the process of being separated from the Nine Clans of *Khyndai Skum* in heaven, the *HynniewTrep – NiawWasa* or the Seven Clans comprising of the Khynriam, Pnar, Bhoi, War, Maram, Lyngngam and the extinct Diko settled across the Khasi-Jaintia Hills. I Find this Highlighted Portion Irrelevant; though it Talks About Oral Tradition, the Context of the Paper is Not About the Origin of the Khasi But Deals with the Emergence of Plague and Resilience. To Introduce The Khasi-Jaintia, this is Important.

Like most indigenous communities the world over, the Khasi-Jaintia have for centuries passed down their knowledge of health, culture, tradition, resilience, rituals and law through oral narratives and expressions for many generations. These observations, especially to invoke the Almighty's blessing and various other social practices over time, have most prominently been showcased in religious events and festivals to develop a sense of belongingness and identity. Easter Syiem is of the opinion that:

> The Khasis have their knowledge system embedded deep in their racial memory and exert an influence parallel to the Western. It has flourished in the crevices of a culture that is mediated between what may be defined as inherited, primary intelligence vis-à-vis imparted knowledge of a secondary nature. This oral intelligence may be harvested from the elders of any village or clan who, by virtue of having interacted in this world longer than others, are the repositories of knowledge and their respective communities.[1]

Over the years, the community has depended on oral traditions when it comes to retelling stories that are associated with significant events. These, over time, became sources for historians to dig into the past and hence use oral history to extract the required information. To stress the significance of oral histories, Paul Thompson emphasises the implications of oral history. He adds that history is recorded from the standpoint of authority, and oral history gives a voice to the voiceless – the common man, the underprivileged and the defeated. Hence, to give voice to the voiceless, "oral history has radical implication for the social message of history as a whole."[2] The history of events is generally written and narrated from "above", which is again sceptical from the common people's standpoint. In giving prominence to the richness of historical sources, anecdotes and oral histories must be considered and given a place. Keeping in mind that most of the indigenous communities in North-East are "oral societies" for many centuries, Jan Vansina, whose area of research is on the Sub-Saharan African societies, states that such communities are "oral civilisations"[3] where the significance is found in 'word of mouth', and this ongoing practice is passed on from one generation to the other.

II

For a broad overview in understanding the Khasi-Jaintia community from the perspective of social history, it becomes pertinent to have a brief look at the conceptual framework relevant to many aspects of the 'once oral-based communities'. In defining social history, Raphael Samuel opines that it "prides itself on being concerned with 'real life' rather than abstractions, with 'ordinary' people rather than privileged elites, with everyday things rather than sensational events."[4] Samuel further emphasised that the dignity of the 'ordinary' people is a unifying theme in this scope of historical enquiry and retrieval, be it a celebration of everyday life or hardships and suffering.[5]

Social history can broadly be understood as a field in history which:

> Had emerged as a trend in the mid-twentieth century as a reaction to older fields—political history, diplomatic history, the history of great men and great ideas—that, in their focus on elites, failed to address the historical experiences of the vast majority of the human population. Social historians, committed to understanding the lives of ordinary people, have faced particular challenges in locating sources. Over time, most non-elites have had little access to the written word; most of the textual sources that do yield information about them were created by those who governed or employed them. Rather than being discouraged by these challenges, social historians have responded creatively, turning to quantitative data, material and visual culture, the built environment, and oral histories to supplement more traditional archival and printed sources.[6]

From the broad concept of social history, it is, therefore, a task for historians to relook into the events of importance which had affected the lives and settlements of the people, which came in many forms, such as plagues, natural calamities, and others. It was the people who were affected, and through their resilience, that victory over the plagues was achieved. Therefore, with regards to the engagement of the Khasi-Jaintia with various plagues, diseases, healing practices and rituals related to the same, we need to study these encounters based on oral traditions and oral histories, which at the same time could bring up a social history, of this particular community. The Merriam Webster dictionary defines a plague as an epidemic causing a high mortality rate and affecting a disproportionately large number of individuals within a population, community or region at the same time. Mary Lowth, in explaining the differences between a plague, epidemic and a pandemic, cites that:

> The terms plague, epidemic and pandemic are used almost interchangeably in the media but mean different things. An epidemic is generally an outbreak of disease widespread enough to affect a whole population – an area, a country or even a continent. The edges blur with the term pandemic, which crosses into other populations and continents globally. The term outbreak is usually synonymous with an epidemic. A plague is an epidemic disease that spreads rapidly to affect populations. It does not need to be global to deserve the term. It usually means a disease with high lethality, and historically has been used to apply to bubonic plague, which has swept the world several times.[7]

The significance of festivals and religious events observed by the people throughout the centuries must be considered when it comes to the study of the endemics that occurred in hill societies. Apart from the colourful festivities and jubilations, the most significant part consists of the solemn prayers of thanksgiving, seeking divine blessings, good health and warding off famines and diseases that may plague the land. However, throughout the chapter, an equivalent term in the vernacular understanding in describing such a plague or equivalent phenomenon will be referred to as "Khlam". *Khlam*, in the Khasi-Jaintia context, also refers not only to diseases contracted among humans but an umbrella term for blights and diseases in the agricultural and animal husbandry sectors.

The Khasi-Jaintia community were largely agriculturalists and traders; therefore, most of their festivals revolved around their occupation and hopes of prosperity, free from sickness/diseases and bountiful harvests. Soumen Sen has stated on the Behdienkhlam festival that social behaviour in indigenous societies relies to a great extent upon ritual events and celebrations involving collective initiatives of a family, clan and the community at large.[8] For centuries, theories of creation, migration, traditions, uprisings and resilience to plagues have been passed down orally through stories, phrases and songs. Another important observation is that these oral-based communities and their belief system strongly associate with nature. In the indigenous faith and spirituality, as God all mighty reigns supreme, the acknowledgement of spirits, both good and evil, who dwell/are present in various forms and elements in nature –mountains, hills, rivers, lakes, forests and animals - is registered. For centuries, the Khasi community have held these elements in high regard and often prayed and offered sacrifices for the well-being of the land and its people, for bountiful harvests at the same time to ward off evils and plagues. With inadequate healthcare measures back in the days when the *khlam*(s) swept the villages, it left the Khasi-Jaintia residents no option but to migrate to safer areas, leaving behind remnants of stone monuments like house/wall foundations, religious megaliths and commemorative stones which stands as testimony to the ongoing oral histories up to the present day.

III

In understanding the world view of the Khasi-Jaintia in the past, apart from acknowledging God the creator, P R T Gurdon, in his observation (i.e. a Western perspective of the people), records that certain evil spirits are both acknowledged by the people ranging from "Ka Rih, the malarial fever devil; ka Khlam, the demon of cholera; Lea Duba, the fever devil which is said to haunt the neighbourhood of Theriaghat"[9] in the southern Khasi foothills bordering Bangladesh. Considering the vast economic dependencies of the Khasi-Jaintia communities with the people of Sylhet,[10] one may have new perspectives if focused on the perspective of epidemics, which resulted from the hill-plain interactions. In most cases (not all), sicknesses and plagues have a pattern of emerging in villages along the foothills or areas where traders shared socio-economic interactions with the plains of Sylhet. Keeping in mind such social interactions of people belonging to different geographies in the past and the development of diseases, for instance, Pranay Lal stated that "the Spanish conquistadors unknowingly carried the smallpox virus in their lungs to the New World, disseminating the natives"[11] leading to the collapse of the mighty Aztec and Inca empires in the 1500s despite the Spaniards being highly outnumbered.

Khasi Hills: Plagues and Resilience

For centuries, the Khasi revered nature in its various forms and elements as their guardian spirits. During the harvesting period, they would offer prayers, perform rituals and offer sacrifices to invoke the blessings of God and the spirits, and at the same time, for protection against plagues and other negativities affecting their livelihood. Gurdon also stated that the duties of the *Lyngdohs* (Priests) regarding leading the community worship and seeking divine intervention offering prayers and sacrifices during cholera and such-like visitations of sickness (jingiapkhlam).[12]As *Khlam*(s) or epidemics swept the settlements, the community practised migration, leaving behind their settlements in search of greener pastures both in terms of slash and burn agricultural practices and the overall well being of the population. In the process, many distinctive natural formations like rocks, hills and rivers have been personified and considered sacred guardians. Therefore, as people left their original settlements in the setting in or prevalence of plagues, the significance of rituals and religious practices was always included. These rituals observed in time began to take shape into awaited annual events, and the activities started to be expressed in feasts and dance and, over the centuries, developed into festivals and community participation. Mentioned below are some of the many instances where migrations due to *Khlam* (s) occurred, and these stories have been passed down through the ages.

We come across the Khlam, which occurred in the Khasi Hills at Twahlongwar, an abandoned settlement under the *Raid* Sawsymper. According to folklore passed through the years, the inhabitants of this village came to the site from a parent village called Twahnongrod which is now under the Mawsynram Civil sub-division. The people of Twahnongrod were masters in the field of trade and commerce. Owing to Twahlongwar's strategic location, it served as a link or a socio-economic corridor between the surrounding highland villages and the border *Haats* (markets) in the plains of Sylhet. The village's popularity grew and attracted people from the neighbouring villages in search of work, labour and settlement. The social interactions between the hills and the plains grew in the process of expansion. During times of plagues, a particular plague known to locals as *Ka Khlam Prie Pynhiar* (Cholera) broke out and devastated the entire settlement of Twahlongwar. The sickness was so severe that families fled the village and wandered to nearby forests far from the affected surroundings. The village, with all its promising aspects of trade and commerce, eventually came to a halt and was abandoned for fear of sickness and death. As recollected in folklore, the inhabitants migrated to establish new settlements around the foothills of *Lum* Symper. Therefore, *Lum* Symper, in time, began to be revered as a guardian spirit, where settlers offered prayers and held rituals in the surrounding sacred forests for protection over any natural calamity and sickness that may befall them.[13]

There is a general belief that the social remnants around the foothills of Lum Symper are sacrificial sites for prayers and offerings. Further, the villagers of the *Raid* Saw Symper considered this peak the abode of a spirit known as *Basa* or the guardian spirit.[14] Occasionally, the residents of the villages recounted tales of observing/encountering the guardian spirit in the form of a tiger roaming on the cliffs of the peak, while others witnessed the spirit appearing in the form of a bright object circling the peak at night. If one visits the abandoned settlement of Twahlongwar, there are still remnants of stone foundations, an iron smelting centre, a unique monolith called 'U Maw Sngi' and various footpaths.

Other oral narratives tell us about the migration of people from one part of the land to another due to the rise of plagues. Focussing on different regions in the Khasi Hills, stories of migration due to plagues were retold by Mrs Relsi Nohriang, an 86 year old village elder.[15] She recollected that histories of migrations and settlements were passed down from her great

Grandmother. A *Khlam* that severely impacted the region of Balat (a village in the Southern foothills of Khasi Hills bordering Bangladesh) led to the abandonment of villages. The villages that were abandoned in the process of establishing new villages, she recollected, were:

(a) The inhabitants of Mawkhmah/Nongpynden migrated to the present village of Kynrang and Rangweng

(b) From Pyndensaw to the village of Nongrim.

(c) From Nongtynhiang to the village of Mawpot

(d) From Dewsaw to Mawkhnai, then to present day Phlangwanbroi.

Similarly, stories embedded in folk narratives were passed to Mrs Adalin Lyndoh Nonglait.[16] She recollects stories of a *Khlam* where the inhabitants had no option but to leave their homes and head to a secluded forest, settling in caves and makeshift shelters. Phriekskila Lyndoh[17] shared the same opinion when *Ka Khlam Prie Pynhiar* (Cholera) rampaged the region, and forest settlements were made to protect themselves from the infected areas.

Local practices and rituals associated with epidemics in the past

In the long tradition of dealing with *khlam*(s), certain annual events began to be observed, and these community initiatives gradually took shape in the form of annual festivals. The people of Wahlong village in the southern Khasi foothills bordering Bangladesh used to practice a festival known as *Ka Beh Khlam*. This annual ritual was mainly practised in warding off plagues from the community. The ritual begins in the morning, in which the men would enter every house and use sticks to ward off any unforeseen negativity that lurks in the household. This act would continue to all the surrounding vicinity of the neighbourhood till they reach the community well. On completing the day's task, the residents would meet for prayers which were followed by the sacrificing of a bull and later feasted by the entire village.[18] We, therefore, see similarities among the regions bordering the plains of Sylhet in Bangladesh – where hardships of the plagues were met with a strong sense of community bonding and resilience, which began to be commemorated as a festival over the decades.

Regarding animal husbandry, stories of *khlam*(s) (context applied to both animals and humans) that consumed the livestock is still a matter of concern and interesting solutions rooted in folk practices/beliefs are still followed. It was said that in the case of domesticated animals, khlam(s) occur during the change of seasons. So when sickness aggravated in the surrounding villages and if two or more fowls fell prey, these particular fowls were cooked and consumed instead of burying them. This practice is believed to stop spreading the sickness to other animals, thereby preventing high mortality rates. There is also a practice where villagers place a piece of burning coal near a poultry shed. This act is performed believing that the smoke emitted is strong enough to cast away any infection from the prevailing *khlam*. Though not scientifically proven, this act is still carried out, especially around the coal belt regions in the Khasi Hills. Another interesting practice was the use of 'millipedes' during *ki aiom khlam* (the epidemic seasons) amongst livestock. Embedded in folklore, millipedes are kept inside a transparent bottle and tied above the shed.[19]

Once upon a time, when humans still communicated with the elements of nature and all dependencies and providence from God, a *khlam* engulfed the Khasi Hills and left the population in despair. According to folklore, a millipede offered help and went to meet the sickness (personified) and questioned the *khlam*'s audacity as to why it brought so much suffering to the people, thus challenging it to a contest. The millipede put to terms that if the *khlam* can count all its legs, it has all the right to destroy and end humankind for good. However, if the *khlam* failed to do so, it should leave the people and never return back. On the day of the contest, the *khlam* started counting the millipede's legs, and as the count neared the end, the millipede moved its body, causing confusion and chaos, which prompted a recount all over again. This act of the millipede continued until the *khlam* lost patience and gave up. Hence from that moment onwards, the sickness and its destruction finally left the hills.[20] So based on such oral traditions, actions and practices that occurred during hardships began to create a trend that eventually led to the inclusion in the belief system and then carried out as a process of healing.

Photo: A millipede in West Khasi Hills

In another series of interviews, many individuals from different parts of the Khasi Hills testify to the use of Marijuana among livestock in dealing with the ongoing sickness that usually occurs once or twice yearly. In rural areas, people rearing fowls and pigs often prepare their livestock for unforeseen epidemics by crushing or cutting marijuana and mixing it with the food/ water until the sickness is over. Similarly, in some places, garlic is used instead of marijuana, where garlic-infused water is fed to the livestock until the threat is over. Interestingly, there is also the practice of mixing rice with alcohol given especially to poultry with the belief that it would build immunity. Indigenous wisdom and practices is an art developed through time, and for such activities to persist to date, there must be significant results and outcome.

Jaintia Hills: from Plagues to Festivals

To understand the advent of the biggest festival (and its primary purpose) in the Jaintia Hills, Dawmanchuh Lamar, who has contributed immensely towards the subject matter, wrote that when the Almighty had given the *U Niawtrep-U Niawskum* (the seven clans) on earth with *Ki Hukum* and *Ki Adong* (directives and proscriptions), *U Tre-Kirot* (Almighty) then made a promise that He will visit the earth and its people and dwell for four days and three nights. In return, He wished for a dance amongst his people. Accordingly, Jowai as a place was chosen and found suitable by *U Syiem Pyrthat* and thirteen Divinities upholding the decree of visitation from God. God then sent forth four sisters named Ka Bon, Ka Tein, Ka Wet and Ka Doh to settle along with the *U Niawtrep-Niawskum* that initiated priestly ranks for the dance. As the years passed, a sturdy population began to settle in Jowai, which mainly comprised four clans – Ki San Syngkong, Challam, Passah and

Chullai, respectively. This group of people in Jowai celebrated the first Behdienkhlam with U Dongsaniriang Paswet as the *Dalloi* and U Het Langdoh as the *Langdoh* (priest). Dawmanchuh Lamar added that the Behdienkhlam Festival as we know it today has its origins rooted deep in the wishes of *U Tre-Kirot* (God Almighty). Before the commencement of the festival, ceremonial rights, prayers and rituals are evoked by the *Khatsoo Waheh* (Council of fourteen priests) to purify the path for the annual arrival of U Tre-Kirot and cast away evil and plagues from the community.[21]

As the population began to grow over the centuries, the people migrated and formed villages around the region and accordingly, Behdienkhlam celebrations were observed by the *Ki Soo Langdoh* (four priestly villages) comprising Chyrmang, Jowai, Tuber and Mukhla in Jaintia Hills. Eventually, as the festival became more extravagant and colourful, *Ki Rong* or decorated structures/beams, were duly incorporated. In the present day celebrations, *Ki Rong* represented each locality decorated with strong social messages. In the early stages of their introduction, *Rong*(s) were made of headless animals to denote the *khlam* or the deadly Cholera epidemic in the region.[22] I. M. Simon gave us an interesting insight into the developments of the celebration, still keeping in mind the original wish of U Tre-Kirot. Simon opines that Cholera took a heavy toll on the people of Jowai at a certain point in time.[23] This narration was further elaborated as:

> The Behdienkhlam festival, at its nascent stage, was known as Ka Chad Soo Sngi-Le Iaw. But at some stage in history during the period of the then Jaintia kingdom, a plague broke out in the plain belt of Jaintiapur and spread to the hills then known as the *Ka Ri Khadar Dolloi*, it became a captivating issue in the minds of the people of the time.

> During the ensuing annual festival, prayers were offered to *U Tre-Kirot* to cast off the disease, and soon it was called 'Ka Behdienkhlam'.[24]

The term Behdienkhlam is derived from the Pnar words 'Beh', meaning to chase/cast away or to get rid of, 'dien' is a tree in the Pnar dialect and 'khlam' is understood as famine or epidemic. I M Simon wrote that, on the third day of the ceremony, using bamboo poles, people would tap their houses in a symbolic gesture to chase away the illness and negativity that may befall the household. In the past (a practice still held to the very day), the central aspect of the ceremony was performed at the centre of the village at a place called Wah Eitnar. Simon wrote: "The entire village would prepare a large beam, and the part of the village on one side of the stream would drag the beam to the stream and place it in the streambed and the other side would take the beam out of the streambed and take it to their part of the village."[25]

Another festival observed in Jaintia Hills is the Tiger Festival at the Nongtalang village in the southern parts of the hills near the Indo-Bangladesh border. H. L. Deb Roy mentions that all the twelve founding clans of the village took responsibility for performing the annual festival in rotation in spring or before the onset of monsoon. Before the auspicious occasion, a tiger is hunted; the flesh and intestines are removed, leaving the skull, skeletons and skin. On the day of the festival, it is placed inside the village boundary. People visit and walk around houses offering prayers and chants, driving away epidemics while ushering good fortunes and is marked by a battle dance before the *Langdoh*'s residence.[26]

On the basis of above discussion, by way of conclusion, it can be said that the study of epidemic through social history perspective provides a comprehensive socio-cultural aspect of society. It also indicates the continuity of the cultural values and social lore despite the increasing education in rural areas and efforts made by the health and veterinary departments to treat livestock, indigenous wisdom and practices throughout the centuries have persisted hand in hand or are never out of sight. Resilience to *khlam*(s) in all forms has undoubtedly brought the community to 'think' and 'act' together.

Notes

1. Easter Syiem, *The Oral Discourse in Khasi Folk Narrative*, Publication: EBH Publishers (India), Guwahati, 2011, p.28.
2. Paul Thompson, *The Voice of the Past: Oral History*, Oxford University Press, New York, 2000, 3rd edition, pp. 6-7.
3. Jan Vansina, "Once Upon a Time: Oral Traditions as History in Africa", in *Daedalus*, Vol. 100, No. 2, p.442, http://www.jstor.org/stable/20024011 , accessed on 15.3.2017.
4. Raphael Samuel, 'What is Social History…?' in *What is History Today…?*, Juliet Gardiner (ed.), The Macmillan Press, London, 1988, p.43.
5. Raphael Samuel, *op.cit.,*, p.46.
6. The Department of History, University of Chicago, 'Social History', https://history.uchicago.edu/content/social-history, accessed on 26.1. 2022.
7. Mary Lowth, "Plagues, Pestilence and Pandemics: Deadly Diseases and Humanity", pp.42-46, https://www.researchgate.net/publication/298130276_Plagues_pestilence_and_pandemics_Deadly_diseases_and_humanity/citation/download, accessed on 25.2.2022.
8. Soumen Sen, "Functions of Community Festivals and a Case Study of Behdienkhlam Festival of Jaintia Hills", http://megartsculture.gov.in/herit-functs-case-study.htm, accessed on the 1.8.2020.

9. P. R. T. Gurdon, *The Khasis*, Akansha Publishing House, New Delhi, 2010, reprint, p.107.
10. The frontiers of Sylhet and the abundance of natural resources from the Khasi-Jaintia Hills attracted the Mughals, the Europeans mercantilist interests making it very cosmopolitan.
11. Pranay Lal, *Invisible Empire: The Natural History of Viruses*, Thomson Press India Ltd., New Delhi, 2021, p.87.
12. P. R. T. Gurdon, *op.cit.,* p.121.
13. An Interview with Mr Phording Kharlyngdoh on 31st January 2018 at Saitshiliah Village, South West Khasi Hills.
14. In locating the role and significance of Guardian Spirits in the Khasi community's understanding, Barnes L. Mawrie stated that "The Khasis also believed in the existence of good spirit, the spirits of the mountain and the rivers (*kileilumleiwah*) whom the almighty God has put on earth to be its guardians. It is wrong to conclude that the Khasis worshipped Nature's spirit as if they were gods or goddesses. Instead, these spirits are considered powerful influencing elements in nature. The good spirits as seen as guardians appointed by the almighty who keeps a watch over his creations; over the hills and rivers (*leilumleiwah*), over the villages (*leikhyndopleishnong*), over the trees and forests (*leikhlawleibtap*). These spirits are seen as the extension of God the Almighty, who is omnipresent and omniscient. The Khasis believed that as long a person fears God and does not violate His commandments, he will be looked after and protected by these good spirits, and he can never be affected by the evil forces." See, Barnes L. Mawrie, *The Khasis and their Natural Environment*, Bhabani Offset & Imaging Systems Pvt. Ltd., Guwahati, 2009, pp. 146-147.
15. An Interview with Mrs Relsi Nohriang on 24th May 2020 at Nongstoin Town. She is a native of Pyngdensohsaw, East Khasi Hills District.

16. An Interview with Adalin Lyndoh Nonglait on the 4th of July, 2020, at Tiehsaw Village, West Khasi Hills District. Her native village is Mawkyllei in West Khasi Hills District.
17. A telephonic interview with Mrs Lyngdoh on 6th July 2020. She hails from the village of Kynshi in the West Khasi Hills District.
18. Kyntiewbor War, 'U Luk Sing Syiem' in the souvenir of *The Silver Jubilee Celebration of the Sunjuk War Wahlong*, Shillong, 2016.
19. A telephonic Interview with Mr Rosting Wanniang on 13th July 2020. A resident of Mariot village in West Khasi Hills District. Mr. Wanniang hails from the Mawkynrum Village in the same District.
20. The Plague and the Millipede, a Digital Story by Grace Temsen in Living Tongues Institute for Endangered Languages, 7th February 2011.
21. Dawmanchuh Lamar, *An Insight into Behdienkhlam Festival*, Eastern Panorama Offset, Shillong, 2015, pp. 11-13.
22. *Ibid.*, p.14.
23. I M Simon, *Khasi and Jaintia Tales and Beliefs, Department of Tribal Culture and Folklore Research*, Lakshmi Printing Press, Guwahati, 1966, p.38; P R T Gurdon, *op.cit.*, p. 158.
24. Dawmanchuh Lamar, *op.cit.*, p. 3.
25. I M Simon , *op.cit.*, p. 39.
26. H. L. Deb Roy, *A Tribe in Transition: The Jaintias of Meghalaya*, Cosmo Publications, New Delhi, 1981, pp. 24-25.

9

Festivals and Sports of the Rongmei Naga

Kamei Kabinai

The term *Rongmei* (*Rong* meaning south or southern direction and *Mei* meaning man or people) would mean the people of the fallow lands or the southerners.[1] The Rongmei people inhabit the three north-eastern states of India, namely, Assam, Manipur and Nagaland. Scholars believe that the Rongmei's ancient home is the western portion of Manipur which is extensively covered by the region of Tamenglong.[2] The festivals celebrated by the Rongmei people are associated with almost every agricultural season. Various games and sports were organised during these festivals, providing people with recreation time and relaxation from their daily work. The festivals of the Rongmei are intertwined with indigenous games and sports which form an essential component of their culture, providing an outlet for recreation and enjoyment and bringing a sense of social harmony along with personality development among the people. According to scholars, religion is the foundation for most of the festivals of the Rongmei,[3] therefore, during these activities, the Rongmei also expressed their reverence and adoration to their Gods through rituals which also included prayers, songs, dance, etc. There is a deep sense of social significance attached to the festivals. Therefore, organised games and sports transcend life's immediate needs and impart meaning to the actions, which are considered a special form of activity and a social function. Organised games and sports, such as Taupwang Phaimai, Chwang Phianmei, etc., form a part of the identity and socio-religious as well as cultural fabric of the people.

Recognition of games and sports played by the people of the Rongmei tribe and the need to research, analyse and deconstruct sports and their relationship with festivals is still relatively thin. Some works have been done on the origin, political history, and culture of the Rongmei tribe both by scholars from within as well as from outside. But writings on the relationship and socio-cultural function of games and sports played during the festivals only have a brief entry, if not at all. Colonial ethnographers like W. McCulloch, T. C. Hodson, Johnstone, R. Brown, and R. B. Pemberton have written about the people but have hardly mentioned festivals and sports. Writings from both foreign and local scholars are relatively new in their enquiry and research about the indigenous games and their relationship with festivals which forms a part of their culture and identity. Historically informed scholarship and a serious academic enquiry on traditional games and festivals can make a significant contribution to the social and cultural understanding of the Rongmei tribe. Another useful contribution that can be made is the demonstration of the importance of regional and local identities, which sports and festivals help to shape and sustain the people. However, there is a lack of effort to bring out the nature and significance of these games and sports. Much acknowledgement is due to be given by academicians towards the study of the games as mentioned above and sports of the Rongmei. In light of the above, this paper attempts to study the relationship, socio-cultural values, nature and characteristics of the indigenous games and sports of the Rongmei.

Every community allotted certain days to commemorate any important event in which cohesiveness is provided to an individual's religious, political, or socio-economic relation with the society. Such days or periods generally originated in religious celebrations or ritual commendations that usually included sacred community meals are called feasts or festivals."[4] Therefore, a festival is a community event in which members of a particular social or religious group take part. It serves as a marker of historical or mythological events and commemorates the legends and heroes intrinsic to the identity of a particular community. It can also mark the beginning or end of a season of an important phase in the solar/ lunar or agrarian cycle. The celebration of festivals involves specific ceremonies, the use of special crafts, songs and dances, ritual motifs, symbols, ritualistic games and sports, or ceremonial preparation of particular food items. Game/Sport[5] would denote a pleasant pastime, a diversion and an athletic contest[6] and offers a 'dynamic accessible window into politics, economics, gender, race, class formation, ideology, religion and virtually any discipline.'[7]

Ancient people had many festivals, which were mostly religious in nature. Whenever they celebrated any good fortune, they believed they had to share part of what they enjoyed with their Gods. Their festivals were intended to promote the flourishing of nature and fertility in humans and animals.[8] The ancient Romans celebrated several festivals which were of diverse origins. The important festivals were Lupercalia, a fertility festival, and the Ferelia, an annual public ceremony in honour of the dead and games also were held in this connection. The Regifugium was celebrated on the event of the overthrow of the kings and establishment of the republic in 510 B.C.[9] Knowledge of the primitive festivals of Greece has derived mainly from the epic poems of the Ancient Greek poet Homer. The Iliad has referred to many festivals, such as Panathenaca, the oldest and most important festival of Athens, held in honour of Athena, patron goddess of the city, and the Odyssey alludes to a festival that was held at the new moon. They also celebrated a harvest festival. The nemesis festival, held in honour of the dead, originated in Asiatic ancestor worship rituals. In commemorating great historical events, the Athenians held festivals- such as the victory over the Persians at the Marathon in 490 B.C. In celebration of festivals, they held athletic contests known as the Isthmian, Olympian, Pythian, and Nemean games, etc.[10] In Japan, the agriculturists celebrated Tasobi (rice-field ritual) festivals at the beginning of the year to ensure a plentiful harvest. They performed dances, songs sung with a Sasara (musician instrument), sowing of seeds, and feasting. These played important roles in securing the aid kami (gods or spirits). They also performed divination using archery, in which the angle of the arrow on the target is significant, which had been used in shrines to help determine the methods that should be used to secure a good crop.[11]

According to Gangmumei Kamei, "Festivals are a vehicle of religion and the Zeliangrong religion is sustained by their colourful festivals accompanied by religious rites and prayers, dance and music and feasting during different months of the year."[12] R. Brown writes, "The festive occasions among the *kowpois* are numerous, and are characterised by feasting, drinking, dancing and singing, and un-moderate amount of haw-haw or peculiar cry of the hill-men without which no entertainment of any kind would be complete."[13] The Kowpois (kabuki/rongmei) are very particular in observing their various festivals and celebrating them with all their might. According to him, the following are the chief festivals of the Rongmei; first, the Enghan (Gaan Ngai), which happens in or about December. During the five days of its continuance, all the village inhabitants dressed in their best attire, keeping up the dance and song. They were interrupted only by short intervals of repose and broke dedicated to feasting. Next, the Ringnai (Rih Ngai) festival, celebrated in or about January, lasts three days. During this festival, the men and women fetch the water separately for their use. The men, having killed pigs, take a portion for themselves, and give a portion to the women, and having cooked them separately, they eat them separately, the men in the house of the head of the family, the women each in her own house. An effigy of a man made of plantain is hung on a tree, and they throw pointed bamboo or sticks at it. Should the javelin strike it on the head, the thrower, it is said, will kill an enemy; but if it lodges in the belly, the thrower is to be blessed with plenty of good. This festival is said to be in honour of their ancestors, but the only visible sign of this is sprinkling their graves with their particular drink. It is then also customary to choose a man to go at midnight to the outer entrance of the village to take the omens regarding their welfare in the ensuing year. If, whilst at the entrance, he hears anything like the dragging of wood, tigers will make mischief; if the falling of leaves, there will be much sickness. On these occasions, young men have been known to cause the omen-taker no small fright, but such pranks are considered sure to bring punishment on their performers, and not long ago, a young man, after having played the tiger, died on his way to the valley; his death was universally attributed to his having incurred the anger of the deity on occasion. In February, there is a festival of three days' continuance, in which the ears of the children born after the last festival of this nature are pierced. This festival is known as the Nahnu Ngai, i.e. (Ear piercing festival). He also mentioned that after the festival of the Oodui Yung" (Gudui Ngai) or Mahlong," (Maleng Ngai) as it is also called, when the cutting down of the jungle on the rooms is finished, a curious ceremony takes place. All the people bathe after the work is completed, and, in addition, their agricultural implements are also dipped in a running stream, as they also are supposed to be exhausted by their labours; thus refreshed, the tools are hung up in their houses until again required for use.[14] With regards to games played by the Rongmei tribe, the juvenile population is fond of kang Canada of the Manipuris, only however, played with the seed of the Gaa creeper. This game is known as the *Gaa towmei/pinmei* among the Rongmei. He also opines that the Rongmei have the spinning top, spun with a string, exactly like those used amongst English boys. For the adults, javelin throw is most played and practised to make them efficient with the spear.

Regarding the festivals, E. T. Dalton observes, "There are first *Engan*, which happens in December. During the five days of its continuance, all the inhabitants of the village dressed in their best attire keep up the dance and song interrupted only by short intervals of response and breaks dedicated to feasting. Next is *Reing-nai* in or about January, which lasted for three days. During this festival, men and women separately fetch the water that each may require. In these festivals, the ancestors' graves are sprinkled with the national drink, and on its termination omen are sought for the selection of land for cultivation and the general welfare in the ensuing years."[15] According to Kamei Budha Kabui 'their rejoining of festivals have expressed through prayer and thanksgiving to God for his blessing of good harvest and welfare and protection against disease and hardship. The honour and farewell to the ancestors are also reflected in the festival. The social and cultural values, the aesthetic and creative sense, their love of beauty and colour are expressed in these festivals." L. Jeyaseelan mentions, "It is believed that the ritual dance and music are a form of worship of God. Dancing, singing, eating and drinking are the four main highlights of festivals among the tribal's of Manipur."

The Rongmei vocabulary for the word festivals is *Ngai* meaning to 'rejoin or celebrate.'[16] while the word *Talimei, Palupmei and Palup Akhiamei* would mean play, games and sports. An individual Rongmei citizen has two ways of passing through time- the sacred and the profane. Throughout history, the sacred time has been interconnected with sports, religious celebrations, and festivals.[17] Like other communities, they also celebrate all their festivals based on the different stages of agricultural operations; pre-operation and post-harvest. The festivals' time and mode of celebration may slightly differ from one area to another due to their agricultural timings and influences of the locality.[18] Different festivals or festivities have different purposes. Some festivals are celebrated for the propitiation of gods and supernatural powers, while others are meant to get protection from natural calamities. Among the Rongmei tribe, certain festivals, such as the *Gaan Ngai*, are celebrated to appease the ancestors who are dead and for the family's welfare. Some other festivals are secular or social in nature, giving the people an opportunity for enjoyment and merry-making. The social and cultural values, the aesthetics and creative sense, and their love of beauty and colours are expressed in these festivals. Games and sports associated with the major festivals of the Rongmei tribe are discussed in this paper.

Gaan Ngai

Gaan Ngai is the most important and greatest festival of the Rongmei tribe, which inhibits in Assam, Manipur and Nagaland. Gaan Ngai means festival of the winter season; Gaan means winter or dry season, and *Ngai* means festival.[19] It is a post-harvest festival celebrated for five days. Each day has its name and speciality having its significance. It is celebrated when the granaries are full, the landscape is dry, and the whole village is free from all agricultural works by worshipping God and honouring the dead.[20] The Enghan festival, or Guai-guai, as some of the *Kowpois* name it, is held in honour of their ancestors.[21] Two or three months before the observance of Gaan Ngai, boys from the male dormitory will set out to the nearest jungle to find the thin bamboo known as *Gu*, which, when dried, will be made into headgears known as *Gupikam*. This will be used on the first day of the Gann Ngai festival, particularly during the *Huai Gammei* procession. The head of the *Pei* (village council) announces the coming of the festival after deliberation with the village elders. The *men of the Khangchu (*boy's dormitory) perform what is known as *Gaan Shaanmei*, where the male from the boy's dormitory blows the horn of *Mithun* or cow (*Guaichei Kapitmei*) at the village jumping ground. It is believed that through this *gaan sha*me, all lower realm Gods are invited to participate in the festival. It also acts as an information and urges all the villagers to be prepared for the festival. The youths from the boy's dormitory dig the jumping ground and prepare the *Daanshanpung* (playground/ village jumping ground) for all kinds of sporting activities during the celebration. For an athlete, the sacred time happens when they perform a sport different from the one they are used to in their everyday profane lives. In ancient Greece, sports served as a means of communication with Gods.[22]

Taupwang Phaimei

Taupwang Phaimei (stone throwing/shot put) is one of the major sports played on the inaugural day of Gaan Ngai, known as *the Ngai ga*me. On the morning of the inaugural day, a rite called Gucheng Phaimei (omen by using ginger) is performed at the northern village gate (*Kaipi Bambu*) by *Muh* or priest, followed by the heralding of Gaan Ngai by drum beating, extraction of fresh fire from the *Daanshanpung* (jumping ground), *Guakpai Jaomei* (omen taking rite through observation of pig spleen) and *Napkaomei* (padding calling ritual). These rites are performed by an elder member of the village *Pei* (council) invoking the intervention of God *Tingkao Ragwang* to prevent any violence, injuries, sufferings, a disorder in dance, music, and discipline and protect them from dangers and evils during the entire festival. After all these rites, all the male members of the Khangchu marched a procession through the length and breadth of the village, shouting *Huai* along with drums and gongs. This is known as *Huai Gammei*, which is an invocation to God and an act of expressing the strength and power of men over water, land, air and evil spirits. Then, the *Nampou, Namngakpou* or a *Banja* (Old Aged man) will be the first to throw the *Taupwang* (round shape stone) by chanting a relevant hymn, and thus, the competition was opened. The hymn of the *Taupwang Phaimei* goes like this:

> We are about to carry out the act of Taupwang Phaimei.
> When we throw it *Au Haipou Tingkao Ragwang*, enable us
> to throw the stone like *langduai* (thread ball).

No one was allowed to touch or throw the *Taupwang* before the village elder as the stone is considered sacred and not be polluted. I interviewed Chaoba Kamson at his residence in Imphal in November 2021, where he narrated the following:

> It is to be a precaution that the elder (Nampou, Namngakpou or Banja) who is the first person to throw the stone is not a widower as it was considered a bad omen for the entire village. It is believed among the rongmei that if the first thrower of the Tawang is a maipu (widower), then the whole male community of the village will follow suit and remain widowers too. Agricultural productivity and poultry will be bad, and there will be famine in the entire village.

The stone, usually round, was collected from a nearby river by the *Khangchu* men by performing a rite known as *j*apan time, which is an oblation of holy wine to *Tingkao Ragwang* and was kept sacred at the *Changchun kai* (boys dormitory) the entire year. It is also practised in some villages that the stone (*taupwang*) is kept covered under the *Daanpan* (stone boulder). The *Tawang* is considered sacred, and it is taboo for young boys to touch or play with the stone. *Taupwang Phaimei* was contested only by members of the dormitory from *Gaana* (adult boys) and Khangbon (manhood) *thien*. The one who throws the longest distance from the starting point is generally declared the winner by the elders or *Banja*, who are present to witness and judge the competition. The Rongmei did not adopt any standardised unit of measurement as it is a competition held in the spirit of traditional and customary values where common brotherhood and community oneness were promoted rather than efficiency ethos as seen in today's modern sports. The winners were not given a prize as per the tradition of the Rongmei customary practices. Instead, they are to pay a fee called *swan* for declaring him a winner by the elders and acknowledging his ability and strength in front of all the villagers. Girls were usually not allowed to participate in the *Taupwang Phaimei* competition.

Daanjwangmei

Daanjwanigmei (long jump) is also one of the most fiercely participated traditional sports played during the festivals of *Gaan Ngai, Tun Ngai* and other occasions. During the *Gaan Ngai* festival, it is played after the *Huai Gammei* (traditional invocation to God) procession from the northern village to the southern gate accompanied by drums and gongs on the first day of the festival at the village *Danshanpung* (village jumping ground). *Danshanpung* is a sacred playing ground where rituals are performed by *Muh* (priest), sanctifying from evil spirits on the first day of the arrival of the festival.[23] This game is contested after the conclusion of *taupwang phaimei* sports. The village elder, a member of *Banja* dormitory, will be the first to land his foot on the newly dug soil, chanting a relevant hymn, and thus, the competition will be opened. The hymn goes like this;

> Today is the day of the festival of our village when the act of long jump begins; *Au Apou Tingkao Ragwang* enables us to jump like the grasshopper (*kah*).

Then the village elders jump a distance which is quite challenging for the young athletes. Widowers are not allowed to inaugurate the game as it is considered a bad omen for the entire village. No one was allowed to jump on the soil before the village elder, as the ground and the *daanpan* (stone boulder) are believed to be sacred and not be polluted. Anyone violating is considered to disrespect the entire villagers and the community's customary practices and traditional values. The competition was contested according to their *Thien* (dormitory). First, it was contested among the *gaana* (teenage boys), then came the *gap* (adult youth), and finally among the khangbon (manhood). This game is to be opened by *Nampou* (village owner), *Namngakpou* (village chief) or *Banja* (elder) as per the customary practices, and no one is to defile the ground. The one who jumps the longest distance is declared the winner by elders who are the judges of the competition. And the declared winner pays a *swan* fee to the elders.

Gudui Ngai (Ginger Soup Drinking Festival)

Luaipinmei (pulling of rope) is the main sporting activity during the festivals of *Gudui Ngai* (Ginger Soup Drinking festivals). This is, in some ways, similar to the modern game of tug-of-war. Ginger, known as *Gu* in the Rongmei vernacular, is considered to be the most important food item in the life of the Rongmei as it is used in different rites, rituals and occasions. It is believed to be the feet of God by the people. Ginger soup mixed with chicken meat is served to every member of the family to nourish health and longevity, which signifies the deliverance of life from hunger during scarcity or famine.[24] *Gudui Ngai* is celebrated after the completion of seed sowing in the field. It is one of the most popular festivals though it is celebrated just for a day in the month of May. The purpose of the celebration of the festival is to pray to God, *Tingkao Ragwang*, for the seeds to root in the soil firmly, to sprout their buds, paddy flowers to bloom, grant plentiful harvest and also protect the paddy plants from insecticides and pesticides. The rite, known as *Maleng Keimei*, is performed early morning on the day of the festival by a village elder or *Mhu* (priest). A traditional agricultural song known as *Katu Lu* is sung for a plentiful harvest in this festival. A day before the arrival of the festivals, the boys from *Khangchu* will go and collect a creeper known as *Kongshu* to be used as a rope for the competition of *Luaipinmei* (tug of war).[25] The material used for this game differs whereby some villages use long thin bamboo while other uses *Maja luai* (a creeper). It is played between the boys' and girls' dormitories to grant plentiful harvests and to ward off insects and pesticides. Ritually girls winning the contests depicts that there would be plenty of food and grains in the entire village. This game shows social norms and respect for women, though Rongmei society practices patriarchy. It is generally believed that had the rope should break, it is a bad omen for the entire village, and so all the rituals are started fresh from the beginning.[26]

Rih Ngai (War Festival)

Chwang Phianmei/ *Kaapmei* (Taking Omen by throwing a bamboo spear) is one of the most important games played by taking omen among the Rongmei in the festivals of *Rih-Ngai* (war festival). It is celebrated for two days in February and is military in nature. In the *Rih Ngai* festival, "*Kavouna*', '*Ritaak Ganmei*' is also performed, and the elderly man recites warrior talks, war hymns, war, etc.[27] Rituals are performed to purify one's body, soul and mind, thereby making one fortunate for every life challenge like war, hunting, cultivation, etc. On this festival, men and women sleep separately and cook food and drink separately. In the evening, members of *Khangchu* armed with spears and dao performed a ceremonial procession of *Ho-hoping* chorus (invocation to the God) throughout the village, followed by a competition of games like *Danjwangmei* (long jump) and Taupwang Phaimei, which is equivalent to shot-put etc. Just before playing these games, the ritual competition of *Chwang Phianmei* is held at the village *Raeng* (village gate). It is an important rite for the participating individual and the entire village for the upcoming year, where an omen is interpreted based on where the *tian* (bamboo spear) hit the painted human figurine installed. R. Brown writes, "An effigy of a man made of the plaintiff is hung on a tree, and at it, they throw pointed bamboo or sticks. Should the javelin hit it on the head, it is said that the thrower will kill an enemy, but if it lodges in the belly, the thrower is to be blessed with plenty of goods." [28]

Role of dormitory

There is a need to mention the important role of the dormitory system as practised by the Rongmei tribe in understanding the festivals and their relationship with games and sports being played during these festivals. The vernacular word for dormitory is known as *Thien*. It is a well-organised traditional social institution found in every village inhibited by the Rongmei people. In ancient traditional Rongmei village, every major activity was operated through this dormitory. The village life of a Rongmei tribe has a separate institution for every member according to their age, group and sex. Ursula Graham [29]opines that dormitories are an admirable institution that disciplines and educates the young and unites the householder. The bachelor's dormitory is known as *Khangchu* while the girls are called *Luchu*. Besides these two important dormitories, there are other institutions like the *Ganchang Kaibang* and *Mathenmei Kaibang*. Among the Rongmei, unlike some other Naga tribes, the *Changchu*n is usually housed by rich and influential individuals who own big houses. Dormitories are considered the custody of cultural and traditional wealth of the Rongmei people. All public items which are attached to cultural and traditional values are preserved with great care, such as mithun (Bos Frontalis) horns, big drums, and musical instruments like cymbals, flutes and violin, known as *Raa*. It also preserves weapons like spears, daos, shields, bows and arrows and important materials related to games. *Khangchu* provides a community sleeping hall for the boys and other members of the dormitory where all kinds of traditional practices and activities such as warfare, songs, dance and games are imparted to the young boys by the elders. Other social activities extended by the *Khangchu* involve major public works like the construction of footpaths, cleaning of village ponds, and rendering help to families in times of sickness and natural calamities. The dormitory acts as a centre of cultural activities. The Khangchu organises all the celebrations and festivals of the village or individual. They dictate and regulate any matter related to holding events and rules during the festivals. The flow of the celebration depends on their wise adjustment of the events needed to be accomplished during the festivals. Members of *Ganchang Kaibang*, especially the *Banjas* (upgraded from *Ganchang* based on seniority), play an important role by performing every religious duty for the entire village. They are also members of the village council called Peikai, where all administrative and judicial duties are looked into. As such, *Thien*, or the traditional dormitory system in a Rongmei village, is the life vein of their cultural and traditional activities where sports occupy an important place in it.

Conclusion

The indigenous games and sports of the Rongmei played during the festivals bring out the identity, culture and social fabric binding the people of the Rongmei tribe in Manipur. The jumping ground, or *Danshanpung*, is usually set up at the centre of the village through a ritual where offerings of *Guam* (ginger chutney) and holy wine are given to God; Tingkao Ragwang occupies a special centre for all socio-religious events, athletic events during the festivals and is considered sacred by the people. The purpose of the game, which is played during the festival, in addition to maintaining physical fitness, not only demonstrates the physical strength of the athletes but is also the unique experience of performing something sacred. Some games and sports played during the festivals are played skilfully as part of the rites, pleasing Gods and themselves at the same time. *Taupwang*, or throwing of the stone, would mean that all evils and dangers are thrown out of the village. This game is also performed on the belief that this competition of stone-throwing would break the heavenly granary's door of God, Tingkao Ragwang. If the said paddy is used for seed sowing, then it is believed by the people that there will be a plentiful harvest for the entire village. Games like *Danjwangmei*, on the other hand, are played for the welfare and prosperity of the people during the festival of Gaan Ngai.[30] It is also contested to prove and be recognised as the strongest and bravest among the member of their community. Other competition like *Chwang Phianmei* (spear throwing) is an important game of predicting an omen for the entire village. It is military in nature as well, where the contestants learned the art of spear-throwing. Agricultural activities of the Rongmei are closely associated with a series of rituals and festivals where games and sporting activities go hand in hand, extending to rejoining and merry-making, thereby giving the people an opportunity for enjoyment through revelry too. This community participation in games and sports during festivals accelerates integration and reinforcement of social relations. It also acts as an educational mechanism among the youth. One of the unique features of these sports among the Rongmei is that the winners of any of these sports will not be given prizes, but they are required to pay fees called *Shon* or *Shwan* for declaring and acknowledging their power and ability.[31] Thus we find that the rich heritage of indigenous games and sports of the Rongmei, which is practised today, continues as the life-vein of their culture, tradition and religion, which is skillfully expressed in the festivals. By studying the Rongmei indigenous games, one will be able to understand how sports have contributed to the wider understanding of their society and culture. Sport is very much a part of the fabric of the socio-religious and cultural lives of the Rongmei society and, thus, makes a significant contribution to an understanding of the everyday life of the people, what they did for fun, how they behaved, what mattered to them and how they thought of their lives and the world they live in.

Notes

1. Gangmumei Kamei, *The History of the Zeliangrong Nagas: From Makhel to Rani Giadinlu*, Spectrum Publications, Guwahati, 2010, p. 37.
2. It is situated west of Manipur and lies between the Imphal and the Cachar valley, south by the Peren sub-division of Nagaland and the Senapati district of Manipur. See, S.C. Batt and Gopal K Bhargava (eds.), *Land and People of Indian States and Union Territories in 30 Volumes, Manipur, Vol-17*, Kalpaz Publications Delhi, 2016, p. 231.
3 G. Lanbilung, "The Religious Aspect of Gaan-Ngai" in Lal Dena (ed.) *History and Society*, Calcutta, 2000, p.114.
4. *The New Encyclopedia Britannica in 30 Volumes*, vol-vii, 15th Edition, University of Chicago, 1980, p. 197.
5. Play is a non-utilitarian activity performed for its sake. Organised play is called games, and it is further divided into competitive and non-competitive games, with competitive games called contests. The contest is again divided into intellectual and physical, with a physical contest called Sports.
6. *Webster New American Dictionary*, Smithmark Publication, 1995, p.435.
7. Steven W. Pope (ed.), *The New American Sports History*, Urbana, University of Illinois Press, 1997, p. 3.

8. *The Encyclopedia Americana International Edition,* vol-xiv, American Corporation, 1973, p. 290.
9. Funk and Wagnalls, *New Encyclopedia,* vol-ix, Funk and Wagnalls, New York, p. 432.
10. *Ibid.,* p. 431.
11. The New Encyclopedia Britannica in 30 volume, vol-vii, 15th Edition, University of Chicago, 1980, p. 200.
12. Gangmumei Kamei, *op. cit.*, p. 274.
13 R. Brown, *Statistical Account of Manipur*, Mittal Publications, New Delhi, 2001, p. 28 (reprint).
14. *Ibid.*, p. 29.
15. E.T. Dalton,.*Tribal History of Eastern India*, New Delhi, 1973 (Reprinted), p. 52.
16. Budha Kamei Kabui, "Historical Traditions, Religious Beliefs And Practices of the Rongmei Tribe", PhD. Thesis, M.U, Imphal, 2008, p. 120.
17. Jan Reznik, *Proceedings of the 2016 meeting of the International Association for the Philosophy of Sport at the International Olympic Academy*, Parnassos Press, 2017, p. 95.
18. Dichamang Pamei, *Liberty to Captives*, A ZBCC Platinum Jubilee Publication, Tamenglong, 1985, p. 24.
19. Budha Kamei Kabui, *op. cit.*, p. 122.
20. Chaoba Kamson, (ed.), *Gaan Ngai A Festival of Zeliangrong of North India*, Imphal, 2003, p. 1.
21. R. Brown, *Statistical Account of Manipur*, Mittal Publications, New Delhi, 2001, p. 29.
22. *Ibid.*, p. 95.
23. Chaoba Kamson, *The Zeliangrong Social System and Culture*, Imphal, 2015, p. 264.
24. R. Brown, *op.cit.*, p. 29.

25. Budha Kamei, *op. cit.*, p. 135.
26. *Ibid.*, p. 135.
27. G. Makuga, *Introduction of the Rongmei Nagas*, Imphal, 1994, p.116.
28. R. Brown, *op. cit.*, p. 28.
29. Ursula Graham Bower, *Naga Path*, Spectrum Publications, New Delhi, 1968, p. 81.
30. Chaoba Kamson, *The Zeliangrong Social System and Culture*, Imphal, 2015, p. 98.
31. Budha Kamei Kabui, *op. cit.*, p. 125.

10

The Impact of Western Music on Khasi Traditional Music: An Analysis

Mitchell Reeves Thongni

Introduction

Through its different genres, Western music has extensively flourished in almost all the fronts and corners of every culture and society in the world. Its impact is massive and stimulative. Khasi Traditional Music (KTM) has also been subjected to this impact and it required be properly addressing and analysing. One should note that the impact of Western music on Khasi Music is synonym with the factors which strongly affected the Khasi society and its culture such as colonisation, Christianity, modernisation and globalisation. The paper aims to study the impact it has on Khasi music from secular and religious perspectives.

To understand the notion of Western Music, one may quote Padma Iyer's statement in her book *History of Music*:

> Music in Western Culture is the result of various influences, including the formalisation of improvised traditions; the growth of notation; the development of tuning systems; the treatment of text; innovative approaches to form; the role of patronage; the absorption of various cultures

> into the style; the growth of technology; investigations of performance practice; and various other factors.[1]

This statement conveys a notion that Western Music was not confined only to the three elements of music – rhythm, melody and harmony. It encompasses certain facets such as culture, traditions, technology, improvisation, patronage of music and aesthetics in a very inclusive way. One may see that music is well-organised, complex and developed. It incorporates many factors contributing to its growth and development. One may infer that the scope of Western Music is boundless, especially in this era of globalisation. Western Music has a long history and has continually had an effect on the music of different societies and cultures of the world till today, such as its impact on KTM.

Some scholars point out that the earliest contact of the Khasi with the West may have occurred during the latter half of the 18th century.[2] However, the complete annexation of Khasi native states into the hands of the British took place after 1839. Eventually, the British sought their vested interests and their supremacy changed the socio-economic and political scenario, leading to their control over the Khasi. Around the same period, Christianity sprung out of the West, landed in the Khasi Hills and transformed the Khasi scenario in many spheres. Christian missionaries not only propagated their agenda of faith but were also involved in other social, cultural and economic activities. We may argue that both colonialism and Christianity brought about Modernization in Khasi society. Different sectors which include language, education, trade and commerce, transport and communication, new ideologies, new food habits, concept of maintaining hygiene, dress and fashion, etc. were introduced to the indigenous people. The changes also motivated for the rise of urban and semi-urban towns and markets in which cross cultural interaction taken place between the Khasi and other communities. There has been a paradigm shift in migration from rural to urban areas. Literacy pushed the younger generation to white-collar jobs. Also, there was a replacement of traditional leaders by educated people.[3] During the modernisation process, some printing presses, such as Ri Khasi Press, was established in 1896.[4] However, scholars like Barnes L. Mawrie asserted that such impact has also brought the loss of many moral and ethical values. People have become greedy, selfish and unhelpful. Moreover, crimes such as theft, murder, adultery, rape, and sexual violence against their own children have become rampant day by day.[5] As a result, immigration of the rural masses to a growing urban centre like Shillong interrupts the social set-up of the erstwhile population and may lead to slums, thus creating a lot of stir in given urban centres. The opinion of S. N. Eisenstadt is relevant in this regard:

> The very fact that modernisation entails continual changes in all major spheres of society means of necessity that it involves processes of disorganisation and dislocation... social problems...conflicts between various groups, and movements of protest, and resistance to change.[6]

Culturally, P. M. Passah critically argues that through the impact of Western education, various aspects of culture have become affected, such as their traditional dances, music and festivals. Most of these were substituted by Western songs, dances and hymns.[7] Nevertheless, the most significant impact of Modernisation in the Khasi society was the emergence of intellectual groups in the early years of the twentieth century coupled with the development of Khasi literature. This group resolved that the preservation and protection of traditional culture and indigenous religion was a must to sustain the Khasi identity amidst the influence of the West.[8] Finally, the twentieth and twenty first centuries saw the exposure of Khasi society to globalisation in which the ideas of materialism, privatisation and personalisation influence the people in many aspects of their life. It seems that even the taste in music among the people, especially in Shillong, is determined by the Western artists who are more popular and accepted by the people. The top chart songs of *Billboard* or *Grammy* can also be heard on radio stations and in music workshops of the Khasi. This impact the production, circulation and overall preservation of KTM which are produced or performed by local artists.

The Growth of the Impact

Western culture has had tremendous impact on the life and the society of the Khasi. Western Music, as part and parcel of Western culture, has extensively influenced many Khasi musicians and listeners of music in general. One may not doubt the reality that the Khasi are not only influenced by Western thought, appearance and behaviour which subtly permeate the entire gamut of Khasi life, particularly in urban areas like Shillong. The singing of hymns and carols by missionaries must also have influenced the Khasi, who imitated and developed a love for the Western style of music.[9] One of the Blues musicians of Shillong, Rudy Wallang, opines that the basis of the impact of Western Music among the Khasi was prevalent mostly during the time of British colonisation. He asserted that some of the Khasi who mingled with the British or the Americans were influenced mostly by the tea planters and soldiers. One can understand here that during their stay in their provinces, the colonisers also brought with them various aspects of Western lifestyle; and among these, hobbies and music were more prominent. Looking at the impact of Western music, he also expresses that the radio plays a very important role during those days. Various stations such as *Voice of America*, *BBC*, *Radio*

Ceylon and others were the most popular. Through these radio stations, which the Khasi could hear during the colonisation period, Western Music gained popularity among the Khasi. On the other hand, he also opines a profound feeling regarding the contribution made by the Welsh and Catholic missionaries.[10] J. F. Jyrwa added, "The Presbyterian missionaries taught tonic sol-fa notation, and the Catholics produced a good number of musicians and pipers who learned the use of staff notation."[11] One may say that missionaries replaced KTM with choir music sung in Western tunes and with particular Welsh accents and cadences. E. W. Kharsohnoh stated that the first impact of Western Music was by the Missionaries when one of the music schools for tonic sol-fa was started during the 1860s or 1870s.[12]

Secular Western Music

We may also note that the impact of Western culture and the Khasi's fondness for music goes hand in hand. One observes that during the 1940s, the Khasi youth of Shillong crowded into music halls to listen to and enjoy the free, rhythmic electronic sounds belted out by the latest tribal beat group. Khasi musicians and composers gained new status in the field of popular Western music. Amongst those, some pioneers are Beriwell Kyndiah, who went to Bombay to play Western instruments in the Hindi film industry. Late Hedronelle Nonglait of Laban, Shillong also gained prominence in composing Western numbers, including composing lyrics released from London. We also find many artists interested in performing Western styles of music. Besides male artists, there were female artists like the *Tham Sisters* of Jaiaw, and Shillong, who most proficiently rendered the songs of the *Andrew Sisters*.

Moreover, there were various groups which held concerts not only in Shillong but outside, like *The Dynamite Boys* in

Assam Tea Gardens and Clubs in Assam Valley and *The Vanguards*, who were on a regular contract basis in night clubs and restaurants of Calcutta. In 1972, a landmark was achieved when one of the local groups called *Fentones* earned the All India Bristol Best Beat Group prize in Bombay. During this period, there were flourishing local bands like *Swing Quartet, Blue Voices, The Rockers, The Vaudevilles,* etc. Over and above this, it is noteworthy to state that another Khasi youth by the name of Austin Reade Majaw, under the professional name of Kim Kozens, played and sang in a one-man show in England for more than half a decade and travelled up to Ireland.[13]

Music knowledge and literature are one of the main impacts of Western Music on KTM. The Khasi have raw materials of their own, but to materialise these into reality, in the beginning, they adopted the Western knowledge imparted by the missionaries. E.W. Kharsohnoh states that the Khasi first assimilated and then adopted the knowledge of the Western world in rendering, refining, digging and sorting out their music.[14] Many techniques like the modes, forms, measurements, pitch, scale and other ornaments were adopted through Tonic Sol-fa and Staff Notation. Hence, proper notation of music could be maintained. This was the landmark in the history of KTM in the sense that music literature could be developed and documented. Ellerine Diengdoh also observes that Western Music has helped KTM in terms of notation. KTM can now be studied as a separate subject because of it.[15] Nalini Natarajan observes, "As a consequence, musical compositions of the post-missionary period leaned towards a Western mode not only in form and melody but in harmony and counterpart as well."[16] Recently, there has been an increasing trend in music schools, colleges and universities where music knowledge and literature can be developed. One can perceive the publication of songbooks with proper notation. The impact of Western Music can also be traced from the incorporation of Western Musical instruments in accompanying Khasi Traditional songs. Some of these instruments are the guitar,[17] piano, violin, mandolin, drums, mouth organ, percussions, etc. P. R. Kyndiah, even during his time, voiced that Some artists are outstanding soloists in instruments like violin, piano, guitar, saxophone, etc. Thus, when observing the impact of Western music on KTM, one may conform to P. R. Kyndiah when he says, "In short, [W]esternized music has not only made its influence felt but appears to have come to stay as one of the important schools of music,"[18]

Devotional Western Music (DWM)

In the colonial times, due to the specific need for public worship, the missionaries taught devotional songs like hymns to the Khasi in churches. They would conduct *Ki Jingiaseng Rwai* (Singing Worship Services)[19] and they also produced translations of Western hymns in the Khasi language with proper notation.[20] The intention of the missionaries was to propagate their faith, but, on the other hand, it served as spiritual satisfaction for the Khasi converts. If one measures the influence of devotional songs such as those in *The Khasi Hymn Book*, they have had a marked effect on the spiritual life of Khasi Christians till today. Besides hymns, DWM choirs and other gospel songs[21] also influence people's lives in many ways through public worship. Though many Christian churches do not practice or sing these kinds of songs, but in the churches that do practice, one can see the enormous impact in fulfilling the congregations' spiritual needs. Thus, DWM has immense significance on KTM in terms of spiritual thirst. In the context of the influence of Western music on the church in Khasi hills irrespective of any denomination, the views of Jacob Joseph seems right and appropriate to mention here:

> One of the greatest challenges of the Indian Christian church is its Western heritage. Most mainline denominations follow a Westernized liturgy and music in their worship. When missionaries came to India they translated the Bible and their own hymns into the local languages for use in worship. But now even a century later, churches still use the same hymnal and the translated Book of Common Prayer for worship. In addition, the Indian church has largely adopted Western pews and postures, with newer generation churches increasingly adopting songs from Euro-American contemporary Christian music, making the worship of the church even more Western.[22]

Negative Impact

Besides the positive facet of Western Music, one can also point out the negative dimension, too. Loistimai Syiemlieh,[23] daughter of Listrimai Syiemlieh[24] asserted that today what we see is the fusion of KTM with Western Music. She contended that if KTM were to be fused with Indian Classical Music, it would be acceptable because it is still in India. However, she strongly disagreed that if it was totally influenced by Western Music, which resorted to the use of drums, electronic instruments, etc., it would devalue the nature of KTM.[25] Nalini Nataranjan observes that with the growing popularity of Western songs and music among the Khasi, the fear is that many of the original songs and music may disappear.[26] Barnes L. Mawrie strongly pointed out:

> It is a cause for lamentation that today's urbanisation and city life has created a cacophony of noises that drown the beautiful and melodious sounds of nature. The craze for

> Western culture and the adoption of Western electronic musical instruments has led to the abandonment of traditional musical instruments. The Khasi youth today take great interest in learning Western musical instruments like the guitar, keyboard, jazz drums, etc., while they disdain their own traditional instruments.[27]

The negative impact of Western Music, when critically analysed from the perspective of the originality of KTM, can be seen as *Ka Rongphong/Ka Tynneng/Ka Pynbud* (imitation). Most of the KTM are influenced by the open doors of globalisation, pop culture, media, etc. Shibani Roy observes: "Today's youth is more inclined towards pop music, accompanied by the guitar or the bongo, though the songs are written in Khasi."[28] Namita Catherine Shadap Sen also remarks:

> However, Khasi music is now so influenced by other peoples that it is impossible for anyone but a professional musicologist, after a long study, to trace the truly indigenous elements. But even an untrained ear can recognise in the so-called Khasi folk songs of the present day (usually sung, incidentally, to verse of which the structure of metre and rhyme is clearly that of English poetry) the influence of Bengali and Assamese folk music, Indian film music and even the *Rabindragit* on one hand, and that of Protestant hymnology, Welsh folk song (learnt no doubt from the Baptist missionaries) and western popular and film music on the other. The guitar is rapidly replacing the *guitar* as the Khasi's national instrument. The usual style of singing is that of India; the singer makes little attempt to throw his [sic] voice forward in the European manner, and he embroiders his melody with quarter tones and grace notes.[29]

From the above discussion, one may note that Western Music has had an impact on KTM in many ways. Keeping in mind the negative aspects, some say that Western Music has diluted the nature of KTM. Others say that KTM has a strong root and origin – it can never be diluted. The following are some observations to point out the negative impact of Western Music on KTM.

Affecting the Tune and Accent

Many Khasi songs, both in the devotional and secular realms, are now very influenced by Western tunes. Though they may sing the lyrics in Khasi, there is a tendency to distance themselves from the original traditional tune. Here, the different genres of music are a matter of argument. The genres that Western Music brought in re-arranged the doorsteps of KTM by affecting its mode, form and style. Such a situation may also lead to hybridisation or fusion of music.[30] Ellerine Diengdoh asserts that when some of the Khasi people are now Westernised, the end product was not a beautiful fusion but an ugly popular product.[31] Though such a process might help in the improvisation of KTM, beyond this, it may lead to the depletion of traditional tunes. Thus, as a developed form of music, Western Music will have the capacity to influence more on KTM.[32] Due to the impact of Western culture, one may note the changes in pronunciation and expression during the performance of KTM. It affects the originality of KTM. Subsequently, the inaccuracy of KTM may be conveyed to a stranger who hears the KTM for the first time. Therefore, when there is so much exposition of KTM to Western Music, musicians should be alert that the genuine essence of KTM should not be lost.

Market Value

Due to the impact of Western Music, one may observe that the commercialisation of KTM is lacking. KTM cannot supersede

Western Music in terms of marketing. People's tastes are more inclined towards Western rather than traditional music. People are favouring more to taste those music incline Western rather traditional. Loistimai Syiemlieh stated that due to the commercialisation of music nowadays, KTM is weakened. She argued that during the olden days, during the 1950s, KTM purely maintained its originality and uniqueness, but now it is otherwise.[33] Western artists' commercialisation influences through homogenisation of globalisation totally ruined the significance of KTM. Like Western artists, most Khasi artists are influenced by the luxuries, whims and fancies of the globalised world. Some Khasi musicians compose music by excessively assimilating Western Music into their music in order to do well in marketing. In this regard, Rudy Wallang pointed out that music, in reality, is not fast-food music where it can entertain others for the time being and then fade away; instead, it is home food music which contains ingredients that can never be degraded.[34] One must note that KTM is a piece of music with a purpose and not only for commercialisation. KTM conveys the ethical and moral values which are handed down through generations. Commercialisation should not be a barrier but a step to promote KTM in the context of the homogenisation of globalisation. The quality of KTM is more important than the quantity. Excess commercialisation may lead to self-vested interests rather than a communitarian music approach.

Conclusion

From the above discussion, one may conclude that Western culture has affected some aspects of culture, such as food, clothing, speaking and recreation, and KTM to a large extent. Western Music, no doubt, has brought immense development in terms of preservation and equipping KTM. Still, the core concepts and valuable traditions of KTM, which are inherent, are also vulnerable to change. As part of a culture, music is one of the areas of concern that Western culture is influencing at an alarmingly fast pace. Hence, proper examination, conscientisation and sustainability are the immediate need of the hour to safeguard KTM from dwindling depletion and total extinction.

Notes

1. Padma Iyer, *History of Music,* Vishvabharti Publications, New Delhi, 2004, p.269.
2. P. N. Dutta, *Impact of the West on Khasis and Jaintia,* Cosmo Publications, New Delhi, 1982, p.28.
3. Jayanta B. Bhattacharjee, "Changing Khasis: A Historical Account," in Sebastian Karotemprel (ed.) *The Tribes of Northeast India,* Centre for Indigenous Cultures, Shillong, 1998, p.342.
4. R. Tokin Roy Rymbai, "Evolution of Modern Khasi Society: Babu Jeebon Roy," in Hipshon Roy (ed.) *Khasi Heritage: A Collection of Essays on Khasi Religion & Culture,* Seng Khasi, Shillong, 1979, p.69.
5. Barnes L. Mawrie, *Introduction to Khasi Ethics,* DBCIC Publications, Shillong, 2005, pp. 87-88.
6. S. N. Eisenstadt, *Comparative Social Problems,* Free Press, New York, 1964, as cited in Bibhas Dhar, "Shillong 1991-2001: An Observation," in S. Sengupta & Bibhas Dhar (eds.), *Shillong: A Tribal Town in Transition*, Reliance Publishing House, New Delhi, 2004, p.4.
7. P. M. Passah, "British Colonization Impact on the Socio-Economic Life of the Khasis-Jaintias before India's Independence," in *Pre-Historic Meghalaya and Social Formation in Khasi-Jaintia History,* Directorate of Art and Culture, State Museum Branch Meghalaya, Shillong, 1996, p.16.

8. M. P. R. Lyngdoh, *The Festivals in the History of the Khasis,* Har-Anand Publications & Vikas Publishing House Pvt. Ltd., New Delhi, p.1991, 174. For more readings on this see, Kynpham Singh, "Seng Khasi," in Hipshon Roy (ed.) *Where Lies the Soul of our Race*, Shillong, 1982, p.7; Panbor Tariang, *The Inter-Faith Dialogue between Christianity and Indigenous Religion,* published by Banshai and Badapbiang Tariang Dkhar, Shillong, 2003, p.4.
9. S. H. M. Rizvi and Shibani Roy, *Khasi Tribe of Meghalaya*, B. R. Publishing Corporation, Delhi, 2006, p.29.
10. Information gathered from Rudy Wallang, Blues Musician, Shillong, 28, May 2014. (hereafter Rudy Wallang, 2014).
11. J. F. Jyrwa, *Christianity in Khasi Culture,* Mrs. M. B. Jyrwa, Shillong, 2011, p.142. Also, see Nalini Natarajan, *The Missionary Among the Khasi,* Sterling Publishers Pvt. Ltd., New Delhi, 1977, pp.127-128.
12. It was said that the Shillong School of Tonic Sol-fa was the first teaching place started by J.P. Jones. In this school, there were 11 Khasi students. The book they used then was *Ka Kot Jingkynud,* written by Rev. Hugh Roberts. Around 1875, Sir Philip in Cherra Theological College also taught Toni Sol-fa to the students. *cf.* Information gathered from E. W. Kharsohnoh, Music Instructor, Assembly Institute of Music Shillong, 25 June 2014 (hereafter E. W. Kharshohnoh 2014).
13. S. H. M. Rizvi and Shibani Roy, *op.cit.,* pp. 28-29.
14. E. W. Kharsohnoh, 2014.
15. Information gathered from Ellerine Diengdoh, Asst. Professor St. Mary's College, Shillong, 20, June 2014. (hereafter Ellerine Diengdoh, 2014)
16. N. Natarajan, *op.cit.*, p.127.
17. Guitar includes Acoustic, Electric and Bass.

18. P. Ripple. Kyndiah, "A Peep into Khasi and Jaintia Music," in in Hipshon Roy (ed.) *Khasi Heritage: A Collection of Essays on Khasi Religion & Culture,* Seng Khasi, Shillong, 1979, p.154.

19 Usually, such worship is for the purpose of learning new songs. *cf.* (E. W. Kharsohnoh, 2014).

20. Nalini Natarajan, *op.cit.*, p.27.

21. Gospel songs include different kinds of songs sung in different genres, but here, it has been clubbed together for the convenience of the study.

22. Jacob Joseph, "Indigenized Christian Worship in India: Some Considerations", *Mission Frontiers*, Sept/oct issue 201, p.30.

23 Loistimai Syiemlieh is Khasi folk singer. She was involved in musical features in Shillong such as the famous play *U Manik Raitong.*(hereafter Loistimai Syiemlieh)

24 Listrimai Syiemlieh is the first Khasi traditional female composer. *cf.* Loissimai Syiemlieh, *Ka Phalang*, published by the author, Shillong, 2009.

25. Loistimai Syiemlieh.

26. Nalini Natarajan, *op.cit.*, 128.

27. Barnes L. Mawrie, *The Khasi and Their Natural Environment,* Vendrame Institute Publication, Shillong, p.113.

28 Shibani Roy, "The Communities: Khasi," in K. S. Singh (ed.) *People of India: Meghalaya, vol. XXXII,* Anthropological Survey of India, Calcutta, 1994, p.34.

29. N. C. Shadap-Sen, *The Origin and the Early History of the Khasi-Synteng People,* Firma KLM Pvt. Ltd., Calcutta, 1981, p.267.

30. This is what P. R. Kyndiah says, "A new class of modern Khasi-Jaiñtia songs which blend indigenous notes and the harmony of Western music is getting extremely popular and catching." *cf.* P. Ripple Kyndiah, "A Peep into Khasi and Jaiñtia Music," *op.cit.*, p. 154.

31. Ellerine Diengdoh, 2014.

32. Rudy Wallang opines that in the fusion process between the two, he saw that KTM lacks chords or harmonisation. He illustrated that *Ka Duitara* or *Ka Besli* cannot fuse automatically on the spot if a piece or a song has to change into another chord progression or transposition. It can be good in a studio recording, but in a live performance, it would not be possible. He stated that most Khasi songs played with stringed instruments like *Ka Duitara and Ka Marynthing* follow the one-chord progression. *cf.* Rudy Wallang, 2014.

33. Loistimai Syiemlieh, 2014.

34. Rudy Wallang, 2014.

11

The Philosophical Values in the Indigenous Culture of Tripura

Pradeep Kumar Deepak

About nineteen tribal communities residing in Tripura practices their religious beliefs. The indigenous tribal communities of Tripura can be categorised into two major groups - Aboriginals and Immigrants. Among the aboriginal are - Tripuri, Reang, Jamatia, Noatia, Lusai, Uchoi, Chaimal, Halam, Kuki, Garo, Mog and Chakma. The immigrants include the Bhil, Munda, Orang, Santhal, Lepcha, Khasia and Bhutia. Most of the tribes of Tripura follow Hinduism while the Lusai and Kuki are mostly Christians. The tribal communities of Chakma and Mog follow Buddhism. One of them are the Tipras who are substantial followers of Vaishnava Dharma and Sakta Dharma and have devotion to Brahmanical Gods and Goddesses. Therefore it is important to analyse ancient philosophical values and their impact on the Indigenous culture of people of Tripura. This paper makes a comparative study of the Indigenous culture and other cultures of our Indian sub-continent. It also critically analyses Tripura's different indigenous cultures and finds out the significant influence of Indian Philosophical values.

Several works have been done on the history and culture of Tripura and its various communities. Nalini Ranjan

Roychoudhury's work *Tripura through the Ages* contains the history and polity of Tripura from the earliest times to 1947.[1] It describes the growth of the socio-economic condition of the tribes in Tripura; Jagdis Gan-Chaudhuri's *A Cultural History of Tripura* also provides valuable explanations for my research paper.[2] The book by S N Guha Thakurata and Bani Guha Thakurta also discusses various issues of Tripura's past.[3] *Sri Rajmala* (Vol- 1 to 4), translated into English by N. C Nath, covers the main events of the royal kings.[4] Priyabrata Bhattacharjee's *Tribal Pujas and Festivals in Tripura* explains in detail the history of the tribal religious cults of Tripura, Pujas and festivals of the tribal communities of Tripura, Brahmanical pujas and rituals, religious mantras and religious songs.[5] Dipak Kumar Chaudhuri's *Reflections on the History of Tripura* provides significant knowledge about the prohibition of Sati in tribal societies and the British policy and the Maharajas of Tripura but does not discuss the topic of the philosophical values.[6] The book *Customary Laws and Practices- Riangs of Tripura* by Bibhas Kanti Kilikdar, describes in detail the traditional institutions, social customs, usages and customary laws and practices of the Riang. K. B. Jamatia has explained in a better manner the historical study of the Jamatia of Tripura in his book *Modernity in Tradition*.[7] Susmita Banerjee in her article laid emphasis on the indigenous knowledge and practices of the ethnic communities of Tripura.[8] These works are useful for understanding the history of the communities of Tripura and provide insightful knowledge to researchers and general readers; however, they did not talk about the philosophical values of the indigenous people of Tripura. Hence, an attempt is made to bridge the gap between the philosophical values in the indigenous culture of Tripura in this paper.

Ethnic culture plays a significant role in developing the socio-philosophical way of life. Pre-colonial societies in Tripura depict the adoption of animism as one of the religious belief systems and it seems they worshipped a number of deities which have influence over their daily life. The Halam believe in the existence and activities of the soul in man, animals and plants. In the Halam society, the soul is called 'Ratha'. The Reang believe in the soul and its separate existence. Like the Tipra, they also call it 'Fala'. So far as the soul is considered in the Reang society, it has been found that they believe sleep is the temporary departure of the soul and death means permanent departure. In the case of the Jamatia tribe of Tripura, animism is of unique factor. They worship supernatural spirits and forces, and although they succumb to Hinduism, the essence of animism is one of the characteristic features of their religion, like the Tipras, Reangs and others. The spirit of God or Deity is indicated by the word 'Matai', and according to the anthropological point of view, "All their primitive deities are nothing, but the nature deities and spirits only".[9] Animism also prevailed among the Uchai tribe of Tripura. The Mundas prefer to call themselves Hindus while they retain the cult of their tribal deities, and animism plays a significant role in their religious life. The Chakma, Mog, Khashi, Garo, Munda and Kuki also believe in animism.[10]

The Hindu methods of philosophical investigation consist of the study of Sruti (Vedic evidence), Yukti (reasoning) and Anubhava (experience). If we look at tribal philosophy, we find that tribal philosophy or way of life is no exception to this. Swami Vivekananda opines that Man does not proceed from error to truth, but from truth to truth— from lower truth to higher truth.[11] This is why, in the tribal way of life, we find less emphasis on reasoning and more on experiences, as we know that religion is based mostly on intuition and often fed and inspired by faith and belief.[12] The worship of trees, fire and water and the figures of various animals might be symbols or carriers of deities who were the real objects of worship.[13] Professor Nirmal Kumar Bose rightly observes that all men have their hopes and fears, and to single out a few elements of tribal religions and to say that the latter is born only of fear is doing great injustice to them.[14] In Tripura, we find the expression of some of the highest qualities of the Indo-Mongoloid people under Hindu inspiration. Like other Bodo groups, the Tripuri had their tribal religion influenced by Hinduism. At the same time, under the patronage of the Tripura Rajas, a good deal of their faith and its rituals are preserved as a part of their religion and still occupy an exalted position in society as the Brahmins in the Hindu society.[15] The Tripuri, Jamatia, Noatia and Halam practice all the Hindu religious rites. Similarly, the worship and festivities connected with harvesting the new crop by the Reang closely resemble the savanna festival of the Bengalis.[16] The Halam and the Noatia follow the Sakta Cult, whereas most of the people from the Kalai and Rupini sections of the former tribe follow Viashnavism. The forms of worship of their deities are similar to those of the Hindus.

The tribal communities' faith is also animistic in nature and they believe in God's presence in all elements of nature. They believe in the existence of spirits possessing the supernatural power of doing harm. All places are holy as they are the seats of either good or bad spirits and, therefore, have to be appeased separately. The appeasement of the spirit is necessary (sometimes with the sacrifice of animals held dear to the devotees) so that the people are saved from calamity in the forms of failure of crop, famine, flood or epidemic.[17] The following are the names of various Gods (including those of the fourteen Gods) worshipped by the Tripuris and other major tribes of the state.[18]

(i) Matai - Katar —- The supreme deity of Tripuri is identified with Siva Mahadeva. The term 'Matai' means God, and 'Katar' means Great or Supreme.

(ii) & (iii) Lam-pra —- The twin deity of sky and sea. The Tripuri word 'Lam' means sky or earth, and 'pra' means the sea or water.

(iv) San - grama or the Himalayan mountains, along with Lam-pra, are looked upon as the most potent or living deities personifying the sky, the sea and the mountains.

(v) Tuima or Ganga (The Ganges river) is especially worshipped in the month of Agrahayana and generally at other times. The priests of Tuima declare the cause of illness after consulting the deity while performing worship in her honour. Tuima denotes the meaning of water- mother or water- Goddess.

For example:-- The Reangs worship the streamlet that flows by the side of their dwelling. This is also regarded as a religious festival to them.

(vi) Mailu - ma or the Goddess of Corn is identified with Sri or Lakshmi.

(vii) Khuluma, or the Goddess of the cotton plant, is worshipped because cotton happens to be an important cash crop for the people.

(viii) Burha-cha or the God who is worshipped especially to cure illnesses.

(ix) & (x) Bani-rao and Thani-rao are the two sons of Burha-cha.

(xi - xvii) The seven Goddesses of witchcraft. Six of them are married, and the seventh is a Goddess who seems to be the Goddess of love in many mythologies, attracting men and granting them her favour. Even the Muslims of Tripura regard them as seven pari sisters and the Hindus as 'Dakinis' or 'Yogiris'.

(xviii to xix) The two brothers Garaiya and Kataiya, which mean the Fair one and the Dark one, are worshipped on the last day of the Hindu year (Chaitra Sankranti). The Tripuris drink rice beer in their honour for 2-3 days.[19]

The indigenous people of Tripura celebrate many religious ceremonies or festivals, just as the Hindus celebrate them in other parts of India. Here are some of the important religious ceremonies of the tribal community of Tripura:--

Bara Puja: This is the most important religious festival of the Halam tribe of Tripura. Generally, it is celebrated once in four or five years in a collective form of this puja is the Halams, Animals are sacrificed in large numbers, and plenty of liquor is also served.

Kharchi Puja: So far as Tripura is concerned, the Kharchi Puja is one of the most popular festivals of the Tipras and the swellers in Tripura. However, it is said to have been influenced by the Brahmanical Hindu. This festival is associated with the indigenous tribal deities. The Puja is celebrated before all the fourteen Gods, viz. Hara, Uma, Hari, Ma (Lakshmi), Bani, Kartikeya, Ganapati, Bidhi or Brahma, Abadhi (the God of ocean or water), Ganga, Agni, Kama and Himadri. Sunil Kumar Chatterjee observes, "The way in which those fourteen main deities of this Kirana people have been identified with the major deities of the Brahmanical Pantheon, probably or early as the 13th Century."

Ker Puja: Ker Puja is one of the main important festivals of Tripura. This is performed according to the chief Priest's 'chant' command. Fearing supernatural forces, the chanter strictly follows some rules, and there is a proclamation that the person who breaks these taboos shall be punished by supernatural powers. Lots of purity is observed during this Puja, just like other Hindu worships. The Ker Puja is celebrated after the fourteen days of Kharchi Puja. This Puja is a must for the Halam tribe, initiated by the Tripuri rajas and celebrated in the Bengali month of Ashada with a view to wording off all dangers.

Garia Puja: The indigenous people of Tripura perform Garia Puja on the seventh day of the month of Baisakh, the opening month of the Hindu Calendar Year. Generally, the God without a head is worshipped. This is made of Bamboo by the tribal people of Tripura. Both men and women perform this Puja to propitiate the deity for blessings.

Actually, this Gariya is the worship of Gouriya (son of Goddess Gauri), meaning Lord Ganesha, who is worshipped by all Hindus of other parts of India.

Worship of Tripureswari Mata: Tribal communities, just like non-tribal people, worship the Goddess Tripureswari Mata, who is regarded as one of the 51 main deities of the Hindus.

Generally, on the auspicious occasion of Diwali, this deity is worshipped with lots of pomp and enthusiasm. Even people from other parts of India also pay a visit to this holy shrine of Mata Tripureswari. The temple of Mata Tripureswari is situated at Udaipur in Tripura, built by Maharaja Dhanya Manikya in 1501 A.D.

Conclusion

Thus, based on above discussion, it can be said that though the philosophical values of the indigenous people of Tripura are varied in nature however they are similar to those of the Hindus of other parts of India. They followed the worship of nature Gods and Gods like Lord Shiva, Vishnu, Ma Kali, Durga, Lakshami, Ganesha and other Hindu Gods and Goddesses.

Indeed, they are the harbingers of the integrated culture of India as a whole. It is said that once Ishanchandra Manikya was asked the question: "To which religion does your Highness belong?" The Maharaja replied, "As an individual, my humble self is in the service of Vishnu, but as Maharaja, I belong to all religions." This shows that there was a great influence of philosophical values in the indigenous culture of Tripura.

Notes

1. Nalini Ranjan Roychoudhury, *Tripura Through the Ages*, Bureau of Research & Publications on Tripura, Agartala, 1977.
2. Jagdis Gan-Chaudhuri, *A Cultural History of Tripura,* Tribal Research and Cultural Institute, Govt. of Tripura, Agartalal, 2017.
3. S. N. Guha Thakurata and Bani Guha Thakurta, *Tripura*, National Book Trust; 2nd edition, New Delhi, 1999.
4. *Sri Rajmala (Vol-1 to 4),* translated into English by N. C Nath, Tribal Research & Cultural Institute Tripura, Agartala, 1999.
5. Priyabrata Bhattacharjee, *Tribal Pujas and Festivals in Tripura*, Tribal Research Institute, Agartala, 1994.
6. Dipak Kumar Chaudhuri's *Reflections on the History of Tripura,* Kalyanbrata Chakraborti on behalf of Bhasa Prakashani, Agartala, 2006.
7. K. B. Jamatia *Modernity in Tradition: A Historical Study of the Jamatia Tribe of Tripura*, Akshar Publications, Agartala, 2007.
8. Susmita Banerjee, "An Analysis of Tribal Communities' Traditional Knowledge and Cultural Practices in Tripura", *International Journal of Creative Research Thoughts*, Vol. 10, Issue 11 November 2022, pp. 796-803.
9. Priya Brata Bhattacharya, *Tribal Pujas and Festivals in Tripura,* Tripura State Tribal Cultural Research Institute & Museum, Govt. of Tripura, 1994, p.11.

10. *Ibid.*, p. 32.
11. Swami Vivekananda, *Thoughts on Vedanta*, Udbodhan office, Calcutta, 1949, pp.15-16.
12. Haridas Bhattacharya, *The Cultural Heritage of India, Vol. IV*, The Rama Krishnan Mission Institute of Culture, Calcutta, 1975, p. 3.
13. *Ibid.*, p. 32.
14. Nirmal Kumar Bose, *Tribal life in India*, National Book Trust, New Delhi, 1971, p. 64.
15. Suniti Kumar Chatterji, Kirata-Jana-Kriti, "*The Indo-Mongoloids- their contribution to the History and culture of India*", *RASB* Vol. 16, No. 2, 1950, pp. 218-19.
16. S. N. Guha Thakurata and Bani Guha Thakurta, *op.cit.*, p. 52.
17. *Ibid.*, p. 53.
18. Government of Tripura, *Tripura District Gazetteers*, Agartala, 1975, p. 146.
19. S. N. Guha Thakurata and Bani Guha Thakurta, *op.cit.*, p. 54.

12

The Rise of Buddhist Monasteries in Eastern Himalayas: A Study of Pemayagtse

Krishna Kumar Sharma

The Himalayan region is inhabited by people of beliefs, religions and their sub-sects.[1] When we come to Eastern Himalayas, covers the whole geographical area, which spread into Sikkim, Darjeeling area of West Bengal, Bhutan and Arunachal Pradesh.[2] It extends from the Kaligandaki Valley in Central Nepal to Northwest Yunnan in China.[3] Tibetan languages, and Lamaistic Buddhism, characterize Tibetan culture and traditions.[4] The land of the eastern Himalayas, whose socio-economic structure served as a fertilizer for philosophy and its institutional development, proved to be a haven for various Buddhist monasteries in the 16th-17th centuries, in which Pemayangtse was one. Pemayangtse monastery[5] of Sikkim, which is affiliated with NyingmaSchool[6] has been in a commanding position among the respective followers. This monastery not only adjoined the state authority and other religious institutions of Sikkim but interconnected Tibet through its philosophical tradition, which impacted the different parts of the Eastern Himalayas. But what is important here is that historians have paid less attention to the Buddhist sources in undertaking the research, whether in Sikkim, Arunachal Pradesh or India as a whole. It is further important to mention that the writers on Buddhism in India during the colonial period and even after have largely focused either on the life of Buddha or his philosophy or on the early form of Buddhism in India. The case of the study of Buddhism in northeast India, Amrendra Kr. Thakur[7] and others have analyzed Buddhism from this perspective. The studies on Buddhist monasteries in northeast India either concentrated on provincial circumstances for growing to monasteries or the studies have focused on the socio-religious activities of a monastery within the political boundary of a particular state. Sometimes, the edited work on Buddhism becomesa collection of articles that also suffer from the problems mentioned above in the historiography of Buddhism in northeast India. Very few relevant research works and studies have been done on Pemayangtseandthe region-based history of Sikkim. In this regard, one of the most valuable chroniclers is available by the ninth sovereign of Sikkim, Chogyal Thutob Namgyal and Maharani Yeshe Dolma (1860-1914).[8] The "History of Sikkim" is composed partly of hagiographic and historiographic documents. It describes many rituals performed by Tantric Monks in the palace's chapel in front of the king and later in different Nyingma monasteries of Sikkim, symbolizing these strong links between religion, monasteries and state sovereignty. Multiple papers published by the Bulletin of Tibetology of Namgyal Institute of Tibetology help to understand the different aspects of the Buddhist monasteries of Sikkim. Colonial historiography on Eastern Himalayas is available in the form of British trade and military mission reports to Sikkim, Tibet and Bhutan and Gazetteers. I relied on the dual attestation method for this article in which various literary texts have been crossed checked with reports on archaeological materials, and undoubtedly it is authentic for fresh research work on religious institutions. Through this article, an attempt has been made to find the reasons for the rise of monasteries like Pemayangtse at the trans-Himalayan level. This article examines all the socio-economic and political conditions that were inevitable for the origin and development of a monastery like Pemayangtse while also appealing to comparative research to other religious institutions from a different point of view. The first part of this article describes the trans-Himalayan socio-cultural and economic relations, which were important for political ambitions and the dispersion of philosophical waves. The second partelaborates upon the origin and development of the Pemayangtse monastery. The third part is in the form of a conclusion.

I

Position of Eastern Himalayas and Trans – Himalayan Intercommunion in Asia

Buddhism strengthened its hold in Tibet from the seventh-eighth century, while during the eighth-twentieth century, the Eastern Himalayas had a complete depiction of cultural and religious assimilation into the art and ritual practices of various sects of Buddhism, Hinduism and Animism.[9] The transmigration of different races developed the separate cultural pattern in the Eastern Himalayan region. From the north, the Lamaistic Buddhism of Tibet and similar Hinduistic elements and the tantric cults of Hinduism from the south greatly influenced the cultural mosaic of this region during pre- and post-colonial Northeast India. In some areas where the borderlands of the Himalayas meet culturally, we find the amalgamation into the ritualism and worship of deities in Hinduism and Buddhism.[10] From the socio-cultural and economic point of view, the position of the Eastern Himalayas has been greatly interconnected in Asia.

From the early medieval period, the multilateral trans-Himalayan socio-cultural and economic relations became stronger. Eastern Himalayas greatly influenced the exchange of social and cultural traditions within Asia. In Eastern Himalayas, Sikkim[11] and Arunachal Pradesh[12] are two states which have physical contact with Tibet, Bhutan, Nepal and Myanmar. There are two approaches to understanding the volumetric role of the Eastern Himalayas in Asian countries: the 'economic-centric role' and the cultural dispersion' through cross-border linkage. On one side, we see cross–border connectivity through Sikkim and Arunachal Pradesh as we find a free movement of goods and daily needs of the commodities within different Himalayan regions and other Asian countries. Officers of the British government have mentioned the Trans Himalayan commercial activities from India to China and Central Asia via Assam-Sikkim-Nepal-Tibet and Arunachal Pradesh-Bhutan-Tibet. A list of usual articles of commerce between Tibet and surrounding countries, i.e., Nepal, Bhutan, China, Bengal and Ladakh, has been mentioned by Captain Samuel Turner, the second Englishmen to visit Tibet, who submitted his report to the Hon. Warren Hastings, Esq. Governor General of Bengal Dated 2nd March 1784. Samuel Turner's report was published in 1800. The first Englishmen, George Bogle, visited Tibet in 1774. The opening paragraph of Bogle's chapter is on 'Trade of Tibet'.[13] Some scholars have shown that from the second century B.C., there was a regular trade route between India and China through upper Burma and Yunnan.[14] Alberuni has mentioned in his book *Kitab-ul-Hind* the trade route between

Assam, Tibet and China. In his *Tabaqat-i-Nasiri*, Minhaj-us-Siraj also mentioned regular caravan routes of Tibetan pilgrims and Traders through Bhutan and Tawang. We find the use of regular caravan routes through Bhutan and Arunachal Pradesh by pilgrims and traders from Tibet and India since the thirteenth century.[15]

Conversely, we find contacts between the people and the socio-cultural acculturation in the Eastern Himalayas. The regional variations in Eastern Himalayas make it culturally and ideologically prosperous. It must be observed on a macro-regional level. Buddhist heritage can be seen in this region in a broader and larger socio-cultural, ecological and spiritual context. Anyone can analyze the socio-religious activities and commands on the general lifestyle of common Buddhist people through major or minor monasteries and gompas in pre- and post-colonial Eastern Himalayan areas. Therefore, scholars can clearly outline this region's tangible and intangible Buddhist heritage. The tangible Buddhist heritage is the architecture of past Buddhist dominance and beautiful murals, sculptures and vivid textual sources. Buddhism is the living tradition in Eastern Himalayas. Buddhism as a culture constructed the state cultural identity of Sikkim and Arunachal Pradesh. Buddhism has developed a legacy of material and spiritual cultures of the Himalayan people, especially in Sikkim and Arunachal Pradesh. Buddhist monasteries and land ownership patterns in both states catalyzed the material culture of Buddhism. Eventually, Buddhist missionary tradition provided a legal addition to the material culture of Buddhism, where a land-holding monastic network availedthe opportunity through the fascination of Buddhism over the common masses. Due to the Indo-Tibetan cross-border trade, the economic development of Sikkim and Arunachal Pradesh provided the solid ground for the emergence of Buddhist monasteries of different sects in these regions.

The monastery is a general term indicating where Buddhist monks and believers live and perform religious activities. Buddhist monasteries are important in Sikkim and Arunachal Pradesh from both points of view. First, monasteries are the centres of learning and religious rites, rituals, or cultural regeneration. Second, as a centre for practising noble professions and creative arts and cultivating artisans' skills as economic activities.[16] All the Buddhist monasteries flourishing in different parts of the Eastern Himalayas mostly belong to the four main schools of Tibetan Buddhism. *Nyingma*, which meansold (eight century CE),is the oldest school of Tibetan Buddhism. While *Gelugpa*, or system of virtue (1409 CE), is the newest school. The other two schools are *Kagyupa* (eleventh century CE*)*, teaching lineage and *Sakyapa* (1073 CE), which meansgrey earth. Some smaller schools, such as *Jonang* and *Rime* movement, promote non-sectarianism and universalism. One question has arisen here, what are the fundamental differences between these Tibetan Buddhist schools? All four Tibetan schools trace their lineage to particular Indian scholars and emphasize particular translations. There are main differences in their actual tantric practices. But some commonalities in them, as opined by the Dalai Lama, are that the philosophical views of *Nagarjuna* and *Madhyamaka*a refound in all four schools. They have developed separate characteristics, styles, and terminology, but all schools share fundamental assumptions about the path and Buddhist doctrine. All orders of Tibetan Buddhism follow the Vinaya of the *Mula – Sarvastivada* School. Nyingmapa school emphasizes 'great perfection' or 'practice', and their tantric practices are mainly based on the 'old tantras' and instructions found in 'hidden treasures'. The

Kagyupa emphasizes Meditation, especially in the Mahamudra system, which is inherited from the Indian master Tilopa. Its tantric practices are derived from the 'Guhyasamaja Tantra' and the 'Cakrasamvara Tantra'. The Sakyapa emphasizes the development and completion stages of practices. Their tantric theory is based on 'HevajraTantra', the basis of their "path and fruit" system.[17]

Nyingmapa is known as the old order, while three other schools, *Sakyapa*, *Gelukpa* and *Kagyupa* collectively referred to as *Sarma* or new orders. In the 17th-18th centuries, scholars and travellers (mainly Chinese) denoted the Tibetan Buddhist school on various colourful hats, i.e., *Nyingma* school and *Sakyapa*schoolas a red hat; *Kagyupa* school as a white hat; *Karma Kagyupa* (subsect of *Kagyupa*) as a black hat; *Gelugpa* school as a yellow hat. From the above explanation of the different schools of Tibetan Buddhism, it can be inferred that the mahaviharas of the eastern Himalayas, which are affiliated withthe particular school, have under activities, regulations and administrations.

II

Red Hat Tradition and Pemayangtse Monastery

As much as the *Nyingma school* has deeply influenced Pemayangtse monastery, it is equally closely related to the Namgyal royal family of Sikkim, whose dynasty lasted from 1642 until its end in 1973.[18] Pemayangtse monastery was started by the master Lhastsun Namkha Jigme in 1645 as a small shrine called Tsangkhang. However, it was re-established in 1705 under the third king of Sikkim, Chagdor Namgyal (1686-1717).Religion has an important role in the formation of material culture in Sikkim. The ruling class was related to Buddhism, who set out missionaries to different parts of Sikkim to propagate the Dharma through the establishment of Buddhist shrines and gompas.[19] Pemayangtse monastery is located on the hilltop of Gyalshing town (now western Sikkim is known as Gyalshing district, HQ- Geyzing). It has been repaired and renovated from time to time, and the present building was thoroughly repaired and renovated during 1960-1970.[20] Large parts of the building are builtusing concrete, and *toonaciliata* wood has been used in furniture.[21] Architectural design, wall paintings and murals of Pemayangtse are influenced by Tibetan culture. It is a three-storey building with 1500 square feet of asymmetrical built-form prayer hall.[22] Buddha, Bodhisattvas, Deities such as *Vajrakila*, *Heruka*, *Vidarana*, *Vajrabhairava*, *Rahula*, *Virudhaka*, *Virupaksha*, *Dhritrastra*, *Vaisaravana,* etc., lineage trees, religious symbols are the main subjects of the wall paintings and murals in this monastery. Natural pigments have been used in wall paintings which are extracted from plants, minerals and other natural resources. Somewhere the paintings are not apparent due to the old and dilapidated condition of the walls. Geometric patterns and symbols are noteworthy in the Pemayangtse monastery.[23] some of the lamas of Pemayangtse monastery and from other Buddhist centres received special training in Torma sculpture, Thanka Paintings, Mandala, Mural paintings and mask making. They became proficient in these arts for various religious occasions.[24]

One important thing to mention here is the role of the Nyingma school, which was prominent in establishing the Namgyal monarchy in Sikkim. First, Chogyal (King) Phuntsog Namgyal (1742-70) was enthroned with the help of Nyingma saints. The sixteenth century was the period which has characteristics of political fragmentations and sectarian conflicts. Due to own Magico-religious practices, Nyingma school tried to come close to royal authorities in Tibet and everywhere in Eastern Himalayas.From politico-religious alliance with contemporary state authorities of Tibet and other parts of the eastern Himalayas, including Sikkim, Nyingma school managed to buildvarious monasteries. Apart from Pemayangtse of Sikkim, *the rDor monastery* was founded in 1632; *the sMin monastery* was founded in 1676; the *dPalri monastery* was founded in 1571; *Kah monastery* was founded in 1159 and restored in 1656;*thedPal monastery* was founded in 1665; the *rDzongs monastery* founded in 1685. All these monasteries were instituted in different parts of Tibet, known as the mother monasteries of the Nyingma school.[25] With the support and patronage of a particular authority, Nyingmaschool tried to dominate other sects through these institutions in the 16th – 17th centuries.

As Melanie Vandenhelsken[26] has mentioned in her article the functioning principles of the Pemayangtse monastery were setup at the founding time of the Namgyal Monarchy in Sikkim. The lamas from Pemayangtse monastery had a significant role in the court of Chogyal. These lamas were the spiritual master of the king, that why a cleric–patron relationship developed between them. The lamas of the Pemayangtse monastery were not only the spiritual guides of Chogyal; they were the sole lamas responsible for holding the rituals for the king and his family. Only the Pemayangtse lamas are empowered to perform the three major public annual ceremonies at the royal chapel: *Panglhasol* on the seven month, *Dupchen Kagye*, on the tenth month and *Guru Tamar*, on the twelfth month. The Pemayangtse lamas were engagedin political functions also. The lamas who used to sit in the royal council were known as councillors or executive councillors.

Kubgen Lama was the chief lama, selected from Pemayangtse monastery in the Chogyal court. The *Dorje–open* was related to religious matters. Next in order was *Um-dse*, who supervised the whole establishment of the monastery and controlled the discussion. *Chor-tim-ba* was the next position of provost marshal and was appointed by the vote of *Tapas*, a group of learned lamas of the monastery. He was the in-charge of the library. The next office was that of the *chi-year*, who had to power to hear complaints from the *tapas* and communicate to the higher authority. The *u-chho* used to act as the family priest to the Sikkim coal. The next rank was the *ku-nyer*, and he was incharge of image caretaker. *Chab-dren* was the pourer of holy water. The conch shell blower, or the *tapa*, was the lowest rank.[27]

In its early days, Pemayangtse and some of the gompas of Sikkim used to send their young monks for better training and to learn strict discipline and religious rites in Buddhist monasteries such as *Mindrol – Ling* and *Dorji – Dak* in Tibet. After returning to Sikkim, these Buddhist monks provided training to the followers in their monasteries similar to what they had taught in Tibet.[28] As Pemayangtse monastery has been the principal monastery of Sikkim, in almost all other monasteries and gompas belonging to the Nyingma school, the chief lama was deputed from Pemayangtse monastery.[29] A national assembly, assisted by the Maharaja of Sikkim, was called the "Lhade – Mede" in pre-colonial Sikkim. This assembly comprised different ranks of Monks and lay, such as *Chutinpa*, *Lama Dorjee*, *Omze*, *Lahpon*, *Village headmen* and other dignified people of Sikkim. During the British rule in India and even after Independence, this assembly has been active with many changes. When a state council replaced a traditional council, the head lama of Pemayangtse was also a member. The important thing to say here is that the

Pemayangtse monastery's chief lama administered the oath and secrecy among the newly elected council members.[30]

Pemayangtse monastery, also known as the 'Unreformed school', advocates the spiritual and the divine world as well as being in close contact with the mundane realm. As we know, there was a system to send one person from Lhopo (Bhutia) house to Pemayangtse monastery for Lamaism, but due to the labour incentive pastoral farming system in Sikkim, many of the families were incapable of dedicating their son to monastic services. Only twelve noble *Lhopo* clan who directly originated from *Khye Bumsa* (the mythical first inhabitant of Sikkim) was eligible to get admission to this Buddhist institution. Therefore, without hesitance, it can be said that Pemayangtse was founded and funded by the Lhopo aristocrats for their interests. In Sikkim, we find the dominance of two major classes, Lhopo and Lepcha. From land control to the administrative level, we see the hegemony of these two classes. Despite this, the main reason why the Lepcha class did not get selected for an institution like Pemayangtse monastery was that they were not equal to the high self-respecting aristocracy such as the Lhopo, who considered themselves superior among all classes, and with whom the emperor himself considered grateful to share same descendants. As the Lhopo supremacy persisted since the founding of the Pemayangtse monastery, which had imbibed Buddhist culture, the choral was also devoted to Buddhism from its socio-political perspective. Therefore, state authority and the Lhopo aristocracy always retained the monopoly of their high clan. The Lepchas, who later adopted Buddhism, despite their superiority in pastoral – agriculture, always found a lower social status than the Lhopo. Secondly, the reason for the decrease in the incidence of political intrigue in Sikkim is that the position of the choral was only of immense symbolic importance. There was no power struggle among the many sons of the choral as it was different from the court conspiracy of the rest part of India.Real power seems to lie in the huge faction of the Sikkimese elite standing behind the choral. Chogyal was not the chief architect of the suction of the lower classes in Sikkim. The Pemayangtse lamas who were involved in the work of tax collection from the raiyat were also ordered not to harass the raiyat in any way, and they were warned that those who worked against this order would be punished severely.[31] However, we also find instances where Buddhism and Pemayangtse religious monopoly was threatened or competing leaders in Sikkim opposed Chogyal, which was attempted to be suppressed or abolished by the lamas of Pemayangtse monastery. According to the Limboochronicle, *Teyongshi Sirijunga*, a learned Limboo man who revived Kirat literature and taught Kirat people in different parts of Sikkim, put him under arrest, bounded him to a tree and shot him to death by lamas of Pemayangtse. The Limboo leader *Sirijunga*, who had challenged the supremacy of the state and the religious monopoly of Pemayangtse, his assassination sparked outrage in public, resulting in the then Bhutia ruler fleeing to Tibet. The royal monastery of Pemayangtse not only provided a moral and religious justification for the state's social sovereignty but also displayed military-like aggression in the administration of Sikkim to safeguard the interests of Chogyal. The assassination of an official of Nepali origin by Pemayangtse lamas in 1880, reported by His Excellency Thutob Namgyal and Yeshe Dolma himself, in these cases, the reaction can be equated to that of the national army. Pemayangtse lama ranks have counted as the same as the king's army.[32]

The formation of the social structure of Sikkim witnessed a change after the entry of the Nepalese clan in Sikkim challenged the monopoly of the nobility, such as the Lhopoand Lepcha, where Limboos were suppressed. John ClaudeWhite became the Assistant Political Officer of Sikkim in 1889. From 1890 to 1908, White encouraged Nepali settlement to enlarge the tax base and boost agricultural production.[33]In the land dispute, the rugged political situation that had arisen due to the threat to the internal social and economic dominance of the aristocratic class involved the Chogyal and the Pemayangtse lamas on one side and some local edacious mediator and the British government on the other. When we study the Pemayangtse monastery with other Buddhist monasteries of Eastern India and the Hindu – Brahmanical temples of South India, some similarity is markable. It was essential for all these religious institutions to continue to receive political patronage and grants. These religious institutions legitimised the state power at the socio-religious level, which was necessary for the ruler to remain in power for a long time. Same as the Brahmanical temple of south India and Nalanda Monastery of eastern India, Pemayangtse also possessed lands and some other administrative rights related to owning estates. In its early stages, the Pemayangtse monastery did not have state-subsidized lands. However, it had the right to receive grants from some villages for sponsoring the support of religion.[34] According to Thutob Namgyal and Yeshe Dolma's *History of Sikkim*, Chagdor Namgyal, the third chogyal, appointed 108 families as the chief laymen for supporting the 108 lamas (auspicious number of Pemayangtse lamas). These layperson families used to provide religious needs and necessities to these lamas.[35] The first recorded land under the charge of Pemayangtse was the *land of Phulbari* granted by the chogyalGyurmeNamgyal to a lama as a jagir in 1730 A.D., was regranted to Pemayangtse when the lama passed away. This type of grant to the monasteries was not merely a result of the generosity of the authority but to legitimize the choral rule at the social level through its religious function and ritual ceremonies, and this was what the ruling class of Sikkim expected from them. Similarly, in later times the SikyongTulkuNamgyalchoral granted territory to Pemayangtse monastery for the service of one of its senior monks named Chichudar Yap Chiba of Tikchuk to collect taxes from the land between the rivers Khale-chu, Rigne-chu (Rangit), Rathong-chu and Rimbi.

The benefits of land grants and privileges that the Nalanda monastery was enjoying during the period of Pala rulerswerethe same pleasures the Pemayangtsewere getting through the rulers of Sikkim. A Tibetan officer Rabden Sherpa Gyalpo is credited with introducing the taxation system in Sikkim in 1747. Rabden Sherpa made a constitution that defined a fixed system of state revenue, and every raiyat was expected to contribute in the form of different products or kinds. Political officer J. C. White supervised the British land resettlement program in 1889. After a land survey this year, according to the quality of land, leased them out to interested landowners at various rates. The revised regulations strike the golden epoch of Pemayangtse, which was glutted with the graciousness of the choral of Sikkim. Now the monasteries could not proceed with the land acquisition process. However, monasteries like Pemayangtse, Ralong, Rumtek, Phodang and Phensangcould collect taxes on their respective estates, pay taxes to the government or keep the whole collected land revenue for religious activities. *Cheoshi*(support of Dharma) is a term for the regular income of monasteries. The superior lamas of Pemayangtse monastery formed a council called *udorcheotsum*, which used to governthe whole estate of the monastery with the help of tax collector *Mandal*.

The Pemayangtse estates remained under the control of the *Udorcheotsum* council even after 1947, when property rights were withdrawn from other institutions after the abolition of the Zamindari system. Ecclesiastical Affairs Department took over the Pemayangtse estates between 1950 and 1973. However, until 1980, the department paid a portion of the taxes collected from the monastery-owned estates to which the monastery was entitled. From 1990, a group of Pemayangtse lamas lobbied for their right to collect taxes directly and also claimed to elicit taxes that were not reimbursed to Pemayangtse.[36]

III

Conclusion

Sikkimese Buddhist institutions where Pemayangtse is in the leading role could be analyzed at the trans-Himalayan level dispersion of monasteries originating from Tibet. After the diffusion of Buddhism in Tibet, where it achieved the utmost of royal guardianship, its various schools were ready to occupy different places according to their social-economic benefits in the eastern Himalayas. Not only the trade-commerce or economic activities but the social and political condition was also significator for the blossoming of Buddhism in Sikkim and other parts of the eastern Himalayas. Lands were replete with resources, but large tracts were politically vacuumed. Behind the foundation of religious institutions in pre-modern Sikkim was nothing but the expansion of state-monastery relations in Tibet. It was bound to erupt after the mutual relations between the state and religious institutions had attained the peak of momentum. The alignment between the Nyingma school and the royal authority dominated the Sikkimese province from beginning to end. Two things seem to be very important in the history of pre-modern Sikkim first, the division of feudalistic society into the Inferior and superior classes established by the dominant *Lhopho* (Bhutia) clan of Tibetan origin; second, state-monastery resolute static relations which signify the divine concept of rule more than the cleric-patron relations in a modified society. The form of the monastery of Sikkim is closely comported with the state-church relations of European civilization and especially of the kingdom of Byzantine, where the monarch controls the state through church administration.[37] Monastery like Pemayangtse became the basal for the rule of Chogyal. Same as the Buddhist monasteries of north India and Brahmanical temples of south India, Pemayangtse was legitimizing the royal authority at the social level and helping to state in administrative and military work as an autonomous body of contemporary government. At the social level, Pemayangtse's uncontested rights suffered a setback when the Sikkimese elite began to be challenged by the Nepalese class during the colonial period. Britishers encouraged Nepali settlement to enlarge the tax base and boost agricultural production. The system of land leasing by the British affected the economic interests of the ruling class as well as the Pemayangtse monastery of Sikkim. The acquisition of land by Pemayangtse monastery had now come to a halt. Due to the lack of royal patronage in the nineteenth century, Pemayangtse was also facing the same situation as the Nalanda monastery in the twelvth century. Unlike the Nalanda monastery, the people in Sikkimese society were not disillusioned with Pemayangtse. Hence it managed to maintain its existence even after the colonial period. Theroyal philanthropy, which built the background for the upswing of Pemayangtse, where their objectives were interconnected due to its destitution, closed the political and economic level support for this monastery during adverse circumstances. That is the actual cause of the anticlimax of the Pemayangtse.

Notes

1. David Zurick, Julsunpacheco, Basanta Shrestha, Birendra Bajracharya, *Atlas of the Himalaya*, International Centre for Integrated Mountain Development (ICIMOD), Kathmandu, Nepal.
2. S. C. Bose, *Geography of the Himalaya*, National Book Trust, New Delhi, 1972, pp.37-38.
3. E. Sharma, et al., *Climate Change, Impacts and Vulnerability in the Eastern Himalayas*, Eriksson, Kathmandu, 2009.
4. Buddhism has two main schools-Hinayana and Mahayana. Hinayana is mainly followed in Sri Lanka, Thailand, and Burma, and its sacred language is Pali, while the Mahayana form is followed in Sikkim, Arunachal Pradesh, Tibet, China, Mongolia, Japan, Nepal, Bhutan etc., and its sacred language is Sanskrit. Buddhism in Tibet faced and absorbed many non-Buddhist native religious elements. The hybrid Buddhism of Tibet, which contained multiple layers of Bon-Tantric, Yogic or Vedic and Saktist practices, provided its unique flavour, embellished as Lamaism. The word 'Lama' is often applied to Buddhist monks, but more precisely is applied to the most senior and enlightened who have passed rigorous qualifications and are seen as a reincarnation of their previous life. The two more seniors, The Dalai Lama and the Panchen Lama, who hold political and spiritual authority, are prominent figures in Tibetan Buddhist society. See William S. Weedon, *Tibetan Buddhism: A Perspective*, Philosophy East and West, Vol. 17, No. 1, University of Hawai'i Press, Jan 1967, pp.167-172 and Chowang Acharya, *Aspects of Monastic Education In Sikkim*, Bulletin of Tibetology, 1998, pp.1-6.

5. Pemayangtse monastery or Sangchen Pemayangtse Gompa means *'most sacred lotus summit monastery'*.

6. There are three sub-sects of Nyingma school in Sikkim- first, *Lhatsun-pa*, which has influenced most of the Buddhist centres in Sikkim, including Pemayangtse; second, *Kathok-pa*, with monasteries of Kathok and Doling and third, *Ngadak pa* with the monasteries of Namchi, Sinon, Tashiding and Thong-mochhe. These sub-sects emphasise particular spiritual works or translations such as *Lhatsun-pa* highlights *Le-tho Ling pa*; *Long-chenrab-jammg* by *Kathok-pa*; and *Rig-dsin go dem can* by *Ngadak pa*. See, Dadh, Narendra Kumar, *Guru Rin-Po-Che and Lamaism in Sikkim*, Bulletin of Tibetology, pp. 34-42.

7. For details, see the relevant portion in Amrendra Kumar Thakur's *History of Arunachal Pradesh (Early times -1972 AD)*, Institute of Distance Education, Rajiv Gandhi University, Itanagar in association with Vikas Publishing House Pvt. Ltd., New Delhi, 2014 and his recent article "Buddhism in Arunachal Pradesh: A Historical Study" in Cecile A. Mawlong and Tejimala Gurung (eds.), *Religion and Society in Northeast India: An Interface*, DVS Publishers, Guwahati, 2022, pp.133-163.

8. Thutob Namgyal & Yeshe Dolma, *History of Sikkim*, translated by Lama Kazi Sandup, self-publication, 1913.

9. Krishna Kumar Sharma, "Non-Buddhist Elements in Buddhism of Sikkim"in Lanukumla Ao (ed.) *Northeast India Readings in Cultural Life*, Research India Press, Delhi, 2021, pp. 77-93.

10. Pradyumana Karan and William M. Jeankins Jr., *The Himalayan Kingdoms Bhutan, Sikkim and Nepal,* D. Van Nostrand Company Inc, New jersey, 1963, pp. 14-18.

11. In the pre-modern period, Sikkim was pronounced differently among different ethnic groups. *Su-Khyim* (Limbu/Lepcha) where *Su* meaning *new* and *Khyim* meaning *palace or house*, referring to the palace built by the first ruler Phuntsok Namgyal; *Beyul Demazong* (Bhutia), which means *'the hidden valley of rice'*;

Drenjong (Tibetan) which means '*valley of rice*'; Sikim (Nepali pronunciation). The word '*Lho-Mon-Tsong-Tsum*' identifies the origin of three dominant ethnic groups of Sikkim where the term '*Lho*' refers to *Bhutias* (Lhopo), who migrated from southern Tibet, the term '*Mon*' refers to *Lepchas* (Rong) who lived in lower Eastern Himalayas and the term '*Tsong*' refers to *Limbus*.

12. Arunachal Pradesh has been popularly believed to be existence since the pre-historic days of Mahabharata and Kalika Purana. Mountain ranges such as Patkai, Naga, Manipur, Tripura and Mizo hills are collectively called *Purvachal*, where Purva means *east,* and Achal means *mountain*. Some characters of Mahabharata hailed from this region. Between 500 B.C. to 600 A.D., the Monpa kingdom was ruled in this area. We found the recorded history of this state in the chronicles of Assam of the 16th century. From pre-colonial to 1972, this state was popularly called the North Eastern Frontier Agency (N.E.F.A.).
13. Nirmal Chandra Sinha, *Articles of Tibet trade 1784*, Namgyal Institute of Tibetology, Gangtok, Sikkim, 1984, pp. 21-25.
14. Sarah Hilaly, "Trajectory of Region Formation in the Eastern Himalayas", *Indian Historical Review*, 42(2)1-15, 2015, pp.8-9.
15. *Ibid.*, pp. 8-9.
16. Yuvraj Krishan, "Destruction of Cultural Property in War and Ethnic Conflict – Policies for Subsequent Restoration," *The Tibet Journal*, Vol. 24, No. 3, Autumn 1999, pp. 83-86.
17. John Powers, *Introduction To Tibetan Buddhism*, Snow Lion Publication, USA, 2007, pp.355-500.
18. *Census of India 2011*, Sikkim, District Census Handbook, North, West, South and East Districts, Directorate of Census Operations, Sikkim, pp. 8-10.
19. Gary Chopel, "Historic Evolution of the Sikkimese Monastery," *Bulletin of Tibetology*, Vol. 47, No. 1& 2, 2011, pp. 57-64.

20. N. Dorjee, "Monasteries in Sikkim", *Bulletin of Tibetology*, reprint Shunyata, Vol.1, No.1, Sikkim Buddhist Association, Gangtok, 1977, pp.51-52.

21. Mechtild Mertz, Sangeeta Gupta, Yutaka Hirako, Pimpim de Azevedo, Junji Sugiyama, "Wood Selection of ancient temples in the Sikkim Himalayas", *IAWA Journal*, 35(4), 2014, pp. 444-462.

22. Downloaded from, https://www.astrolika.com/monasteries/pemayangtse-monastery.html

23. Krunal Pate, *Divine Depiction: An Inquiry into the Geometrical Proportions of Buddhist Monastery Murals of Nyingma-pa sect of Sikkim*, Undergraduate Interior Design Thesis, Faculty of Design, CEPT University, 2019. Download from, https://issuu.com/krunalpatelkd/docs/ui1113_krunal_patel_screen

24. Kamal Bikash Chaudhury & Maitreyee Choudhury, "The Monastery Arts and Crafts of Sikkim", *Bulletin of Tibetology*, Vol. 37, No. 2, 2002, pp.18-32.

25. Marc-Henri Deroche, "History of the Forgotten Mother-Monasteries of the Rnying Ma School: DPAL RI Monastery in the Tibetan "Valley of The Emperors," *Bulletin of Tibetology*, Vol. 49, No. 1, 2013, pp. 77-111.

26. Melanie Vandenhelsken, "Secularism And The Buddhist Monastery of Pemayangtse In Sikkim," *Bulletin of Tibetology*, Vol. 39, No. 1, 2003, pp. 55-73.

27. Keshav Gautam, "Society And Economy of Sikkim Under Namgyal Rulers (1640-1890)", unpublished PhD thesis, Department of History, Gauhati University, 2014.

28. Dr ChowangAcharya, "Aspects of Monastic Education in Sikkim", *Bulletin of Tibetology*, No. 2, 1998, pp. 1-6.

29. N. Dorjee, *Monasteries in Sikkim, op.cit.,* pp. 51-52.

30. K.R Chkravarthi, "Political Development of Sikkim", unpublished Ph.D. thesis, Department of Political Science, University of North Bengal, 2003.

31. Hong Tran, *Chogyal's Sikkim: Tax, Land & Clan Politics*, Independent Study Project (ISP) Collection 1446, 2012. Downloaded from https://digitalcollections.sit.edu/isp_collection/1446.
32. *Ibid.*
33. *Ibid.*
34. Melanie Vandenhelsken, *Secularism And The Buddhist Monastery, op.cit.*, pp. 67-68.
35. Tran, Hong, *Chogyal's Sikkim, op.cit.*, pp. 13-14.
36. *Ibid.*, pp.14-16.
37. Daniela Kalkandjieva, "A Comparative Analysis on Church-State Relations in Eastern Orthodoxy: Concept, Models and Principles", *Journal of Church and State*, Vol. 53, No. 4, Autumn 2011, pp.587-614.

13

Tulonibiya in Assamese Islamic Society: A Case Study

Kabyashree Sarma

Introduction

Every generation of historians has its priorities of research. In the case of India, Tara Chand, K. M. Ashraf, Mohammad Habib and a host of others represent a school of thought who studied medieval India and, besides other problems, studied Hindu-Muslim relations and influences. In the case of northeast India, especially the valleys of Assam, the impact of Islam on the society and the syncretic tradition among the Hindus, Muslims and others, including the syncretic traditions, have been studied. The focus has been on the centres like the Hajo, Hojai, Goalpara/Suryapahar area, *Jari* and *Jikir* and some other socio-cultural influences of each other in the societies of Brahmaputra valley. The studies on Islam in eastern India, including Assam, have focused on the expansion of Islam in the region, and these larger discourses and influence of a predominantly Hindu ritual related to the adolescent period of girls being adopted by the Muslims of Assam never caught the attention of scholars in the past. This ritual is more important because, so far, there is no trace of Islamic traditions supporting this ritual. Hence, to bridge the gap in the historiography of gender studies and the studies on cultural assimilation, the paper is a humble attempt.

French ethnographer, Arnold van Gennep, mentions that there is no term in the Islamic rituals as "puberty rite", but certain rites attached to puberty can be termed the "rites of passage". Muslims celebrate the introduction to sexuality, adulthood and community membership through these different rites, which are not universal in character. Circumcision in males *(khidtna)* and weddings in females, termed the end of childhood and moving forward to adulthood, are the most widely practised puberty rites. Interestingly, the *Quran* does not mention anything about circumcision, and we find slight references to it here and there, only in the *hadiths*. Male circumcision is mentioned in *Bukhari's hadith* as a practice of pre-Islamic prophets like Abraham or Ibrahim.[1] Female circumcision, also called clitoridectomy (*khatna* or *khafz*), however, is a much controversial concept. Although it is not widely followed, specific Muslim communities in Northeast Africa, south India and Southeast Asia perform this rite.

In South India, the *Ritu Kala Samskara* or the *Ritushuddhi* is performed, where the girl wears a *saree* for the first time when she attains puberty. This is probably done to show her transition from youth towards womanhood, where the symbolic reference of *saree* is used to denote an Indian woman. Such kind of practice can also be seen in Assamese society. Popularly known as *Xantibiya* or *Tulonibiya,* it is a ritualistic marriage ceremony of the girl a few days after she attains puberty. Here the girl is not married to any real groom but *tamul-paan* (beetle leaves and areca nut) or *kol-gos* (banana plant). The term *"xanti"* here denotes "*shanti*" or peace to the parents of the girl since she has attained puberty, and much to the relief of her parents, she can be married off, and the term *"tuloni"* can resemble the idea of "*tulilua*" or uplifting which denotes the transition or the upliftment of the girl towards womanhood.[2] Usually, in Hindu society, for seven days, the girl would not be allowed to touch anything or be touched by someone because she is considered impure. For the first three days, the girl has to live on uncooked food and is kept in isolation, not allowed to cut nails, comb hair, or see men. On the fourth day, she is bathed with *maah-haldi* (gram and turmeric paste), after which she adorns a *mekhela-sador* (Assamese traditional wear) and has to live fasting for four more days, has one boiled solid cooked food in the evening, which she has to cook herself. On the seventh day, her seclusion ends after a similar ritualistic bath followed by grooming her like a typical bride, along with a great feast. As a tradition, people always bring gifts to congratulate the bride on announcing her womanhood.[3]

Methodology

The methodology is qualitative and quantitative research conducted in the Islamic areas of Lakhtokia, Hatigaon and Machkhowa with a semi-structured interview schedule, taking 30 respondents, ten from each area.

Findings and Discussions

This part combines the three objectives, i.e. firstly, is "*Tuloni Biya*" accepted in Muslim society; secondly, if yes, what are the ritualistic practices and finally, is it fading away, divided into three sections along with a detailed discussion.

Section 1

Table 1.1" Ritualistic Practice

Sl No	*Celebration*	*Value in number*
1	Yes	14
2	No	16

Source: Data collected from the field by the author

Diagram 1.1

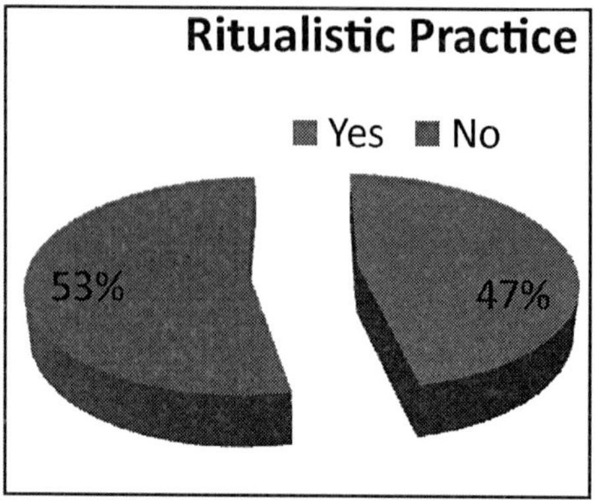

Source: Data collected from the field by the author

The table 1.1 shows that the concept of "*TuloniBiya*" is practised by 47% of the Islamic community, and 53% don't follow such a ritualistic practice. Of the 30 respondents, 16 said they didn't know if such a practice was observed in the Islamic community. Responses like – *"No, I have not heard of any such rituals practised in any Islamic families", "Do these practices exist in our community... I have just heard that such rituals only are observed in Assamese Hindu families"* or *"My parents didn't observed anything as such but I have attended my friends tuloni biya... they belong to Hindu religion"*. Of the 30 respondents, 14 have observed such a practice. Response like- *"Yes. Firstly, I was not allowed to go out of the house for seven days. On the 7th day, they performed rituals along with the dua (prayer). And before the dua, I was bathed with haldi and milk. Along with the rituals, there were certain games played... one I remember was... I was asked to break a clay pot with a leg at a go, and before doing it, I had to think of a name of a girl whom I wanted to have the next period... interestingly within a week or so, that girl got her periods."* was found.

Section 2

This section is divided into two sections which deal with the narratives, tables and diagrams of the respondents who observe such a ritualistic practice.

2.1. Narratives

- Seven days ceremony... bathed with saulguri (powdered rice) and maahhaldi…there was a "Dua in the evening by "Junab"(Priest)…and my friends came…I was decked up like a bride…and three ladies(one being the mother of my Hindu friend) came to my house and sang naam (the devotional song of Assamese Vaishnava)…

  The morning I was bathed with maahhaldi because it was an antiseptic…the water bucket had rings of gold, silver and copper…astradhatu (eight metals)...berry leaves... neem leaves…another bucket had Dettol...I was wearing Mekhela Sador at that time, just like a bride…after that, I wore a lehenga for the evening.
- Firstly I was not allowed to go out of the house for 7 days… On the 7th day, they performed rituals along with the dua… And before the dua I was bathed with haldi and milk. Along with the rituals, there were certain games played…one I remember was…I was asked to break a clay pot with a leg at a go, and before doing it, I had to think of a name of a girl whom I wanted to have the next period… interestingly, within a week or so, that girl got her periods.
- Three days not allowed going out. 4th day went out, and on the 8th day haldi ceremony, dua was performed by a priest, followed by a feast to which people were invited… I was applied gram and turmeric paste and given a bath. I was given a bath with two buckets of water…one had

gold, silver and copper metals and rice powder, and the other had flowers.

- Firstly I was bathed with two buckets of water...one containing gold and silver metals and the second with tulsipaat (basil leaves) and milk, on the 7th day. Before that, I was applied haldi. After two days, the dua was read out, and close family members were invited.
- For 5 days, I was not allowed to go out of the house… on 5th day I was bathed with maah and haldi, and the water had gold and silver in it. I wore my usual clothes, and on the 5th day, a Junab was called…no feasting.
- No, my family did not perform any type of rituals…If a Muslim girl gets her period, she is not allowed to recite and touch the Quran and offer Salah (namaz). On the 7th day of the period, she is supposed to do "ghusl", a purification bath where you have to wash one and clear the pubic hair… It is only after this bath that the woman is allowed to touch and recite Quran and perform Salah… Ghusal and not reciting and praying are the only rituals which I have seen being performed by my other family members.
- I was asked to have a fast like less masala and oil, and on the 11th day was given some haldi and dal paste to wash; then, an older lady performed some puja at my place... She was my neighbour.
- The ritual, which was of 7 days, was done…where I had to take only vegetarian food and was not always allowed to go out. Only after the 7th day they celebrated tulonibiya, and I was allowed to go out and take anything… I was bathed with haldi and maah near a banana tree, and then I had to wear new clothes. Then bunches of fruits were to be seen

by me so that in the future, I would bear children and was not allowed to have non-vegetarian thereafter.

- No such conservative practices were observed in my family… I was allowed to talk to everyone.
- My mother and sister-in-law gifted me gold rings; apart from that, I received gold earrings, clothes and money.

2.2. *Tables and Diagrams*

2.2.1. Composition of the days observed

The table 2.2.1 shows the number of days the ceremonial practice is observed. It is divided into five parts, i.e. 1-3 days, 4-5 days, 6-7 days, more than 7 days and didn't observe. The diagram 2.2.1 shows 54% don't follow it, 37% observe a 6-7 day ritual and 3% each in case of 1-3 days, 4-5 days and more than 7 days.

Table 2.2.1: Days observed

Sl. no	*Days observed*	*Value in number*
1	1-3 days	1
2	4-5 days	1
3	6-7 days	11
4	More than 7 days	1
5	Didn't observe any	16

Source: Data collected from the field by the author

Diagram 2.2.1

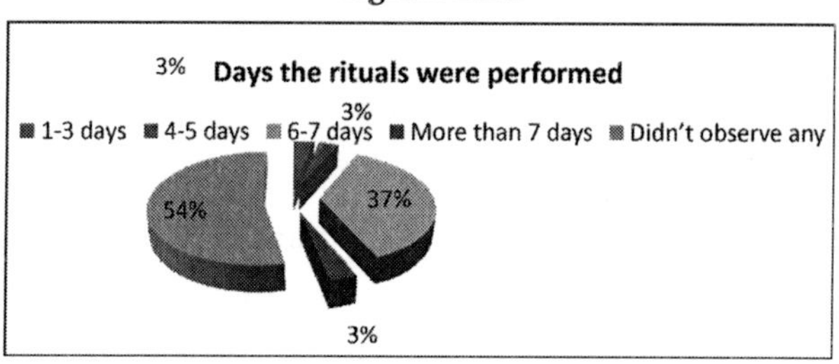

Source: Data collected from the field by the author

2.2.2. Composition of the scale of the ceremony

The table 2.2.2 shows how the ceremony is celebrated, whether big or small. It's divided into three parts big, small and no ceremony. The diagram 2.2.2 shows 53% don't celebrate it and 27% celebrate it on a small scale, and 20% celebrate it on a big scale.

Table 2.2.2 Ceremony

Sl. No	*Ceremony*	*Value in number*
1	Small	8
2	Big	6
3	No	16

Source: Data collected from the field by the author

Diagram 2.2.2

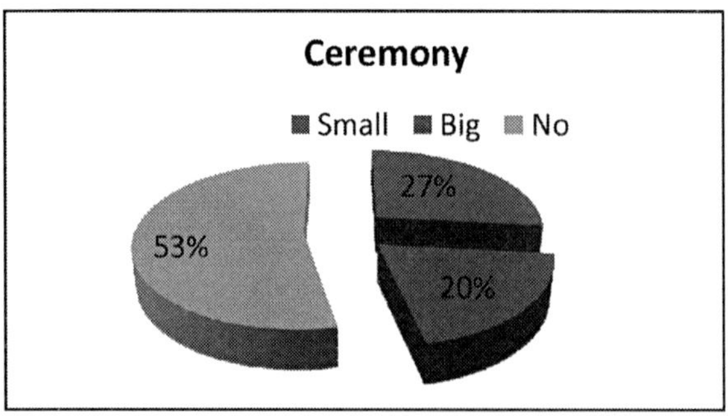

Source: Data collected from the field by the author

2.2.3. Composition of the people invited to the ceremony

The table 2.2.3 shows whether it was a closed celebration or an open one. It's divided into two parts, the first only family members and the second family relatives and neighbours. The diagram 2.2.3 shows 64% invited only family members, and 36% celebrated it with their friends, relatives and neighbours.

Table 2.2.3: People Invited

Sl. No	*People invited*	*Value in number*
1	Only Family Members	9
2	Friends, relatives and neighbours	5

Source: Data collected from the field by the author

Diagram 2.2.3

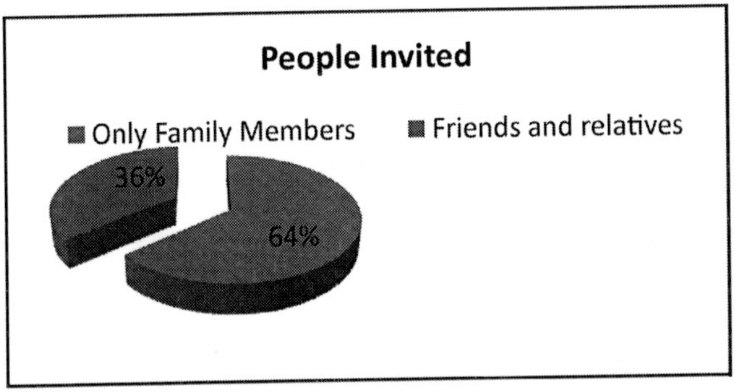

Source: Data collected from the field by the author

2.2.4. *Composition of the different types of attire*

The table 2.2.4 shows the different kinds of dress worn in that period. It's divided into three parts western, traditional and no specifics. The diagram 2.2.4 shows 57% don't have any specific. They wore whatever was comfortable; 10% wore Western attire, and 33% wore traditional clothing.

Table 2.2.4: Attire

Sl. No	*Attire*	*Value in number*
1	Western	3
2	Traditional	10
3	No specific	17

Source: Data collected from the field by the author

Diagram 2.2.4

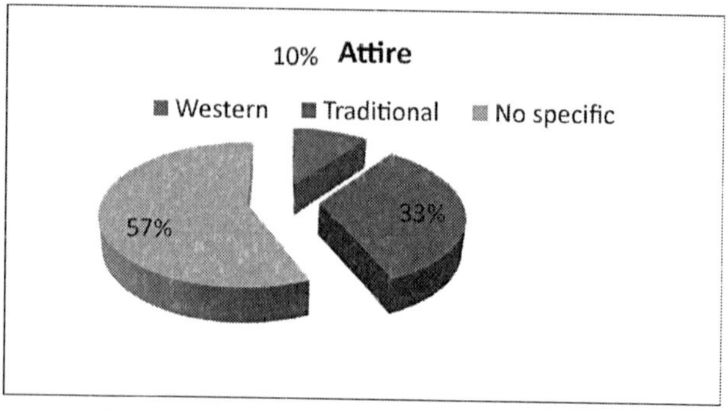

Source: Data collected from the field by the author

2.2.5. Composition of separate rooms

The table 2.2.5 shows whether a separate room was given to the respondent during such ritualistic practice. It is divided into two parts yes or no. The diagram 2.2.5 shows 88% were not given a separate room, and 12% were given so.

Table 2.2.5: Separate rooms

Sl. No	*Separate Rooms*	*Value in number*
1	Yes	2
2	No	14

Source: Data collected from the field by the author

Diagram 2.2.5

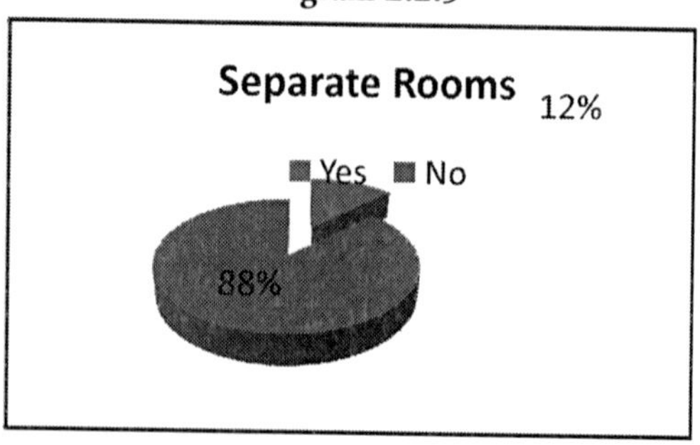

Source: Data collected from the field by the author

2.2.6. Composition of whom they first approached

The table 2.2.6 shows whether the respondent had approached the male or the female of the family. It is divided into two parts male and female. The diagram 2.2.6 shows 97% went to the females and 3% went to the male.

Table 2.2.6: First approached

Sl. No	*First approached*	*Value in number*
1	Male	1
2	Female	29

Source: Data collected from the field by the author

Diagram 2.2.6

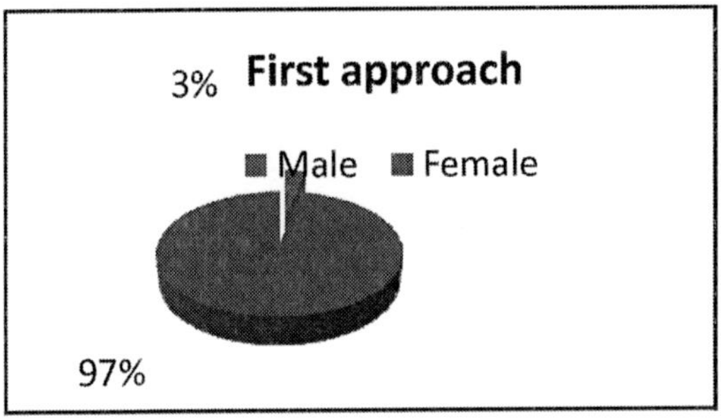

Source: Data collected from the field by the author

2.2.7. Composition of who supervised the rituals

The table 2.2.7 shows who supervised the ritualistic practices. It is divided into two parts male and female. The diagram 2.2.7 shows 93% were supervised by females, and 7% was supervised by male.

Table 2.2.7: Supervision

Sl. No	*Ritual Supervision*	*Value in number*
1	Female	13
2	Male	1

Source: Data collected from the field by the author

Diagram 2.2.7

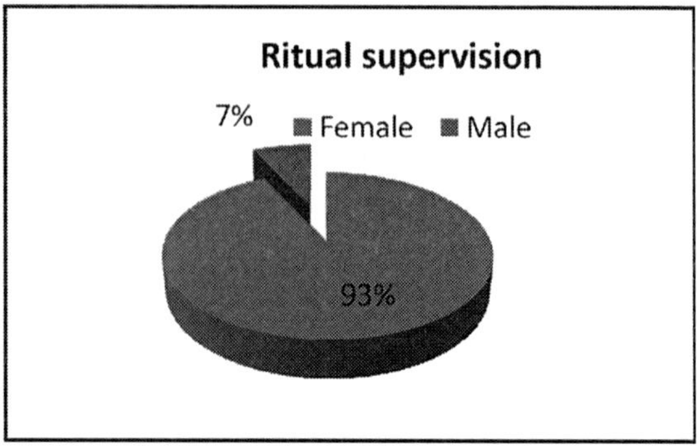

Source: Data collected from the field by the author

Discussion and Elaborations

From the study, it was found that the concept of "*TuloniBiya*" is practised among 47% of the Muslim Assamese society, but from the narratives, it would be seen that there are variations in such rituals. The table 2.2.1 shows the difference in the days the ritualistic practice was observed. Like 37% of the respondents observe it for 6-7 days, and 3% of the respondents follow it for a range of 1-3 days, 4-5 days or more than 7 days. The process of applying *haldi* and *maah* on the skin of the girl who attains puberty was common in all the cases where such a ritualistic practice was celebrated. But the day when it was applied varied from three to eight days. Out of 30, 11 respondents observed the "*Haldi Ceremony*" on the 7th day after the onset of the menstrual cycle. This is done because *haldi* and *maah* are considered auspicious and have antiseptic elements. Just after the "*haldi* ceremony", the girl is bathed with water, rice powder, leaves, flowers or metals; where in one bucket water is mixed either with rice powder; metals like gold, silver or copper; leaves like *Neem*, *Tulsi* or *Bogoripaat* (Jujube leaves) and the other contains water mixed with milk, rose petals or Dettol. Just after that, a "*dua*" is performed by the *junab*, followed by feasting. This feasting can either be a big or a small one. Diagram 2.2.2 shows that 27% celebrate it on a small scale, and 20% celebrate it on a large scale out of those who celebrate it. This celebration involves family members in most cases, which is evident in diagram 2.2.3, where 64% of the people invited were the family members of the respondents, and 36% included relatives, friends and neighbours. 33% wore traditional attire like *MekhelaSador* or *Salwar Suit* during the ceremony, 10% wore western clothing like a shirt, skirt or pants, and 57% said there aren't any restrictions in a dress. A majority of 88% of the respondents were not separated into a single room or given to use separate bathrooms. Instances have been found where the respondent's brother was sent to their grandparent's house, and the father was not allowed to talk to her even if he was in the house. It was found that 97% of the respondent first approached their mother, aunty, sister, grandmother, and sister–in–law and the rituals performed were supervised by the females of the family. Only one respondent out of 30 approached her father, and he supervised the rituals because she stayed with him. No restrictions in communicating with the family's male members were found. Gifts like gold earrings, rings, nose pins, money and clothes are gifted in such celebrations. Foods like vegetarian and non-vegetarian, along with fruits and dry fruits; boiled food; less masala food; intake of less citrus food was found to be taken during that period. Certain games like breaking a clay pot with one leg at a go, and before doing it, the person had to think of a name of a girl whom she wanted to have the following periods and bunches of fruits were to be seen by the girl so that in the future she could bear children were played.

Apart from these, it was found that in two cases, *naam* was sung, and in a single case, it was found out that the *"Haldi Ceremony"* was done near a banana tree.

Respondent 10 said that if a Muslim girl attains her period, she is not allowed to recite and touch the Quran or offer *Salah*. On the 7th day of the period, she is supposed to do "*ghusl*", which is a purification bath where you have to wash one and clear the pubic hair. It is only after this bath that the woman is allowed to touch and recite Quran and perform *Salah*.

Section 3

This section is divided into two parts, which deals with the third objective, including tables, diagrams and narratives for a detailed explanation.

3.1. Narratives

- No, it will fade away with time. I did not like such practices as I was not allowed to leave my home.
- I will like to do the rituals done with me during my daughter's time
- No, these types of rituals are of no use nowadays.
- As I haven't faced any rituals, I cannot say about it…but if there are practices where girls are not allowed to have a meal together, to have food in separate bowls and to wear dirty cloth, then this should be changed…they should not be treated differently as it is part of womanhood and awareness is much needed in this regard.
- I think to an extent.
- I enjoyed it…so I would like my daughter to celebrate it… just to make her feel special about womanhood.

- Yes, but not in Guwahati...attended the puberty marriage in Jorhat, where I saw the girl being bathed after applying haldi and dua recitation after it.

3.2. Tables and Diagrams

The table 3.2.1 shows if such a practice was observed when the respondents' mothers attained their first puberty. The table is divided into two, either yes or no. The diagram 3.2.1 shows that 47% observed such a practice, and 53% didn't celebrate it.

Table 3.2.1: Celebrated during Mother's time

Sl. No	*Celebrated during Mother's time*	*Value in Number*
1	Yes	14
2	No	16

Source: Data collected from the field by the author

Diagram 3.2.1

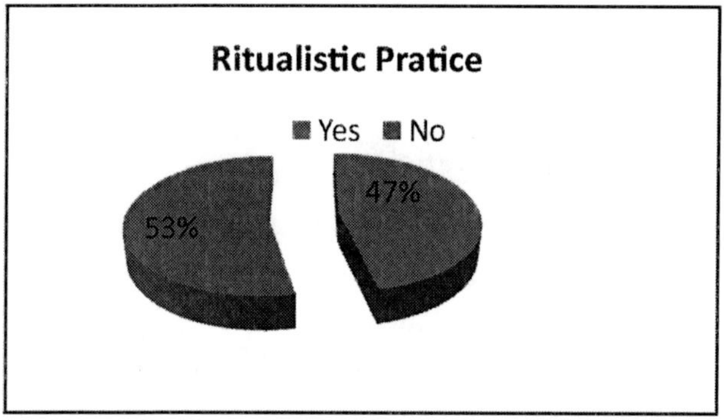

Source: Data collected from the field by the author

The table 3.2.2 shows whether such a practice be carried out by the respondents if they have a girl child. The table is divided into two parts, either yes or no. The diagram reveals that 80% will not be performing such a practice with their daughters, and only 20% will follow it.

Table 3.2.2: Carry Forward

Sl. No	*Carrying forward*	*Value in number*
1	Yes	6
2	No	24

Source: Data collected from the field by the author

Diagram 3.2.2

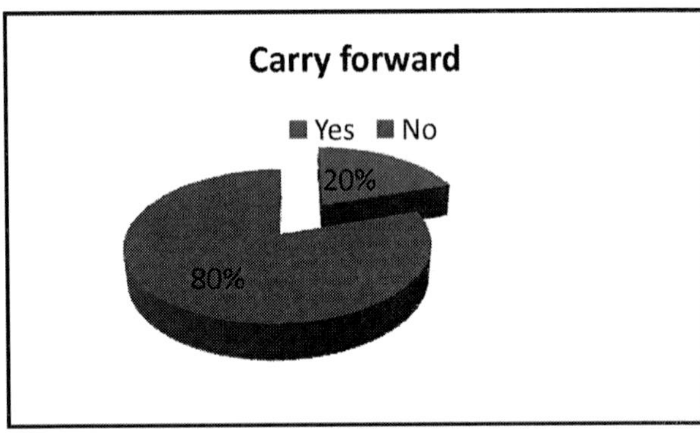

Source: Data collected from the field by the author

Discussion and Elaborations

It has been found that such a ritualistic practice in Muslim society has been carried out earlier in a small number. 14 out of 30 respondents said that such a practice was performed when their mothers first attained puberty. And 16 of them said their mothers didn't undergo such a practice. So if Table 1.1 and Table 3.2.1 are compared, it can be seen that the exact same number celebrated it both during their mother's time and their own; and the same number didn't. So it is something that passes on from one generation to another. 80% of the respondents say they will not perform such a practice if they have a baby girl. And could be seen in Table 3.2.2 that 24 out of 30 said that they would not continue this, and some respondents with whom these were performed don't want to perform it with their daughters. They said that modernisation or their dislike of such a practice and the usual trend of not seeing these rituals among their families or community would lead to fading of these practices.

Conclusion

Muslim *tulonibiya* is not universal, making the divisional line very thin, where few remain indifferent. There is a vast difference in the ritualistic practices; the observing days varied, the celebration being a culmination of the Assamese Hindu and Muslim society since *naam* and *maah-haldi* based ceremonies have been observed. Unlike Hindus, they refrain from the purity concept, being separated only because of hygiene and societal demands. Urbanisation and the rising violence against women have made people refrain from ceremonially observing *tulonibiya*. Again a trend has been found regarding the continuation of such practice. *Tulonibiya* was observed only in families whose mothers have gone through the process. This way, this ritual might carry on, a few being reluctant to carry it forward because they feel ashamed of telling people about the attainment of mensuration.

Notes

1. A. Niaz, *Puberty Rites*, 1, July 2017. Retrieved from islamicus.org: http://islamicus.org/puberty-rites on 18 February 2020.
2. S. Das, "Declining og Tuloni Biya: a Case Study", *Rupkatha Journal on Interdisciplinary Studies in Humanities*, 2017, pp. 242-249.
3. *Ibid.*, pp. 242-249.

References

Ahmed, K. A. *Muslim Contribution to Assamese Culture,* Procreate Prakashan, Guwahati, 2004.

Caplan, A., "Boys' Circumcision and Girls' Puberty Rites among the Swahili of Mafia Island, Tanzania", *Africa: Journal of the International African Institute, Vol. 46, No. 1,* 1976, pp. 21-33,

Das, M., "Menstruation as Pollution: Taboos in Simlitola, Assam", *Indian Anthropologist, Vol. 44, No. 2,* 2014, pp. 47-63.

Das, S., "Declining og Tuloni Biya: a Case Study", *Rupkatha Journal on Interdisciplinary Studies in Humanities,* 2017, pp. 242-249,.

Gennep, A. V., *The Rites of Passage,* M. B. Vizedom, & G. L. Caffee, Trans., London and Henley: Routledge and Kegan Paul, 1960.

Good, A,. "The Female Bridegroom: Rituals of Puberty and Marriage in South India and Sri Lanka", *Social Analysis: The International Journal of Anthropology, No. 11,* 1982, pp. 35-55.

Karunakaran, T., & K. Somasundaran, "Empowering The Young Women0 A Study With Reference To Puberty Rituals". *Paripex-Indian Journal of Research, Vol. 5' Issue 8,* 2016, pp. 134-136.

Khalidi, O., "Indian Muslim Society and Economy", *Islam in South Asia,* 2004, pp. 177-202.

Niaz, A.. "Puberty Rites", from islamicus.org: http://islamicus.org/puberty-rites (2017, July 1), Retrieved 18 February 2020,

Rigby, P., "The Structural Context of Girls' Puberty Rites", *Man, New Seies, Vol. 2, No. 3,* 1967, pp. 47-63.

Webner, P., "The Hidden Lion: Tswapong Girls' Puberty Rituals and the Problem of History", *American Anthropologist, Vol. 36, No. 3,* 2009, pp. 441-458.

14

Village Development Board and Village Council: A Unique Device of Local Governance System in Nagaland

Mahabir Jha

Introduction

It is evident that after India's independence in 1947, the Government of India has gone for notable administrative changes in governance with the marked objective of changing the rural face of the country and helping the poor avail themselves the opportunities for self-development. Under the process of decentralised administration, the government evolved the strategy to constitute Panchayati Raj Institution and empowers the village panchayats to play a vital role in rural development and poverty alleviation programs. Article 40 in theConstitution of India states, "The State shall take steps to organise Village Panchayat and endow them with such powers and authority as may be necessary to enable them to function as units of self-government." The 73rd Constitutional Amendment Act was approved on April 1993.The Act was intended to grant constitutional sanction and set up "democracy at the grass-root level."[1]The village-level democracy turned out to be a real vision for India with the 73rd amendment act of the constitution, but since its laws did not cover the scheduled areas so the Panchayat Extension to the Schedule Areas (PESA) Act came into being, mainly to enable tribal self-rule into these areas in 1996. PESA was a law thatthe Government of India formed to secure self-governance through the traditional Gram Sabha for all the people residing in the Scheduled areas of Andhra Pradesh, Chhattisgarh, Gujarat, Himachal Pradesh, Jharkhand, Madhya Pradesh, Maharashtra, Rajasthan, etc. comes under the scheduled areas.[2]

The problem in northeast India has been how to replace the traditional governance with the new rural administrative pattern under the PRI. The traditional governing village institutions in the tribal areas of the northeast have been playing a vital role in the governance of the villages. The traditional institutions among the tribal people are deeply rooted in their politico-administrative system and hence are not very keen to depart from this tradition and adopt new patterns. The Village Council, the Area Council and the Tribal Council, which are traditional institutions and have been playing dominant roles in village governance, are still significant. On the other hand, the government of India is determined to implement rural development programmes through the three-tier village panchayat system.

The changing economic policy of the Government of India from centralised national planning to decentralise planning following the recommendations of the Mehta Committee paved the way for the growth of Village Panchayati Raj. The Nagaland government had declined to introduce the Panchayati Raj Institution. On the other hand, the government of Nagaland developed a new device to incorporate both the traditional system of village administration and the modern pattern of Village Panchayat. Article 371A of the Constitution makes exclusive provisions for religious or social practices of the Nagas, Naga customary law and procedure, administration of civil and criminal justice involving decisions according to Naga customary law, ownership and transfer of land and its resources within the state of Nagaland. This Act gives recognition to the traditional practices of the Naga people.[3]Under such circumstances, a middle way has been developed in Nagaland. The set-up developed in 1976 to cover rural development programmes is the Village Development Board (VDB). The VDB has emerged as a model in place of the Village Panchayat in Nagaland for rural development.[4] Every recognised village in Nagaland has a Village Council and its development wing, the Village Development Board.It has proved as a policy inthe right direction toward rural development. However, it has to cover a long distance and face new challenges to achieve its purpose. This paper focuses on the establishment, scope and functions of traditional modes of local governance, i.e., Village Councils and their VDBs which have evolved from indigenous practices of the Naga tribes and later regularised through legislation, facilitating their easy assimilation with the existing village system.

Village Councils

Village Councils have administrative, executive and judicial powers and duties vested in them vide the Nagaland Village and Area Councils Act. Anyone above 25 can become a member after being chosen based on consensus following Naga customary law. Traditional village chiefs like Gaon Burahs and Angs are ex-officio members of the Council with voting rights. The Council is responsible for planning the development of the village and ensuring the maintenance of basic amenities like water, roads, forest, education and other welfare activities. It is also the custodian of all the community land and resources within the village. No land within the village's jurisdiction can be transferred for any purpose without the approval of the Council. The Council also has to execute justice according to the customary law of the tribe for any dispute arising within the village limits. The Council can hear and settle civil and criminal cases according to customary law. There are instances where Village Councils have settled murder cases also. In case of disputes between villages, the respective Village Councils can resolve the matter over a joint meeting or refer it to the Area Council or other appropriate authority.

Area Councils

An Area Council has jurisdiction over villages within a mountain range as notified by the state government. Each mountain range has some villages, and a particular tribe usually occupies an area covered by several ranges. These ranges have special significance for people as land, forest, and other resources within the village are the common property of the villages within the range. The Area Council adjudicates disputes arising out of sharing of this common property. The members of the Area Council are elected representatives from the Village Councils in the proportion of one member for a population of 500 and part thereof, not below 250. So, bigger villages have more than one representative in the Area Council.[5]

Role of the Village Councils

Under the Nagaland Village and Area Council Act 1978, every recognised village in the State shall have a Village Council. Its powers and duties, as enshrined in the said Act, provide for the following:

1. To formulate Village Development Schemes to supervise proper maintenance of water supply, roads, forest, education and other welfare activities.
2. To help various government agencies carry out development works in the village.
3. To take development works on its initiative or request by the Govt.
4. To borrow money from the Govt., Banks or financial institutions for application in the development and welfare work of the village and to repay the same with or without interest, as the case may be.
5. To apply for and receive grant-in-aid, donationsand subsidies from the Govt. Or any agency.
6. To provide security for due repayment of loan received by any permanent resident of the village from the Govt., Bank or Financial Institution.
7. To lend money from its funds to deserving permanent residents of the village and to obtain repayment thereof with or without interest.
8. To forfeit the security of the individual borrower on his loan repayment default.
9. advanced to him or on his commission of a breach of any of the terms of the loan
10. agreement he entered into with the Council and to dispose of such security by public auction or private sale.
11. To enter into any loan agreement with the Govt., Bank and Financial Institutions or a permanent village resident.

12. To realise registration fees for each litigation within its jurisdiction.
13. To raise funds for utility service within the village by passing a resolution subject to the approval of the state Govt.
14. Provided that all monetary transactions shall be conducted through a scheduled bank or Nagaland State Coop Bank.
15. To constitute a Village Development Board (VDB).
16. To empower certain Acts in the event of an epidemic.

Village Development Board

The Village Development Board is the offshoot of the Village Council. The institution of the VDBs, synonymous with the concept of decentralised grass root level planning in Nagaland, was first set up in 1976 in Ketsapomi village in Phek District on an experimental basis. The first rural development agency, which appeared in 1976 in Nagaland after such realisation, was called the Village Common Fund Committee. This Committee was given a new terminology, namely, the Village Development Board (VDB).[6] During the early period, the Village Council, as an institution, used to be the single body to maintain order in the village and punctuate discipline among the villagers. It was assigned to perform legislative and judicial functions by interpreting customs and maintaining traditions, which are the founding base of the tribal society. These are deeply rooted in the blood and habit of the tribal people. The Council comprised the village elders who used to meet to decide prominent issues and profitable courses of village life. It was a good model for village development and incorporated traditional wisdom. With time, it also has been found fit in tune with the needs and requirements of present societies.[7] The Village council used to manage common property and common village fund in the interest of the common people. Before India's Independence, the Village council played dominant roles in governing the village affairs and in doing welfare to the villagers. After India's independence, its significance and functions decreased due to the advent of the 'erudite administration'. No doubt, it still exists, and its importance in the village cannot be denied, but its significant roles are confined to "only as a lower court' of the village.

Organisation of VDB

Evidently, the Government of Nagaland formulated the VDB to be the core body in the form of the Gram Sabha, which comprises "all permanent residents of the village" who form the "general body of the VDB."[8] According to the Model Rules (1980 &1989), the meeting of the VDB must be held at least twice a year to discuss and deliberate issues regarding village development and approve the Schemes chalked out by the Management Committee, the most influential organ of the VDB. The Management Committee constituted for three years, has a minimum strength of five and a maximum of twenty-five members. The village council chooses these members from outside of its membership. The provision has been made to include 25 % of women members in both the VDB and the MC. The Deputy Commissioner or the Additional Deputy Commissioner happens to be the Chairman of the Management Committee. The members of the MC select one from among themselves as the Secretary who must be a literate person of the village. If such a literate man or woman is unavailable in the village, the government may appoint one government servant as the Secretary to serve the purpose. It is notable that "No Village Council's Chairman or head Gaon Burahs (GB) or village administration head etc. shall be permitted to hold the post of the Secretary of the VDB's Management Committee (MC). It means the post of the MC Secretary is very significant. The members of the MC itself must hold this rank. The government's power and responsibility bestowed upon the Secretary have made the post very influential and attractive. The Secretary lays before the general body "all details regarding the VDB schemes, money drawn, loans issued against fixed deposit security, the interest of fixed deposit, manner of utilisation of interest amount and other issues." The Secretary is always in close contact with the district authorities related to rural development, including the Deputy Commissioner. The Secretary receives any cheque issued by the district authorities related to rural development or the schemes and programs related to village development. It is he who maintains all records of expenditure. All these provisions have highlighted the rank and position of the Secretary not only among the villagers but also among the government officials related to the VDB's activities.

Sources of Income of VDB

Since the VDB stands in place of the Village Panchayat, it is provided with sufficient funds for rural development through various agencies. The most reliable resource is the Matching Grants given by the Government of Nagaland, which is equal to the amount of the common fund raised by the villagers. However; it has an upper limit of rupees five lahks only. It means the villagers can raise the fund maximum of rupees five lakhs, and the government of Nagaland would give another fund of rupees five lakhs. The villagers raise such fund maximum through labour free of cost done to the development schemes. The labour component generally constitutes 30% of the scheme cost. Another reliable resource is grant-in-aid given by the government of Nagaland annually. Each recognised village receives a grant-in-aid at a specific rate for carrying out community development schemes. In the beginning, the rate of allocation was Rs. 100/- per tax-paying household with a minimum of Rs. 5000/-. At present, the amount has been increased manifolds. Funds allocated by the Central government of India for implementing various centrally sponsored schemes are another viable income resource of the VDB. Since the VDB is a recognised field agency, the subsidy amount is directly released to it, and it is the VDB that sanctions and disperses subsidies to a few selected households to meet 50% of the cost of the scheme taken up.

Management Committee of VDB

The provisions have been made to handle the cash safely to avoid mismanagement or malpractice of the funds under the VDB. Clause 8 of the Model Rules insists on opening bank accounts and their joint operation by the Chairman and the Secretary of the Management Committee (MC). Moreover, "No cheque shall be honoured unless accompanied by a copy of the MC's resolution authorising such withdrawal signed by the members of the MC present."[9] The amount received from the sources must be put in a fixed deposit, which cannot be withdrawn except the interests; otherwise, the VDB "not be eligible for any funds, grants-in-aid, Matching Cash grant, funds available under the JRY and other development funds from the Department of Rural Development."[10] The Secretary of the MC has to maintain complete records of the amount received in the form of grant-in-aid. He also keeps details of drawls of money and disbursals under the running development schemes. The Village Council still has supervisory power over the VDB. Both the MC and the VDB secretaries are responsible to the Village Council. There are also provisions for auditing the accounts for which initiative should be taken from the Village council.

Controlling Officer

Following the decentralised planning system in Nagaland, the planning process begins at the grass-root level under the cooperation of the VDB. The schemes and programmes formulated by the Gram Sabha are sent to the Block Development Officer's (BDO) office. After proper scrutiny, the schemes are forwarded to the District Planning Board (DPB), which sends them to the Rural Development Department for final approval and realising the grants-in-aid. The BDO is the withdrawing officer on behalf of the VDB. The amount sanctioned to meet the expenditure for implementation of schemes is withdrawn from the bank after completing the report of the work where the BDO plays a remarkable role because it is he who ascertains whether the job has been completed or not.

Working Areas & Functions of VDB

Though the villagers have the autonomy to choose the schemes for their village development, the government provides specific model schemes to make the work easy for the villagers. Some of the model schemes/ functions provided by the government are mentioned below:

1. Making each VDB vibrant, with powers to take decisions and implement schemes;
2. Enabling VDBs to mobilise internal resources for investment in various income-generating and economically productive activities;

3. Checking migration of educated unemployed rural youth to towns by ensuring self-employment opportunities;
4. Gradually helping rural areas access basic facilities.
5. Construction of resting shades on kheti, village approach roads, playgrounds, community granaries, common latrines in the village, footsteps, drains, market sheds, waiting sheds, etc.
6. Programmes like community cattle, piggery, goat farming, poultry, fishery, etc.
7. Community fuel wood production, embroidery centres, dairy, fair-price shops, forestry, tea and coffee plantation and running of community buses.
8. Formation of village development schemes.
9. Supervision of various development schemes running in the village.
10. Help other development agencies to carry out development works.
11. Take development works on its initiative or on the request made by the government, borrow money from the government, banksand financial institutions for application in the development and welfare work of the village and repay the same.
12. Apply for or receive grant-in-aid, donations, and subsidies from the government or any agencies.
13. Lend money from its funds to deserving permanent residents of the village and obtain repayment thereof.
14. Forfeit the security of individual borrower on his loan repayment default.

15. Raise funds for utility services within the village by passing resolutions etc.

Before establishing the VDB, development inputs regarding specific resources were generally channelled through individuals rather than the community. Only after the establishment of the VDB "the community is being recognised as the resource-owning unit to a limited extent, even for the flow of development input. This is a breakthrough in the positive direction."[11]

In each recognised Naga village, the VDB is active under the cooperation and supervision of district-level officials, including the Project Director, Project Officer, Block Development Officer and many others. The VDB has assumed the responsibility to utilise the development funds provided through different sources of the Central and state governments. The District Planning Board (DPB) also plays a vital role in rural development. However, the relationship of the District Rural Development Agency (DRDA) with the DPB needs to be clearly defined; the result creates confusion among the villagers on the one hand and brings about specific difficulties in the implementation process of programmes.

Evaluation of the Performances of the VDB

The performances of the VDB in respect of rural development have been appreciable, no doubt, but several shortcomings have been found in the proper formation of development schemes, their successful implementation and the correct utilisation of funds provided for development. The objective of the VDB has been to draw the direct participation or involvement of the villagers in development programmes. In formulating and implementing the poverty alleviation programmes, the VDBs try to evolve a balanced approach through trial and error. Being rooted in the soil, it responds to the demands of the situation almost as a reflex action. As a field agency for rural development, the VDB in Nagaland has "appeared as a shining shine and a novel model innovation in the process of rural development creating new hopes and aspirations among the people, no doubt, but it has to cover a long distance to change the rural people's economic conditions and rural face..."[12]Appreciating the role of the VDB, Mr Hello, the Project Director of Rural Development of Mokokchung District, said that the problems of the state in implementing the SGSY and other related poverty alleviation programmes, the "VDB play a vital role, and it may be a self-supporting institution relating to the rural development programmes."[13]

The works of development which have taken place in Nagaland are better than in other states of India, no doubt, but the target fixed is still far away. The main priority of development works in Nagaland has been to construct community halls, playgrounds, community latrines, waiting sheds, village approach roads, primary school buildings, running community buses, dairy forms, piggery and poultry forms and development of small-scale industries. There is a provision to grant sufficient loans to the villagers for initiating personal schemes like tea and coffee plantations, etc. All the schemes and programmes for generating self-employment are run in the state. Under the Indira Aawas Yojana and Samagra Aawas Yojana, corers of rupees have been allotted. The objective of the Matching Grants is not only the "resource that the VDB could mobiles but also the judicious utilisation of resources for gainful purposes." In Nagaland, the VDB has assumed the status of a non-banking financial institution and has become a popular agency to effect newly launched multi-dimensional programmes like JRY, JGSY, SGSY and IAY, etc. The state has received an enormous amount for the development of rural areas and rural people.[14]

Before launching the Integrated Rural Development Programme (IRDP), most of the agencies related to rural development "neither exercised proper care in electing beneficiaries nor in ensuring the extension of services or supporting facilities in the matter of credit." Moreover, there needed to be more sufficient funds and required technical skills. When the IRDP came into being, not only were adequate funds provided, but special care was paid to develop the Scheduled Castes and the Scheduled Tribes. Sufficient amounts have been provided free of cost from the government to construct new *pucca* houses. All these programmes are centrally sponsored and funded on a cost-sharing basis between the government of India and the government of the state in a ratio of 75:25.

During the last few years,foremost priority has been accorded to development in rural areas. The rural development programmes have been streamlined and strengthened. The Ministry of Rural Development has taken several initiatives to create social and economic infrastructure in rural areas to bridge the urban-rural divide, provide food security, and fulfil other basic needs of the rural poor. To meet the requirement of funds for rural development, the allocation of funds for implementing various schemes has been enhanced to Rs. 76,774 crores as against Rs. 42,874 cores during the Ninth Plan.[15]

For the development to align with the people's wishes and aspirations, the emphasis has also been shifted towards the participation of people in the development process through self-help groups and Panchayati Raj Institutions. The Gram Sabha has been assigned important responsibilities, and the aim is to make it a vibrant forum of self-governance. Two main schemes, one for providing ways employment- Sampoorna Gramin Rojgar Yojana (SGRY) and the other for providing self-employment 'Swaranjayanti Gram Swarozgar Yojana (SGSY) to the rural poor, are under implementation to face the biggest challenge of unemployment in the rural areas.[16]

Ensuring rural connectivity is an important and integral part of the overall development strategy of the development of villages. Pradhan Mantri Gram Sadak Yojana (PMGSY), a hundred per cent centrally sponsored scheme, was launched on 25th December 2000. As per the latest estimate, about 1.72 lahks unconnected habitation in the country is to be taken up under the PMGSY, covering a total length of 3, 68,500 kilometres.

Nagaland state, as part of the Indian federal system, is entitled to get its shares in all the development schemes which have been launched so far. Besides that, Nagaland has been given particular preferences keeping in view the backwardness of the area and the people. When Atal Bihari Bajpayee, the Prime Minister of India, arrived in Nagaland in 2003 to attend the convocation Programme of the Nagaland University, he sanctioned crores of rupees for the construction of four-lane roads from Dimapur to Kohima.The VDB, the main agency for rural development, has to play a significant role in developing the state and its people.

Speaking at the silver jubilee celebration of Kohima block Village Development Board at Ura academy hall as the chief guest on 10th August 2005, Dr Shurhozelie, the Chairman of the governing body, DRDA Kohima, stated that "with help of VDBs Nagas can once again be self-sufficient and independent."[17] He also stated that "VDBs was formed to let the grass-root villagers have an equal and active participation in the policy and decision making functions of the government, which he also termed as decentralisation of power". Calling upon the VDBs to cooperate and support rural areas' development, he urged the VDB functionaries to strive hard for economic progress and self-sufficiency.[18] Dr Shurhozelie, while appreciating the role of the VDBs, said that the development, which has taken place in the state, "has been a rolemodel for the rest of states of the country." He further stated that "The formation of the VDBs in Nagaland led to the implementation of Panchayati Raj while MP's Local Area Development Fund has also been started after the Compact Area Development fund in Nagaland."[19]He suggested that peoplebe 'hard-working and self-sufficient'. Simultaneously, the Director of Rural Development, Metsubo Jamir, urged the VDBs "to have broader outlook and perspective to fulfil various developmental programmes entrusted by the government and for judicious utilisation of the VDB deposited an amount of Rs. 45 crores.

Challenges/Findings

1. The VDB and VC faced challenges such as corruption, political influence, the dominance of the few, etc., encompassing the social, economic and political spheres.
2. Except for a few literate and capable members, most of the members of VDB and VC are illiterate; therefore, the degree of expertise and technological knowledge with clear visionary ideas is very much lacking.
3. The selfishness and narrow-mindedness of the VDB members often create confusion, disputes, misunderstanding and jealousy amongst the people, and there is an invariable clash between the VDB and VC members as the Village Council members feel that they were neglected and ignored in many decisions making.

It is often also alleged that the broad leaders and their relatives enjoy the maximum benefits.

4. Though 25% of seats are reserved for women in VDBs and VCs, women hardly get space to participate in decision-making in the Village Administration.
5. There is a lack of democratic spirit. The Chairman and members are selected, not elected. The village is just like a kingdom having everything with the village chairman, who acts as the ruler or administrator.[20]

Conclusion

Despite the challenges mentioned above, the Village Councils, along with the Village Development Boards, have been playing an important role in the smooth progress of livelihood and economic growth of the community and the village as a whole. The VC and VDBs can perform better if proper management and administrative discipline can be introduced at all levels through proper utilisation of its funds. The local governance systems of the Village Councils are mostly based on the Naga customary laws. Each Naga village possesses and rules its funds and also prepares development actions to preserve rule, organise, in carrying out justice and secure protection. In many ways, the traditional self-governance of the Nagas is quite similar to that of Gandhi's view of “Village Swaraj” and also similar to the opinion of Charles Metcalfe, who called the village panchayats a "little republic".[21]The State has nearly1355 villages (1280 recognised, 75 unrecognised and 111 hamlets in 2021), and each village has its Village council and Village development board. No developmental activity takes place without the active participation of VC and VDB at the village level.

Notes and References

1. D. C., Bhattacharyya, *Indian Government & Politics*, Vijoya Publishing House, Kolkata, 2014, p.371.
2. https://mha.gov.in/sites/default/files/PESAAct1996_0.pdf pp.-9-16
3. Amba Jamir, "Understanding Local Self Governance in Nagaland: An essence of the institutions and their activities" 2010, retrieved from ftp://solutionexchange-un.net.in/public/decn/comm_update/res-55-030311-20.pdf as on Nov 26.16.
4. Chandrika Singh, "Functioning of Village Development Board in Nagaland", *Dialogue*, Vol. 5, No. 3, January- March 2004, p. 187.
5. Joya Chakraborty, "Local Self Governance as Democratic Participation: The Unique Case of the Nagas", *Journal of Business Management & Social Sciences Research*, Volume 1, No.2, November (2012), pp.101-102.
6. Neikonuo Sekhose, "Local Governing Institutions in Nagaland with special reference to Village Council and Village Development Board (A Case Study of Dimapur)", A Dissertation Report, Submitted to the School of Arts and Languages, LPU, Phagwara, 2017, p.19.
7. Maithani and Rizwana, *Decentralized Development, National Institute of Rural Development*, Hyderabad, 1991, p.4.
8. Village Development Board (VDB), (revised in 1989), Government notification dated 21st November 1989, Government of Nagaland, Kohima.
9. *Ibid.* Clause 8 (a)
10. *Ibid.* Clause 10.
11. B. K. Roy Burman, *Towards Poverty Alleviation Programme in Nagaland and Manipur,* Mittal Publications, New Delhi, 1984, p. xi.

12. Chandrika Singh, "Functioning of Village Development Board in Nagaland", *Dialogue*, Vol. 5, No. 3, January- March 2004, New Delhi, p.187.

13. Shri Hello Rengma, Director of Rural Development, Government of Nagaland, Mokokchung, issued a Pamphlet.

14. Swarn Gyanti Swarozgar Yojana (SGSY), a manual published by the Government of India, Department of Rural Development, New Delhi, 1999, p.1.

15. B. K. Roy Burman, *Towards Poverty Alleviation Programme in Nagaland and Manipur*, Mittal Publications, New Delhi, 1984, p. xxvi.

16. Swarn Gyanti Swarozgar Yojana (SGSY), *op.cit.* p.1

17. North East Herald, 11th August 2005, Dimapur, p.2.

18. *Ibid.*

19. *Ibid.*

20. Neikonuo Sekhose, *op. cit*, pp.41-42.

21. D.C. Bhattacharyya, *op. cit.* p.370.

15

Print Media and Consciousness in Manipur

V. Mancy Baite

Today, the impact of Media, as Marshall McLuhan describes, has turned the whole world into a "global village", whereby countries of the world are closer to each other because of the advances in mass communication.[1] Before introducing new media technologies, like radio, television etc., the notion of "mass media" was restricted to print media. By the mid-nineteenth century, print media became the primary source of information, spreading and generating public opinion. Given its ability to reach the masses, with its immense influence, it penetrates society generating individual, socio-political and economic consciousness. In this background of the nature and role of print media, this paper aims to study the role of print media in generating consciousness in Manipur, a state in the Northeastern region of India. The paper has been divided into three; the first part of the paper will conceptualise print media and consciousness. The second part of the paper will discuss the beginning and development of print media in Manipur, highlighting the role of print media in bringing socio-political and national consciousness; the third part will be in the form of a conclusion.

I

Print media is a means of mass communication through printed publications, such as newspapers and magazines. Newspapers form an important component of journalism. Newspapers mean publications with titles and newsprint. It has been since the fourteenth century in Europe and the invention of the movable printing by the machinery of the 'press' that literate societies have come to rely upon print as the chief means of communication and, as a direct outcome of the Industrial Revolution, the print media have become a major source of information.[2] The word 'journalism' was originally applied to the reportage of current events in print forms. But, with the advent of radio and television in the 20th century, the use of the term has broadened.[3] Journalism, by definition, is "the activity or profession of writing for newspapers, magazines, or news websites or preparing news to be broadcast" (Oxford Languages). C. Northcote Parkinson views it as "... the ability to write and to convey thoughts in a way that people will understand quickly. It means being able to trim long meandering articles into shape. ... Journalism also means a nose for news and a feel for words, respect for truth, and a sense of mission. It means being able to size up a situation on the spot. And it means developing deep insight into human conditions."[4] Today, Journalism, with the new media technologies, shoulders a big responsibility of reporting information and building public opinion on media platforms, be it newspapers, radio or television, as media is believed to be the moral compass of society. Journalism is used interchangeably with other terms such as press, news, newspaper, etc. The term "press" is often used as a collective word for the activities involved in producing news; initially, it denoted print media but has now been extended to electric forms as well.[5] The study of the histories of journalism, newspapers and press are not studied separately, and, in most works, these are simultaneously discussed.

The *Cambridge Dictionary* describes Consciousness as the state of being awake, thinking, and knowing what is happening around you; it is also described as being aware of and responsive to one's surroundings. In the 1980s, consciousness was studied in several scholarly disciplines, such as psychology, philosophy, neuroscience, linguistics, medicine, etc. In the late 1990s, with the birth of two scholarly journals, Consciousness and Cognitive and the Journal of Consciousness Studies, considerable interdisciplinary cooperation evolved in consciousness studies and has since become cross-disciplinary. Scholars have analysed the concept of consciousness, and a number of approaches to its implications have evolved in the historical and social sciences discourses.[6]

Sigmund Freud, a neurologist and the founder of psychoanalysis is of the view that "feelings, perceptions, thoughts and desire cannot occur without being conscious. Whereas, philosophers Thomas Negel and John R. Searle hold that non-conscious states occur in ways similar to conscious states but deny that those non-conscious states are full-fledged feelings, perceptions or thoughts. By the mid-1990s, it was accepted that individuals could be in some mental states of which they are wholly unaware.

John Locke, who is regarded as one of the most influential Enlightenment thinkers, in his work, *Essay Concerning Human Understanding*, talks about personal identity; he puts forth that "Since consciousness always accompanies thinking and it is that which makes everyone to be what he calls self, and thereby distinguishes himself from all other thinking things, in this alone consists personal identity, i.e., the sameness of a rational being" .[7]

There is a curious asymmetry between the assessment of conscious and unconscious processes. Mental processes are conscious if people claim them to be conscious and can be reported and acted upon with verifiable accuracy. The term conscious marked the contrast between those mental processes one is conscious of and those not.

Conscious events experienced in the brain and outside the brain are interlinked. Conscious experiences depend in a direct way on a set of events outside the brain and in the past; for events outside the brain, social relations are important. The social environment shapes much of the architecture of the brain.[8] Media greatly influences the content of consciousness perceived and shared by individuals. Marshall McLuhan, in his book *The Medium is the Message*, reiterates that the role of media is so pervasive in the personal, political, economic, aesthetic, psychological, moral, ethical and social consequences that they leave no part of us "untouched, unaffected or unaltered."[9] Hence, the concept of consciousness cannot be detached from understanding the processes of change.

Print media, the earliest means of mass communication, stands as a catalyst for generating consciousness among people throughout the past. Newspapers by the mid-nineteenth century appeared in various parts of the world; newspapers at that time became the sole means of communication and expression which provided nationwide coverage. Newspapers were also used to serve revolutionary propaganda; one crucial example is *Iskra* (The Spark), published by Vladimir Lenin in 1900; it was a political newspaper of the Russian socialist emigrants; the newspaper is known for its satirical nature, which played an important role in spreading narrations for political freedom and a socialist revolution.[10] Another prominent example is *Thanh Nien* (Young People's Newspaper), a Vietnamese newspaper which focused on social affairs, introducing Marxism to the country and providing information on revolutionary strategies. These newspapers proved impactful in generating a sense of unity and national consciousness among the people.

Les Switzer and Donna Switzer, in their work, *The Black Press in South Africa and Lesotho*, start their discussion by briefly explaining the words like 'Black', 'Press' etc., used in their work's title. In this book, the authors discuss the origin and history of the various newspapers and distinguish these newspapers as catering to different sections of society. The Black Press has been defined as a readership directed primarily at an African, Indian and coloured audience. Besides publishing other news, these newspapers were also used as a voice to let out the grievances of the people marginalised by the white populace. These newspapers also reveal the common people's viewpoint towards developments in their society.[11]

The credit for the advent of journalism in India goes to the British. James Augustus Hicky, who served under the British, started the first weekly newspaper in Calcutta in 1780, named the *Bengal Gazette*. After this, some other newspapers, both English and vernacular, made their appearance in India during the British period. In 1789, the first newspaper from Bombay (Mumbai), the *Bombay Herald,* was started, and another newspaper, the *Bombay Courier*, was brought out in the same year. Other newspapers, such as *The Indian Gazette, The Calcutta Gazette, and The Madras Courier,* soon followed. These newspapers played a pivotal role in spreading news and ideas under the British rule.[12]

In the larger Indian context, journalist N. Ram in the foreword to R. Parthasarthy's book, *Journalism in India*, has identified four stages of journalism during the pre-Independence period of the country. He said the period between 1780 and

1818 was the "preparatory phase." Stage I (1818-1868) starts off with pioneering works in the field of journalism. Stage II (1868-1919) observes the rise of the Indian press as part of the nationalist struggle and the appearance of two trends in the press. One trend is supportive towards colonial rule and its policies, and the other is criticism and opposition to the Raj. This stage also saw the growth of Indian presses owned by Indians. Some notable events in this respect are the foundation of the *Amrita Bazar Patrika* (1868), *The Hindu* (1878) and the pro-Raj newspaper, *The Statesman,* in 1875. Stage III (1919-1937) saw the delineation of the Indian press into "moderate" and "radical" tendencies in relation to the strategy and tactics adopted for the freedom movement. The struggle between the nationalist and pro-British press continues thereafter. The struggle for the freedom of the press and for wider civil liberties, too, acquired a fuller voice. Stage IV (1937-1947) saw a mature Indian press, and during this stage, the Indian press as a whole took up a new role in independent India.[13]

Commenting on the importance of the printing press, including newspapers, A. R. Desai, in his book, *Social Background of Indian Nationalism*, writes, "The printing press played a big role in the history of a number of peoples, in their national awakening, in their imbibing progressive ideas, and in their being drawn as active forces into great social, political and cultural movements." His opinion explains the significance of newspapers in providing facts and figures that relate to the various aspects of historical developments. A number of other scholars have identified this link between journalism and socio-political consciousness in India and abroad through their studies.[14]

Hence, on the one hand, the post-Independence period witnessed the publication of new newspapers; on the other, the history of journalism in India began to be studied. Most of these works substantially focus on newspapers in the context of socio-economic, cultural and political developments.

II

Coming to the second part of the paper, it is to be noted that in the Northeastern region of India, the introduction of print media and the beginning of journalism can be traced twenty-five years later from the publication of the *Bengal Gazette* in 1780. The first newspaper in North-east India, the *Orunodoi*, was published in Assam in 1846.[15] Newspapers in the region also depicted national consciousness; one crucial example here can be drawn during the partition of Bengal, the *Weekly Chronicle*, a newspaper from Assam expressed objection to the partition, stating, "the professed advantage of the partition is that the District Officers will have more leisure and therefore more opportunities of doing good or evil. The administration may be stronger and more vigorous, but that means no good to the people. The plea for administrative efficiency does not appeal to the people these days when efficient administration does not necessarily mean suppression and detection of crime or more strenuous efforts for furthering the local interests and aspirations of the people. Moreover, efficient administration is currently a menace to the popular cause. For Government is anti-nationalist, and no devotee of nationalism in India can wish that the Government may be stronger and more efficient and far less than it is more popular."[16]

The *Times of Assam*, in 1911, reported on the racial inequalities committed by Mr Vickers, Assistant Commissioner of Sibsagar, where Mr. Vickers insulted an Indian gentleman for having omitted to shut his umbrella while saluting him. The incident came to be alleged as the "umbrella phobia."[17]

It is evident from the above reporting of the *Weekly Chronicle* and the *Times of Assam* that newspapers addressed the political issues and the racial inequalities, depicting the consciousness of the people towards the racial attitude and exploitative measures taken by the foreign rulers.

Manipur also referred to as the 'jewel of India', occupies a strategic position, surrounded by Nagaland in the north, Mizoram in the south, Assam in the west and an international boundary with Burma in the East. Manipur consists of a diverse set of population; the valley districts are dominated by the non-tribal population who speak 'Meteilon'. The hill districts are occupied mainly by thirty-three different tribes, broadly grouped into Nagas and Kuki-Chin-Mizo.[18]

This part of the paper will discuss the beginning and development of print media in the state, which cannot be ignored in the growth of the writing world in Manipur. The history of Manipur would be incomplete without understanding the history of print media in the state as newspapers in Manipur represent the voice of the people, often used by social reformers to promote socio-cultural and political consciousness, which influenced the masses and helped shape the society. Since accommodating all the journalistic endeavours made during the course of the history of the press in the region is not possible, only the significant journalistic efforts made in Manipur are described in this paper.

It is said that Journalism in Manipur started outside the state in Cachar, with *Meitei Leima,* a handwritten magazine brought out in the year 1917;[19] however, some scholars date it back to the year 1910. The history of Newspapers in Manipur started late; it may have been due to the hilly terrain of the state, which kept it aloof from other states. "Besides, print media has no value to an illiterate," as stated by Achungmei

Kamei.[20] The value of education was recognised very late in Manipur. Education in Manipur started in 1885 through a middle English school started by Sir James Johnstone, the then-political agent; since then, education has been making gradual progress in the state.[21] From 1891, a regency administration of the British operated in Manipur, and during the post-independence in 1972, Manipur became a full-fledged state of India.[22] Throughout these courses, Manipur entered a new phase of history in her political, social and administrative characters in which the role of print cannot be ignored.

After the release of *Meitei Leima* in 1917, Jananeta Hijam Irabot, one of the earliest pioneers of journalism in Manipur and a political leader, started voicing out on socio-political disorders. His first endeavour was brought out in 1922 as a magazine, *Meitei Chanu*, through which news and social and political change messages were spread.[23] This was followed by *Masik Jagran* in 1924; it aimed at educating Manipuris and improving the standard of living. Irabot's literary novel writing was first seen in *Yakairol* (1930), published by Dr Ningthoujam Singh. This monthly magazine encouraged new writers to try new areas of literary fields, promoting Manipuri literature, including journalism.[24] The credit for pioneering print media journalism in the state is awarded to Tonjgam Gokulchandra Singh, who published the *Dainik Manipur Patrika*, a daily newspaper in 1932.[25] The paper critiqued the British Government and presented an anti-British narrative; it also acted as a mouthpiece of the religious and cultural views of the people. The paper presented independent state desires, which created tensions for the then political agent. The paper had three editors. Shri. Thongbam Gokulchandra Singh was its first editor and later handed over the editorship to Shri Hawaibam Lalhari Singh again continued editing the newspaper until Shri

Lalita Madhab Sharma took over charge as an editor on 10 December 1934.29.[26] The paper in its editorial of 23 March 1934, wrote, "In a kingdom, if three organs like the king, the king's law and the man who executed the law carefully observe the rules, there will be peace in the realm. And if one of the three organs is not active, peace will not prevail there. Again, the rulers of the country practised bad characters; its people opposed it. The people will revolt with arms in their hands to rectify the rulers' misdeeds, and they will not be afraid of any punishment. At this time, the people will not obey the rule of law, and there will be chaos and disorder in the state." *Dainik Manipur Patrika* was instrumental in teaching the Manipuri their rights to be citizens and against the monopolist of the then rulers. The anti-colonial consciousness among the people can be seen through the paper's reporting.

In the late 1930s, Irabot endorsed the Swadeshi movement by using indigenous clothes made of *nailing.* With the active involvement of the *Nikhil Manipuri Mahasabha,* Irabot boycotted the cigarette distributors of the Imperial Tobacco Company of India Limited. As a supporter of the Swadeshi agitation, Irabot had also burnt his foreign clothes and made bonfires of the foreign cigarettes at Buri Bazar and Oinam Bazar as the Swadeshi movement gained momentum in an all-India character. The annual session of the congress, held in Calcutta in 1906, laid down Swaraj as its goal.[27] In 1933, *Lalit Manjuri Patrika,* edited by Arambam Deorendrajit was published. The monthly paper contained literature, philosophy, history, economics, and science. In this magazine Irabot greatly influenced by the political ideology of Bal Gangadhar Tilak, published his serialised biography.[28] The *Lalit Manjuri Patrika* was also a mouth piece of the then Congress party of India and supported the views of the Nikhil Manipuri Hindu Mahasabha.

In 1935, the Manipuri Sahitya Parishad was established by a group of educated notable literary figures such as Irabot, Dorendrajit, Nabadwipchandra, Shyamsundar, Khwairakpam Chaoba and others. The main objectives of the Parishad were to develop the Manipuri language and literature, encouraging young writers to produce and publish standard work. It also started the *Manipuri Sahitya Parishad Patrika*, mainly to convey information, views, speeches and resolutions of the Parishad.[29]

The use of print media was not just limited to political fields, a monthly health journal *Metei Maiba,* Shri Sagolshem Indramani Singh was its editor, and Shri Ninggombam Mangi Singh was its publisher. It was printed at the Thabal Printing Works at Uripok. The paper mainly focuses on issues related to health and hygiene.

The paper was designed to update the masses on health care, the need for a good dispensary and the availability of medicines. In the editorial pages of September 1938, the editor wrote, "A fruit is the most precious and inalienable medicine of human life, fruits are tremendously useful for the body, child, pregnant women, tuberculosis patient, growth child etc. It is also useful for everyone and also for the old and weak people… However, rotten fruits should not be eaten."[30]

Women in Manipur have played an important role in the state, more remarkably during British rule. The second *Nupi Lan,* which means women's war, marks a distinction in channelling a national consciousness. The second *Nupi Lan* erupted as a mass agitation against the combined feudalistic-colonial rule in 1939 which continued till 1941. When heavy rainfalls struck the state of Manipur, it affected the production of crops and led to a scarcity of food,[31] rendering many unemployed; on top of the ongoing crisis, the price of food grains hiked, and during this serious crisis, the Marwaris who had established a monopoly in the food grain business continued the export of rice, and the state Durbar did take any measures to secure the people. As the existing taxes already overburdened the people, the unsympathetic and inconsiderate attitude of the exploiters raged a sense of rebellion, and as a result, women came in unison, protested and demanded an immediate stoppage of rice exports, during which a clash between the Assam Rifles and the protesting women took place.[32] This mass agitation is also regarded as a fight for independence in Manipur. The Amrita Bazar Patrika, which was based in Calcutta in 1940, showed concern regarding the treatment of women during the protest. The editorial of 11 March 1940 reported that "two women agitators were injured following a clash between a group of women and the State Civil Police. In that incident, the women surrounded the Durbar Hall with the Durbar members and President Sharpe inside, demanding immediate disposal of a case in which an Inspector of Police of Imphal was charged with assaulting a woman…" [33] This report on the mass agitation did not only point towards the discontentment of the people but also to the growing anti-colonial consciousness in the state and in the other parts of the country, where a sense of oneness erupts. This further emphasised, importantly, the need to introduce new political and economic reforms in the state.

In August 1938, a weekly journal known as *Tarun Manipur* was published. It was printed at the Churachand Printing Works. Shri. Rajkumar Shitaljit Singh was its editor, and Arambam Dorendrajit Singh was the publisher. Shitaljit edited both *Lalit Manjaree Patrika* (*Masik Manipur*) and *Manipur Matam*.[34] He was associated with the then news agency, the *Press of India*. Shitaljit wanted to elevate the status of women in Manipuri society. In his editorials of 11 September 1938, he wrote, "a man may divorce his wife anytime when he feels so, whereas women had no such rights." It shows that polygamy was widespread in Manipuri society, not polyandry.

Women's issues, in particular, were highlighted by *Manipuri Mahila,* which started in 1939. The *Manipuri Mahila* is the first-ever publication dedicated to women. After this, in 1969, a magazine titled *Yaipha Yumbanda Nupi* (the Role of Women in family welfare) was published, and *Macha Leima*was also a paper focused on women, published in the same year by the Chanura Marup (Women organisation). The editor and all the writers of this particular magazine were females, and their articles were based on issues related to Manipuri women. The publication of this woman-oriented magazine was an important milestone in Manipuri Journalism. The Family Planning Association, Manipur branch and the Mahila Kalyan Samiti published many Manipuri journals on International Year of Women, 1975.[35]

A cyclostyled weekly *Anouba Jug* was published in April 1947, edited by Hijam Irabot, who inspired the peasants, farmers and oppressed people to fight for their emancipation.[36] The journal's main objective was to reform the Manipuri society, removing social stereotypes of the caste system, untouchability, and superstitions, which were quite prevalent at that time. It also aimed at improving the condition of peasants, objecting to the implementation of forced taxes like bridge tax, road tax, and river tax. The paper also stood against forced religious conversion and the concept of purity. It also proved instrumental in creating consciousness of the value of democracy. Irabot also attempted to strengthen the relationship between the hills and the valley population. Irabot explained all these possible reforms in his weekly and convinced the people. Irabot's Anouba Jug won a number of young followers.[37] The paper aimed at building a socialistic egalitarian society.

Though the beginning of Print media or Print journalism began very late in the hills due to the topography of the region, which kept it unreached for a long period and hence delayed educational and technological advancements, what contributed to the growth of journalism in the hills was the existing consciousness to protect and preserve their culture, society and identity, where the print media proved instrumental in communicating the same.

In the hill areas of Manipur, the development of print media began with the development of Christianity in the early twentieth century; the first printed publications were in the form of Bibles and church journals. Christianity also became an institution for introducing education in the hill areas.[38] The first tribal printed publication appeared in 1941 with a cultural magazine in the Hmar dialect, *Hmaswamna*, which Zathuoi edited; the journal was published from a Mission Compound in Churachandpur. In the same year, *Lhangsam*, a Thadou-Kuki journal, was published from Motbung in Sadar Hills; it was edited by S.L. Lunneh, who was a pioneer of Christianity and a tribalizer. The paper carried multi-perspective content on Christianity, society, and culture. Subsequently, a number of vernaculars appeared, like in 1952, Zingsol, a monthly Gangte dialect magazine; the editor of this magazine Lamzasoi Gangte was the first graduate among the Gangtes. In the following year, *Sim le Mal*, *Penna Gam*, *Zouzam*, and Thadou-Kuki magazines were brought up; these magazines could not survive long due to financial problems and also journalism as a profession was not popular during those days. However, most of the publications were produced with the intention and content to create awareness among the people as a need to address social issues was strongly felt.

Maithomi, a Tangkul month magazine, was published in 1948 and continued upto 1965, *Zingram* was also a Tangkul daily in 1964, and both these papers were published in the Ukhrul district. The Kom, a monthly journal from Bishenpur, *Chongsem*, was brought out in the year 1959; the paper focused on the importance of culture and religion. In 1969, *Known*, a Hmar journal which means light, was published in Churachandpur, *Sikhawar*; a Hmar church journal was also produced at the same time in Assam. Prof. Gangumei Kamei, in 1958 edited a monthly journal on social and cultural aspects of the time, named *Mairam* (Torch Flame) in the Kabui language. *Chamdin* is another Kabui journal from Tamenglong located in the western part of Manipur in 1950. Most of the print media published in the initial years in the hills showed a cultural, religious, political, academic, and social awakening trend.

The student bodies, like the Hmar Students Association and the Gangte Students Organisation, started publishing magazines in English in the 1960s. Papers like the *Siamsin Pawl*, which was published both in Paite dialect and English in 1962 from Churachandpur, and the *League Tribune*, published both in English and Zoumi language in 1962, are examples of an attempt to expand the readership and also a voice for exposure. *The Young Democratic*, in 1961, is a half-monthly publication of the Naga Students Union Association, where the political thoughts on the state policies were discussed; it also aimed at unifying the Naga population in Manipur.

More newspapers were published subsequently, such as *Thuthang* (1971), *Sikni-eng* (1977-78), *Sumkawn* (1980), *Manipuri Express* (1981), *Thinglhang Post* (1982), *Hmaswamna Thar* (1987), *Aja* (1992) and many others.[39]

The post-Independence period saw an increase in the development of print media in the hill and valley areas. The publication of newspapers, magazines pertaining to a community, the state and the nation began.

III

From the above discussions, it can be observed that print media being the earliest means of mass communication, became the primary source of spreading and receiving information, imbibing progressive ideas, and most significantly, the sentiments of the people. Given the content and trends of reporting related to political activities and social change, the contents of consciousness perceived and shared by individuals in a society are greatly influenced by print media. Hence, the theoretical application of the concept of consciousness is viable in understanding the role and impact of print media. It is also seen in the case of Manipur; since the beginning and development of print media in the state In Manipur, starting from the publication of the Dainik Manipur Patrika in 1933 to subsequent publications, print media has been utilised as a means of information, which stood as a catalyst for building public opinion and social change. Despite the fact that the education system was introduced very late in the state, both the hills and the valley have encouraged the growth and development of print media in the state. The existing consciousness of the need to preserve language, identity, and culture and eradicate social evils has been reflected through the papers introduced, in which social reformers and educated sections of the people have contributed immensely. Significant attempts to promote education and writing have also been observed. Women-related consciousness has also been a focus in the journey of the development of print media in the state. It is evident through the trends of newspapers, magazines that Manipur did not remain aloof from the growing anti-colonial consciousness. Therefore, the role of print media in generating consciousness of the need for social and political reformations must be addressed in studying the history of Manipur.

Notes and References

1. Marshall McLuhan, *Understanding Media: The Extensions of Man*, The MIT Press, London, 2001, p.7.
2. Helen Geracimos Chapin, *Shaping History the Role of Newspapers in Hawai'i*, University of Hawai Press, Honolulu, 1996, p.1.
3. *The New Encyclopaedia Britannica*, Volume 6, University of Chicago, Chicago, 1989, p.627.
4. Cited in K. C. Sharma's *Journalism in India: History, Growth, Development*, Regal Publications, New Delhi, 2007, p.3.
5. Denis Mcquail, *Journalism and Society*, Sage, New Delhi, 2013, pp.1-2.
6. Philip David Zelazo, Marris Mascovitch, and Evan Thompson (eds.), *The Cambridge Handbook of Consciousness*, Cambridge University Press, New York, 2007, pp.177-178.
7. Rocco. J. Gennaro, *The Routledge Handbook of Consciousness,* Routledge, New York, 2018, pp.11-12.
8. Philip David Zelazo, Marris Mascovitch, and Evan Thompson(eds.), *op. cit.*, p.863.
9. Marshall McLuhan, *The Medium is the Message*, Penguin Books, London, 2001, pp.8-22.
10. Helen Rappaport, *Conspirator: Lenin in Exile*, Basic Books, New York, 2012, p.35.
11. Les Switzer and Donna Switzer, *The Black Press in South Africa and Lesotho*, G. K. Hall & Co, Boston, 1979.
12. Rangaswami Parthasarthy, *Journalism in India*, Sterling Publishers, New Delhi, 1989, p.3.
13. *Ibid*, pp.7-16.
14. A. R. Desai, *Social Background of Indian Nationalism*, Popular Prakash, Mumbai Reprint, 2005, p.207.
15. B. K. Baruah, *History of Journalism in Assam*, Sahitya Academy, New Delhi, 1964, p.4.

16. Home Department Political, *Part B proceedings, January, No. 83*, 1910, p. 10.
17. Home Department Political, *Part B proceedings, September, No. 105*, 1911, p. 158.
18. S. M. A. W. Chishti, *Political Developments in Manipur 1919-1949*, Kalpaz Publications, Delhi, 2005, pp. 13-14.
19. Rajkumar Sanahal Singh, *Meitei Chefong*, Rajkumar Publications, Imphal, 1982, pp. 9-12.
20. Aheibam Koireng Singh, Shukhedeba Sharma Hanjabam, and Ksh Chitrabhanu Devi, (eds.), *Media in Manipur, Volume I*, Akansha Publishing House, New Delhi, 2020, p.116.
21. Shanti Devi, *Development of Education in Manipur*, Rajesh Publications, New Delhi, 2001, p.8.
22. S. M. A. W. Chishti, *op. cit.*, p.13.
23. Karam Manmohan Singh, *Hijam Irabot Singh and Political Movements in Manipur*, B. R. Publishing Corporation, Delhi, 1989, p.39.
24. R. K. Maipaksana, *Journalism in Manipur*, Imphal Press, Imphal, 1990, p.87.
25. Aheibam Koireng Singh, Shukhedeba Sharma Hanjabam, and Ksh Chitrabhanu Devi, (eds.), *op. cit.*, pp.116-117.
26. M. Kriti Singh, *Manipurda Journalisingi Eithas*, Imphal Press, Imphal, 1980, p.10.
27. *Azad*, Bengali Weekly, Silchar, 5 March 1963 cited in Jayanta Bhusan Bhattacharjee, *Cachar Under British Rule in North East India*, Radiant Publishers, New Delhi, 1977, p.255.
28. Arambam Dorendrajit Singh, (ed.) *Lalit Manjuri Patrika*, 2nd Issue, October 1933.
29. Karam Manmohan Singh, *op. cit.*, p.43.
30. M. Kriti Singh, *op. cit.*, pp.55-57.

31. E. E. Lyndall, *Administrative Report, Manipur State, 1930-40*, State Printing Press, Imphal, 1943, p.1.
32. Home Department, Political, National Archives of India, New Delhi, *File No. 26 (23)*, 1940.
33. S. M. A. W. Chishti, *op. cit.*, p.85.
34. Rajkumar Sanahal Singh, *op. cit.*, pp.48-49.
35. M. Kriti Singh, *op. cit.*, pp. 60-64.
36. Rajkumar Sanahal Singh, *op. cit.*, pp.60.
37. M. Saratchandra, *Irabot Manipur Favourite Hero*, Imphal Press, Imphal, 1983, p.6.
38. M. Kamla Devi, "Print Media Journalism in Manipur, (Past and Present)" in *Manipur Today, Journal*, 1998, pp.57-58.
39. Aheibam Koireng Singh, Shukhedeba Sharma Hanjabam, and Ksh Chitrabhanu Devi, (eds.) *op. cit.*, pp. 123-143.

16

Bodo Students' Movement: An Introspection

Sudev Chandra Basumatary and Junmani Basumatary

In general terms, students' movements can be categorised as social movements and had played a significant role in some Asian and African national struggle for Independence. These sort of movements have contributed to the political, social, and economic growth of a country in which students were involved in a variety of political and social issues.[1] Students' involvement in India can be traced back to the establishment of the Indian National Congress. During the colonial era, the Bihar Chatra Sanmilan (1906) was regarded as the first student organisation at the provincial level, and in Northeast India the Assam Chatra Sanmilan (1916) was the first of its sort.[2] According to records, Boro Chatra Sanmilan (1919) is next to Asom Chatra Sanmilan in Assam. In this paper, an attempt is made to study the rise and growth of students' movement among the Bodo community of Assam and also introspect the various aspects which directly and indirectly deals with them.

Relative Deprivation Theory and Bodo Movement

The lack of tangible benefits regarded as necessities in society defines deprivation. Deprivation refers to being short of or deprived of something. Therefore, according to the Relative Deprivation Theory, when people are deprived of their basic requirements, they compare themselves to others, frequently resulting in conflict. It is not just a comparison of the groups themselves but also the groups over time. This thesis, which is a social movement theory, explains or attempts to justify the idea that social movements and conflicts arise from feelings of deprivation that are largely brought on by the perception of scarcity of things that are regarded as necessities. The phrase "Relative Deprivation" was initially used by Samuel Stouffer, and Robert K. Merton, an American sociologist, expanded on the study by providing context based on American soldiers serving in World War II. Many academics have submitted their justifications.

Ted Robert Gurr, an American author and political scientist, in his book *Why Men Rebel* (1971), examines the connection between relative deprivation and political violence. Gurr has tried to prove that "Relative Deprivation", mostly as a result of unequal distribution in society, is the main cause of political violence in society. Even if many important factors contribute to crises, violence, movements, and other related phenomena, according to him, Relative Deprivation in Collectiveness is the main cause of crises, violence, and movements in society. According to Gurr, conflict is a necessary component of human experience and cannot be eliminated from a person's existence. It is a belief that although poverty cannot be isolated from conflict, the latter is more likely to have an impact on impoverished groups of society (whether they be individuals or communities). He developed the idea that value expectations and value capabilities are related to relative deprivation. Gurr believed that Relative Deprivation accounts for the difference in the men's disparity between Value Expectation and Value

Capabilities because Value Expectation refers to materialistic conditions they believed should be theirs, and Value Capabilities refer to materials and conditions they can afford.[3] Considering this, Gurr advocates for sensitivity from relative deprivation and emphasises it as a key factor in the diversity of opinions among social groups.

The Bodo movement, which turned into the Bodoland Movement after the formation of ABSU in 1967, was an outcome of relative deprivation of the Bodos. The Bodos, an aboriginal tribe of the region, were subjected to various exploitation and deprivation. However, as a result of internal and external migration, the population of the Bodos dropped.[4] Despite the creation of tribal belts and blocks by the government, there has been an increase in the number of non-tribal populations in Bodo-inhabited areas. On the other hand, tribals residing in forest lands for many years were ordered to be evicted by the AGP Government, although forest law was amended in the legislative assembly in 1980 stating that the rights of the tribal, residing in forest land since 1979, were to be protected.[5] Moreover, there has been an example of eviction of the tribal from their land by the then AGP Government. This is evident from complaints made by Late Upendra Nath Brahma and his delegation team to then Home Minister Buta Singh. They complained that 14000 were served notice by the government, and many of those orders were executed in Darrang and Kokrajhar districts.[6] Thus, the problem of land alienation aggravated the situation and hit the economic condition of the Bodos.

The Boro Chatra Sanmilan[7] as an architect of Bodo nationality

It may be difficult to imagine that a student community had a key role in guiding a civilisation away from antiquated traditions and leading towards modernity. The student body frequently stood up for its members' rights. It is interesting to note that this occurred in Bodo society in the early twentieth century. The Boro Chatra Sanmilan is the earliest student organisation among the Bodo. Some concerned Bodo youths began organising themselves to regain what they supposedly thought were lost socio-cultural and political spaces. This effort led to the creation of Boro Chatra Sanmiloni. In 1919, Gurudev Kalicharan Brahma provided direction and inspiration for the creation of the Chatra Sanmmilan. The creation of Chatra Sanmilan has sparked great zeal and rebirth among the conscious and educated members of Bodo society. It was the beginning of a new, conscious generation to work for the broken social order. A significant contribution to the development of Boro nationalism was thus made by the Boro Chatras anmilan.[8] At that time, educated Bodo people found it embarrassing to be presented as belonging to the Bodo community and were embarrassed to talk in Bodo in front of other community members. Some enlightened Bodo households even altered their surnames, such as Boro to Bora or Hazowary to Hazarika (Assamese title), to blend in with other progressive societies.[9] Under such circumstances, the Boro Chatra Sanmilan realised that social change could not be anticipated unless the light of higher education reaches the traditional society's common folk. Instead, the entire Bodo society tended to completely disintegrate.

The Sanmilan also understood that with the onset of the Company rule, the so-called Indian middle class and Assamese middle class began to possess the majority of privileges and the best petty positions in Bodo-dominated districts. The emergence of the middle class in various regions of then-combined India and neighbouring communities like the Assamese society gave them the opportunity to apply for some of the clerical and lower-level administrative positions in the then-colonial administration. They appear to be more developed than other tribal societies as a result. The Bodo people, who were cognizant and educated, were forced by the surrounding development to consider their social advancement for the sake of larger interests. Therefore, there had no choice but to educate their population in order for them to compete with other communities in the struggle for existence.

Under the direction of Gurudev Kalicharan Brahma, the Boro Chatra Sanmilan implemented certain action programmes to develop the Boro community as a composite society. They started two of the most difficult tasks to complete to complete their objective. First, the ChatraSanmilan needed to create policies to help the average Boro person comprehend education's value and draw them into learning. Second, to produce literature in Bodo to elevate the language to the level of other highly developed languages, removing any social stigma associated with speaking Bodo and preventing the conversion of Bodo speakers to other communities and titles. The Sanmilan established the "Daridra Boro Chatra Bhandar" fund as a first step in promoting education among the Bodos to assist the underprivileged but bright kids in furthering their education. The Trust had decided to use the money for students who demonstrated academic excellence and moral integrity and qualified for the Trust's scholarship.

The Boro Chatra Sanmilan's fifth session made a momentous decision to grant primary scholarships at the primary level to deserving kids to encourage them to continue their studies. The Sanmilan did not fall short in its efforts to support female elementary school students, and prizes were given to the top female students. In addition, the Sanmilani used to plan gatherings at various locations from year to year as well as ceremonies for distributing things like mandatory reading materials, pen papers, and other study aids, etc. In addition, the Sanmilan had taken steps to secure financial support from kind and wealthy people to assist talented Bodo students in pursuing further education. A greater number of students attended school as a result of Sanmilan's significant efforts, and more Primary and Middle Schools were built in the following years in Bodo-dominated areas. The Bodo Chatra Sanmilan successfully transformed the thinking of the Bodo culture as a whole, which undoubtedly opened the door for further advancement.

After the Chatra Sanmilan's tremendous effort, the Bodo literature in the truest sense of the word starts. The Sanmilan felt that in order to preserve and further their culture and customs, Bodo language literature was an absolute necessity. In terms of language and culture, the Bodo civilisation was in a pitiful state; it was on the verge of extinction. The Bodo language and culture, on the other hand, were under attack from the dominant Indo-Aryan languages and civilisation, and it appeared that they would soon vanish. In order to continue with their goal of publishing all forms of creative literature in the Bodo language, the Sanmilan took the initiative, and in 1924 the first edition of the periodical magazine "Bibar" was published. The inaugural issue's editorial clearly outlined Sanmilan's goal, which was to establish a common stage for the performance of skills such as songs, poems, essays, and lectures. Bodo literature was greatly enhanced by the brilliant poetry, novels, and plays that the literary platform motivated the younger generation to produce. Thus, it can be said that the Bodos' current language and literature have a strong foundation due to Sanmilan's admirable endeavour.

Given the aforementioned circumstances, it is appropriate to note that the Boro Chatra Sanmilan, which was a by-product of Gurudev Kslicharan Brahma's socio-religious movement, did an amazing job of recreating the Bodo nationality as Gurudev wished. In order to realise his dream, the Chatra Sanmilan was essential.

Kachari Jubok Sanmiloni and Boro Jubak Sanmiloni

In the early years of the twentieth century when Bodo delegations met the Simon Commission and other British parliamentary and constitutional groups to ask to be recognised as a separate entity from the other mainstream, the seeds of division between the Bodos and other communities were planted. It was interesting to see that the young Bodo people had already taken steps to search for their lost identity. In 1928 and 1929, the Assam Kachari Jubok Sanmiloni, led by Mr. Jadav Khakhlary as its General Secretary, and the Boro Jubok Sanmiloni joined together and sent a letter to Mr John Simon, who was in charge of the Simon Commission. The demand was to recognise their unique identities and help them get what they wanted. The demands were: (i) putting together a Bodo Regiment in the British (Indian) Army; (ii) giving seats to tribal people in the Assam Provincial Council and the Local Bodies; and (iii) putting them on the Electoral Roll and Census Report of India as Bodo, not Hindus. Through the Government of India Act of 1935, the British Government in India gave in to some of these demands. One of the most important requests that the British government gave in to was giving the plains tribes of Assam their own electorate and four assembly constituencies.

The team was more interested in moving forward, and the memorandum had been sent to the Simon Commission. The

Bodos and other plains tribal people in Assam decided to push for more political power. Therefore, in 1933, Mr BhimbarDeuri and Mr Rupnath Brahma led to form the Assam Tribal League, a political group made up of tribal people. The main goals of this political group were to protect the language, culture, and identity of the tribes by making the areas where they lived a "Schedule Area."

The Tribal League and other tribal groups in Assam fought not only for their survival and growth but also for India's freedom. Some were Bodo leaders, such as Jogendra Kumar Basumatary and Rupnath Brahma. After India attained its freedom, the then-Chief Minister of Assam and leader of the Indian National Congress (INC), Gopinath Bordoloi, promised to give in to all Tribal League's main demands. Chapter X of the Assam Land and Revenue Regulation, 1886, was changed in 1947 to protect Tribal Land.[10] This part of the Act made it possible for Tribal Belts and Blocks to be made to protect tribal land, culture, and identity.

The tribal leaders were overjoyed by the promises made by INC leaders at the time. Then, in 1953, they decided to keep the Assam Tribal League out of politics and changed its name to "All Assam Tribal Sangha." After giving up on politics, the All-Assam Tribal Sangha became a social and cultural organisation. This left the tribal people of Assam with almost no political power. In the meantime, hill tribes wanted some of the hilly districts of the state of Assam to be made into their own separate state. The Naga National Council and the Mizo National Front fought to make the Naga Hill District and the Lusai Hill District of Assam independent states. While the hill tribes of Assam fought harder for their political rights through peaceful and violent means, the plain tribal leaders were busy joining the political parties of their choice, leaving the

All-Assam Tribal Sangha to fight for its survival. Tribal leaders like Rupnath Brahma got involved in the politics of Assam. In his life, he had worked in many ways with his capacity in politics.

Therefore, Bodo people, who feel they are missing out on everything, learn to gear up with new energy. Compared to other communities at the time, the Bodos were not as educated as they should have been. Still, the Bodo people knew that improving education was one of the most important aspects they could do, so they joined together to do good things for the community. Thus, in 1952, Bodo Sahitya Sabha was set to work for the community. The main goal of Bodo Sahitya Sabha was to protect and improve the language, literature, and culture of the Bodo people. The Bodo Sahitya Sabha took an inspiring lead in improving the Bodo language and asked that it be taught in primary schools. Even though the Sahitya Sabha worked hard to obtain what they wanted, their journey was not a smooth one. Bodo Sahitya Sabha is a strong support for the Bodo people because of what it does and how it works.

Genesis of All Bodo Students Union

There were various socio-political organisations formed before the formation of the All Bodo Students Union.'However, district, sub-divisional and local student organisations were also formed. Some of the local organisations formed by the Bodo students were Parbatjhara Chatra Sanmilan, Gangia-Saralbhanga Chatra Sanmilan, Ripu Anchalik Chatra Sanmilan, Goalpara District Bodo Students' Union.[11] The existence of several organisations before the formation of ABSU reveals that it was the formative stage of consciousness of the Bodos. This rise of consciousness among the Bodo youths made the formation of ABSU in 1967 inevitable. Thus, it is not much difficult to trace the genesis of the formation of ABSU. The origin of the formation of ABSU can be attributed to the Goalpara District Bodo Students Union in 1966, as under the banner of this organisation, the Bodo youths unanimously decided to form ABSU in 1967.[12] Indeed, the demand for a separate state for the plains tribal people of Assam was also begun by the Goalpara District Bodo Students Union in January 1967 when Smt.Indira Gandhi, the then Prime Minister of India, declared the policy of reorganisation of Assam on the federal structure.[13]

There is no doubt that the establishment of the Bodo Sahitya Sabha undoubtedly filled a void, primarily in the fields of language and literature, but the political side was overlooked. However, this could not address the issues of the Bodos fully. Soon, the plain tribes, particularly the Bodos, became dissatisfied with the lack of a strong organisation to represent the plain tribes struggles. The establishment of Nagaland State on 1 December 1963, carving apart the Naga Hill District of Assam, was a new scramble for plain tribes, particularly the Bodos, at the time. The Bodo youths were incited when the then-Indian Prime Minister, Indira Gandhi, pledged the All Part Hills Leaders Conference (APHLC) delegation to rebuild Assam into a federal structure on 13 January 1967.[14]As a result, leaders such as Kanakeswar Narzary, Baneswar Basumatary, and others convened an urgent conference of like-minded Bodo youths on 15 February 1967 at the Kokrajhar Tribal Rest House, culminating in the formation of ABSU.[15] The gathering concluded with a solemn revolutionary resolution to establish the All Bodo Students Union, also known as ABSU, in order to create a Bodo nation under the strong motto "unity, struggle, and prosperity".[16] The organisation was founded with the intention of advancing "Justice, Dignity, and Peace." ABSU stated in its Golden Jubilee celebration that its ultimate goal is to "unite the Bodos living around the world to form an organisation that will help them get to know each other better and protect and improve the Bodo nation's economy, education, culture, traditions, language, and literature."[17]

The Bodos and other tribal leaders in Assam believed that the state's various governments' policies were chauvinistic and discriminatory. Because the ruling class believed they were superior to everyone else, the majority of the tribes were incensed. The plain tribes had several political groupings, whereas the hill tribes were tightly organised. Taking advantage of internal dissension among the tribes and their organisations, the exploitative governing class used harsh methods to suppress the approaching revolutionary movements of the Bodos and other tribes in Assam.[18]

Two influential organisations were founded in the Kokrajhar district of Assam in 1967: the All-Bodo Students Union and the Plains Tribal Council of Assam (PTCA).[19] Immediately after its formation, PTCA began to lead the political struggle of Assam's plains tribals.[20] The PTCA-led movement grew stronger, and on 2 December 1972, they launched a political movement for the construction of a separate state called "Udayachal." The primary objective of the PTCA was to end land alienation, marginalisation, and discrimination against the tribes by successive Assam state governments.

In addition, from 1967 to 1986, ABSU maintained its apolitical stance and served mostly as a youth force in various Bodo movements. In 1972, the Bodos initiated a new push for the introduction of Roman script for the Bodo language. As a new organisation comprised of young leaders, ABSU sponsored and actively participated in the Roman Script movement. Parallel to this was the Udayachal movement, when ABSU firmly backed the drive for the carving out of Assam to create the Udayachal state.[21] ABSU, in addition to mobilising Bodo youths for comprehensive socio-cultural and economic development, served as a strong support base for the political battles of Bodos and other indigenous communities.

Since the colonial regime onwards, different student bodies have launched movements for the betterment of the community. These movements ranged from political issues to literature, language and social reforms. During the colonial period, social reforms were carried under the banner of students' organisation, and literature began to flourish. The initiation of Boro Chatra Sanmilani for the dream of restoration of identity, language, culture, and tradition as a tribal got fulfilled on their part by awakening the young generations.

However, post-independence student organisations worked for the all-around development of the community. The formation of the All Bodo Students' Union in 1967 ushered in a new era for the community. This organisation began to work for language and gradually turned to demand for a separate state, launching the Bodoland movement, which would resolve all the problems of the Bodos. This movement for a separate state has culminated in three different Accords with the government for the upliftment of the community.

Notes

1. Philip G. Altbach, "The Transformation of the Student Movement" , *Asian Survey*, Vol. 6, No. 8 (1966), pp.448-460.
2. Meeta Deka, "A Historical Perspective of the Years of Students' Protest in Assam 1905-1972: An Exploration of Its Root", Ph.D. Thesis, Department of History, North-Eastern Hill University, Shillong, 1991, p.71.
3. Ted Robert Gurr, *Why Men Rebel*, Princeton University Press, New Jersey, 1971, pp.123-134

4. Sudhir Jacob George, "The Bodo Movement in Assam: Unrest to Accord", *Asian Survey,* Vol. 34, No. 10, 1994, pp. 878-892.
5. Dainik Assam, December 4, 1986, Guwahati.
6. Tribals' Grievances to be Examined in *The Statesman*, 29 January 1986, New Delhi
7. Note: In the case of BoroChatraSanmilan, to denote Bodo will be used as "Boro".
8. Rahul Kalita and Hemashree Gogoi, "Traditional Beliefs of Bodo Community: A Study on Lakhimpur District", *International Journal of Multidisciplinary Educational Research* Vol. 11 No. 3(2), 22 March, pp.98-102.
9. Sekhar Brahma, in *Mugani Sakhi*, p. 244.
10. As mentioned by Charan Narzary in His Book titled Dream for Udayachal and The History of The Plains Tribals Council of Assam (PTCA, 1967-93), "In the pre-independence elections held in the year 1046, the Congress returned with a majority to form its government and the Assam Tribal League joined hands with the Congress. Accordingly, the Congress Ministry headed by Gopinath Bordoloi was again installed. And, BhimbarDeori was introduced in the Bordoloi Ministry as a representative of the Assam Tribal League in September 1946. As a partner in the Congress Ministry, the Assam Tribal League succeeded in amending certain provisions of the Assam Land and Revenue Regulation Act of 1886. Accordingly, to give effect to the spirit of the Line System, Chapter X was incorporated into the Assam Land and Revenue Regulation Act of 1886, and the Tribal Belts and Blocks were constituted under the provisions of Chapter X.
11. This is informed by Surath Narzary, Retired Principal of Kokrajhar Government College, who happens to be one of the founders of the All Bodo Students Union.
12. Surath Narzary, Retired Principal of Kokrajhar Government College, informed that he was the General Secretary of Goalpara District Bodo Students Union. He stated that it was formed in

1966, and the members decided to form ABSU in one of the meetings held at the Tribal Guest House of Kokrajhar town, which culminated in the formation of ABSU on 15 February 1967. This meeting was attended by Bodo youth leaders, viz., Tarun Ram Basumatary (President, Goalpara District Bodo Students Union), Lahendra Nath Basumatary, Ranjit Bargayary, Kanakeswar Narzary, Orup Gwra Basumatary, Surath Narzary and many other Bodo youths.

13. Why Separate State? A Memorandum submitted to the President of India by All Bodo Students' Union, HQ, Kokrajhar, 10 November 1987.
14. *History in Glimpse, All Bodo Students Union (1967-1917): A Journey of Struggle*, published by All Bodo Students Union, Bodofa House, Kokrajhar, 1917.
15. *History in Glimpse, All Bodo Students Union (1967-1917): A Journey of Struggle*, published by All Bodo Students Union, Bodofa House, Kokrajhar, 2017.
16. See *History in Glimpse, All Bodo Students Union (1967-1917): A Journey of Struggle*, published by All Bodo Students Union, Bodofa House, Kokrajhar, 1917; The Motto of ABSU while inception was "Unity, Struggle and Prosperity", later changed to "Unity, Survival and Prosperity". Apart from the motto, ABSU bears a strong vision of the organisation, the Vision: Live, Work and Prosper. Life symbolises Existence, Security and Dignity; Work symbolises Work Culture and Ideology; and prosper symbolises All Round Prosperity.
17. 50th anniversary of ABSU at *JangkhrithaiFwthar* Kokrajhar from 12th to 15th of February, 2017.
18. *History in Glimpse, All Bodo Students Union (1967-1917): A Journey of Struggle*, published by All Bodo Students Union, Bodofa House, Kokrajhar, 2017.
19. Sankar Das, *Bodoland Statehood Movement: A Study on the Role of All Bodo Students Union (ABSU)*, M.Phil. Dissertation submitted to Mizoram University, 2017.

20. Charan Narzary, in His Book, Dream for Udayachal and History of the Plains Tribals of Assam (PTCA 1967-1993), addressed who constitute the Plains Tribals of Assam quoting, "The Barmans of Cachar, the Bodo-Kacharis, the Deoris, the Hojais, the Kacharis including the Sonowals, the Lalungs, the Meches, the Miris or Misings and the Rabhas constitute the Plains Tribal Community of Assam. The percentage of their population to the total population of Assam is small; in the areas where they are more concentrated, their percentage is more than fifty per cent. Such areas are the tribal belts and blocks, the tribal sub-plain areas and the integrated Tribal Development Project Areas. These areas are generally called the Plains Tribal Areas.

21. Charan Narzary, *Dream for Udayachal and the History of the Plains Tribals Council of Assam* (PTCA 1967-1993), N.L. Publications, Guwahati, 2011.

17

Dooars of the Eastern Himalayan Region: Some Aspects

Sanshi Upadhya

The region called Dooars is a geographically descriptive name which denotes the area beneath the foothills of the Bhutan Himalayan Kingdom of Jalpaiguri and Alipurduar Districts of North Bengal. It also forms the Indo-Bhutan boundary. The word 'Dooar' is derived from the Hindoostanee word *dwar*, meaning gate or entrance. These are a series of mountain passes through which communication between Assam's plains and Bhutan's interior takes place.[1] It covers an area of 30 kilometres in breadth and 350 kilometres long, stretching from West Bengal to Assam.[2] However, in the case of Assam Dooars, the breadth is very inconsiderable.[3] This article attempts to study the 'history of spaces' in relation to the fluid geographical area of the Dooars located below the foothills of Bhutan. From an early period, it was an area of mediation between various cultures, people[4] and states[5]. Throughout history, this area had been a bone of contestation between various dynasties until the British annexed the area through war, survey, mappings narrative and state documents.

The total number of Dooars was eighteen, of which eleven were in Bengal, between the river Tista on the west and Manas on the west. Seven were in Assam, lying between the river Manas on the west and Dhansiri on the east. The Eighteen Doors in Bengal are Dalimkot, Chamurchi, Zumerkot or Maynaguri, Luckee or Lakshmi, Buxa or Baxa, Bhalka or Bhulka, Gommar, Repoo, Bagh and Sidli. On the other hand, the seven Assam Dooars comprised of Bijni, Chapakhamar, Chapaguri, Baksha and Gharkola, located in the district of undivided Goalpra and Kamrup, the Boree Goomah and Kalling dooar was situated in the Darrang District and to the east of Darrang another Dooar known as Koriapara Dooar which was under Tibet. It was through the Koriapara Dooar that trade between Assam and Tibet took place.

The studies related to the Bengal and Assam Dooars have mostly been looked into within the framework of the modern notion of state, nation and political boundary. The formation of Dooars as a socio-political space and settlement of various communities likes the Gorkhas, the Bhutias or the Lepchas as such must be studied, keeping aside colonial concepts of boundary and or nation-state in order to get a wider picture of the history of the region. Hence, a trans-national and trans-temporal approach should be adopted for re-writing the history of this area. The main objective of this paper is to study the fluid geo-cultural setting of the region trade routes, which connected and brought together people from various Kingdoms of the Eastern Himalayas to settle in this part of the region and thereby giving rise to various political contests, claim and counterclaim in the region.

Various writers have carried out a wide range of works on the history of Indo-Bhutan relations, where one can find information about the Dooars region. Of such work, mention may be made of Nagendra Singh's *Bhutan: A Kingdom in the Himalayas*,[6] which mentions the early British relation with

Cooch Behar at a time when Cooch Behar sought help from British East India Company against the Bhutias. It also says about various political missions sent by the British via the Dooars to Bhutan, starting from the mission under George Bogle in 1774 to Ashley Eden in 1863. It also provides information about the commencement of the British Political influence over Bhutan.

Nirmala Das, in her book, *The Dragon Country and the General History of Bhutan*,[7] discusses the beginning of Assam's political relations with the East India Company in 1772, the annexation of Assam, including the disputes that took place in the Dooars region, which resulted in the signing of the Treaty of Sinchula in the year 1865.

Manorama Kohli has carried out works on Indo-Bhutan trade in her book *India and Bhutan: A Study in Interrelations 1772-1910*[8] which provides insight into the relationship between the British government and Bhutan, focusing on direct trade and commercial relations and the desire of the British Government to establish relation with Lhasa and through Lhasa with Peking (China). Another work by Arabinda Deb, *Bhutan And India: A Study in Frontier Political Relations: 1772-1855*,[9] writes about British Commercial missions to Bhutan, intending to establish trade relations with Bhutan and Tibet. The work mentions how the British, after signing the Treaty of Sinchula (1865), established free trade with Bhutan, Tibet and Central Asia. Madhu Rajat's work, *Indo-Bhutan Relation Through the Prism of History*,[10] mentions that through repeated attempts, the British tried to establish commercial ties with Bhutan. The work also deals with the Dooars and tribes residing in that region.

In his article "India-Bhutan Relation: An Overview",[11] Joseph C. Mathew describes how East India Company came into close political relations with Bhutan when old trade routes to Tibet and China through Nepal were closed. In search of an alternate trade route, the British discovered a new strategic way through Bhutan and Chumbi Valley to Tibet. After the British conquered Assam, it had to face several disputes with Bhutan on the matter of payment of tribute on the Dooars affair and the border incursion of the Bhutias, which ultimately resulted in the Dooar War and the signing of the Treaty of Sinchula (1865). The after-effects of the treaty gave the British the opportunity to have political control over the external relations of Bhutan. There are several other works on Indo-Bhutan disputes during the British period and the signing of the treaty of Sinchula, one among such is the work of Suranjan Das and Shantanu Chakrabarti's article "India and Bhutan: A Symbiotic Relationship?"[12]

On the history of Assam Dooars, or the Eastern Dooars, its trade relation with Bhutan writers such as Heramba Kanta Barpujari, who in his book *'Problem of the Hill Tribes of North-East Frontier 1822-42, Volume I,* [13] mentions the important trading sites of the Dooars, officials who the Ahom government appointed to maintain trade transaction with Bhutan etc. Swarna Lata Baruah's book *A Comprehensive History of Assam,* [14] N. N. Acharya's book, *North East India on Historical Perspective*, Pratap Chandra Choudhury's book, *The History of Civilization of the People of Assam to the Twelve Century A. D.* [15] speak of the ancient trade routes of Assam of which Dooars played a preeminent role.

Gunnel Cederlof's book *Founding an Empire on India's North Eastern Frontier 1790-1840*[16] speaks about the period before the colonial power conquered Assam and the framing of the policies of East India Company to control the age-old trade routes to establish trade links with Burma and China.

A well-documented book, *The Dooars in Historical Transition*[17] by *Sailen Debnath*, mentions various dynasties that ruled over the Dooars at different periods in history. It also mentions various communities like the Koch, the Bodo, the Lepcha, The Totos, the Rabhas, etc., settled in the Dooars region. It also mentions the introduction of agriculture in the region and the coming of various plantation workers from outside the area.

Sanghamitra Mishra's Book Sanghamitra Mishra, *Becoming a Borderland: The Politics of Space and Identity in Colonial Northeastern India,*[18] highlights the history of Eastern Dooars and the transition it went from the pre-colonial period to the colonial period. Though it specifically deals with the Goalpara region, one also finds in her work mention of the Dooars located in the district of Goalpara along with historical linkages that Goalpara shares with Bhutan, Cooch Behar and parts of Bengal. It also mentions that colonial law gave rise to a hierarchy of contest in the region leading to identity consciousness.

Shymal Chandra Sarkar, in his article "The Condition of the Tea Garden Workers of Jalpaiguri District in Colonial India", [19] writes about the tea garden workers of Jalpaiguri, which comprises the Dooars during the colonial period. Import of tea garden workers in Dooars from the tribal belts of Uplands of India were deprived of basic wages, under-served, exploited and kept as alienated groups. The paper focused on the historical background of the Tea Industry and the origin of tea workers in the Jalpaiguri District. Thus though, we see that although a lot of works have been carried out on the topic of the Dooars region, the works fail to see the region as a transnational zone.

There is a dearth of material on the early history of Dooars. However, epics like Ramayana and Mahabharata mention that the region was inhabited by non-Aryans, namely the Kambojas, Kiratas, Savars and Mutvis. The Kambojas and Kiratas were the same stock of people or akin to each other. The Kirata, in the course of time, came to be known as Koch. This area was a part of Pragjyotishpur in the Vedic period. Later the entire region became a part of ancient western Kamrup. Throughout history, the Dooars saw political ups and down and witnessed the rise and fall of many ruling dynasties and political units, of which Kamatapur was the most prominent. The entire Dooar region was a part of ancient western Kamrup and continued to be so until the middle of the seventh century. In the seventh century, one Sangaldip from Koch (modern Koch Behar) subdued Bengal and Bihar and extended his sway upto Bhutan. After that, for several years, Koch Behar, with Dooars as well as Bhutan, was under Indian Rulers.[20] In 1515 it became a hub of the Koch Kingdom. For some period, Kamatapur and Koch Kingdom gave political distinction to the Dooars, later followed by episodes of vacuum.[21] In 1587 Koch kingdom was divided into Koch Behar (western) and Koch Hajo (Eastern), which led to the division of jurisdiction of the respective kingdoms over the territories together with the passes/Dooars lying in the Bhutan hills. The territory between Sonkosh and Bhoroli, together with the passes, went under the control of Koch King Raghudev of Koch Hajo, and the territories lying to the west of Sonkosh, together with the passes, went under the control of Parikshit. During the time of the Moghul invasion in 1612 A.D., there rose chaos and confusion in the kingdom of Parikhshit, taking advantage of which the Bhutias extended their boundary to the southern part of the foothills and absorbed territories on the northern frontier of Koch Hajjo and later upto Gohain Kamal Ali.[22] By this time, two Dooars of the Darrang district: Buriguma and Killing, came under the possession of Ahoms since Bali Narayan/ Dharmanarayan brother of Parikshit Barman took shelter in the Ahom territory during the Mughal invasion of Koch Kingdom. Bali Narayan was later made the nominal head of Darrang. In the seventeenth century, Bhutan emerged as a distinct political identity under Shbdrung Nawang Namgyel,[23] who bought the various chieftains ruling over the country of Bhutan under his subjugation and divided his country into eastern, western and southern parts, which comprised the Dooars region. These Dooars played a significant role in the emergence of Bhutan as a distinct and unified polity and reinforced the frontier characteristics in the Bhutanese National Character. In 1760 the Bhutanese army overrun the Koch territory, and two Bhutanese Governors, Tongsa Penlop and Paro Penlop, became in charge of the Assam Dooars and Bengal Dooars, respectively. But irrespective of that, the Bhutias had to pay annual tribute to the Ahom king and presents to the Darrang Raja, which included articles such as Yaks, ponytails, gold dust, blankets and knives.[24]. The earliest relations between British India and Bhutan began in 1772. That year, the Bhutanese made a claim to Cooach Behar, invaded the state, and carried off the Raja, Dhirajendra Narayan, and his brother, the Dewan Rao. The East India Company was at the height of its relentless expansion across India when the unsolicited invitation of military intervention came from the Cooch Behar. Warren Hastings was the head of the English East India Company in Calcutta. Even before the appeal from the Cooch Behar arrived, Hastings anticipated the need to pay more attention northward as the Bhutanese invaders and the gangs of Sanyasis ravaged the territories already under British control. For all these reasons, Hastings readily agreed to send the British troops to Cooch Behar when the appeal for military support reached him through Charles Purling, the collector at Rungpoor. British initially supported Dharma Narayan's claim as the king of Koch Behar, setting him on the throne, but later signed an agreement with minor Dharma Narayan to become the sovereign ruler of Koch Behar.[25] Soon after Hasting began his administration in Bengal, he began to look for opportunities to establish commercial relations with Assam, Bhutan and Tibet. The Bhutanese raid of Cooch Behar brought the Company in close contact with not just Bhutan but also Assam, and the Company began to furnish information about the Assam trade. In 1774 Company appointed Hugh Baille as the Company's agent at Goalpara, where he had been an agent of Clive's Society of Trade. The Company was further interested in trade and territorial expansion, which made it look for ways to establish close contact with Sikkim, Bhutan, Tibet, Cooch Behar, Bijni and Assam.[26] When Scott was appointed Governor General Agent to the North Eastern Frontier in addition to his duties as Commissioner of Rangpur in 1823, Assam faced atrocities committed by the Burmese. The Expansionist policy of the Burmese and the British led to war between the two parties, where the British came victorious. As a result of the war, the Treaty of Yandaboo was signed on 24th February 1826, which made the Burmese resign from Assam, and Assam passed under British rule.[27] After the annexation of Assam, the British, to stop the repeated incursions of the Bhutias and to punish them, annexed all of the Assam Dooars by 1841. As Assam Dooar was occupied by the British, the wrath of the Bhutias inevitably fell on the plains adjoining the Dooars in Bengal, and they started carrying atrocities in the Bengal Dooars. Therefore the British, to punish them, occupied all the Bengal Dooars by 1865.[28] In 1865, the British took various recommendations for marking a boundary line between Bhutan and British India, and thus boundary survey began in 1866. It was maintained to include tribal people of the Dooars within India, excluding the Bhutanese cultivator.[29] After the British occupied the Dooars, they even stationed several military garrisons along the Indo-Bhutan frontier, thus altering the area from being an economically strategic space in the pre-colonial period into a closed frontier space after the British acquisition.

The Dooars acted as important pathways through commercial relations in the Eastern Himalayan region.

They were the highway of trans-mountain trade. Several markets were in the foothills of Bhutan, particularly in the Dooars, where trade between hillmen and plains took place every winter. Traders from Bhutan, Tawang, and the neighbouring areas came down to the plains through the Dooars with their merchandise like rock salt, gold dust, musk, woollen blanket, yak tails, ponies, Chinese silk etc., which they barter for cloths, raw silk, yarn, rice, dried fish etc. Annual fairs were also held at certain important Dooars, of which the one in Udalguri in Eastern Dooar was the most popular, which accounted for the maximum volume of trade between Assam and Tibet. The Principal fair of the Bengal Dooar was held at Jalpesh. In Maynaguri Tehsil, people attend it from all parts of the district as also from Dinajpur, Rangpur, and other district of northern Bengal.[30] Bhutias came from Darjeeling, Buxa, Bhutan, with cloth, blankets, ponies, skins and various other articles sold at good profits; they took away cotton and woollen cloths, betelnut, and tobacco.[31] Alipurduar fair, Falakata Dooar, was attended by people of the Dooar and Kuch Bihar and Bhutias. The Bhutia women of Chunbatti made exceedingly pretty cloth with endi silk and cotton and exchanged this with the Kyans of Buxa for rice or any other articles they may require. The Bhutias also grow turnips, radish and other country vegetables, which they sold daily in the cantonment market to the sepoy of the regiment stationed at Buxa. They also sold eggs and milk.[32]

Mules and ponies in the hilly region and bullock carts in the plains were most commonly used for transporting goods in markets and fairs. Occasional instances of raids in the markets and villages in the nearby foothills done by the tribal people living in the hills adjacent to the Dooars disrupted the free flow of trans-Himalayan trade. The raiders not only raided the traders of their goods but also took away villagers for using them as slaves. The Ahom government, in order to solve this problem, started giving in kind an annual grant to the chief of the concerned tribe for preventing such raids and maintaining peace in the Dooars; this system was called Posa. Even some official position was given to such chief. In the Bengal Doors, they were called the 'Jungpens' or 'Soubahs'. And in the Assam Dooars, they were called 'Diaries'. The Ahom government generated substantial revenue for the duties that were levied on goods transacted at the Dooars.[33] The Torsa River initiates from the Chumbi Valley of Tibet Autonomous Territory of China, and then flows into the Bhutan Himalayas, where it is named Amo or Amo River passes through the Indo-Bhutan borderline in the Totopara area of the Bengal Dooars. It is a transnational riverway and comprises a business route from the Chumbi Valley of Tibet, Bhutan and Dooars. The western Teesta-Torsa portion of the river is in Jalpaiguri, and the eastern part falls directly to the Brahmaputra Valley of Northeastern India. The western part is therefore known as Bengal Doors, and the eastern part as Assam Dooars. Using this waterway, from Tibet, Sikkim and Bhutan reach up to the Bay of Bengal. That was probably a transnational trade route in pre-colonial times. And therefore, states and kingdoms like Sikkim, Tibet and Bhutan emerged out[34]. Bhote Community from the Tibeto-Burman region successfully entered this region along with Teesta-Torso waterways (Teesta River originates from Sikkim) which had holistic impacts still in the folk life.

Goods from Bhutan were oranges and spices. To date, oranges, spice and potatoes, as well as the woolly clothes of Bhutan, have their hold in Indo-Bangladesh markets. The Totos were primarily carrying goods from Bhutan to the plains to vice-versa. They were like a community on any ancient trade route dealing in trade and carrying other products like spice, silk, ethno medicine etc. Bhutia traders once got into these plains with their goods on the back of Tangan horses. Also, Bhutia people and women carried goods to river ports and weekly markets of Dooar in Jalpaiguri.[35] During the winter, Bhutanese Sharchop tribes came down to Dooars due to heavy snowfall in the high-altitude Bhutan Himalayan. They brought orange, wool, yak skin, yak milk product like Chhurpi, fermented alcohol, chhang and Tibetan horses and dogs.[36] Both intra-regional and inter-regional trade took place in Dooars. The Meches, Totos, Rabhas, Garos, and Drukpas used to supply cotton, oranges, ginger etc to the people of the plains and on the other hand, people living in the south exported rice and other commodities to the north. The Meches, Totos, Rabhas, Garos, and Drukpas used to supply cotton, oranges, ginger etc, to the people of the plains. On the other hand, people living in the south exported rice and other commodities to the north. International trade relations among Tibet-Bhutan-Rangpur existed throughout Dooars.[37]

It is to be noted here that due to various geographical, political and climatic reasons, Dooars was sparsely populated. But after the British occupied the region after the Sinchula Treaty in 1865, they adopted various measures to bring political stability to the region and came up with various economic activities.[38] Commercialization of agriculture by mainly opening vast tea plantation sites led to a change in the region's demography. Sponsored migration by the British made people from various parts of India and the Sub-Himalayan region settle in this land, altering human ecology and society.[39] The early settlers of the region were Mongoloid tribal people such as the Garos, Toto, mech, Drukpa, Rabha, Dhimals etc. On the other hand, Santhals, Oroan, and Mundas were immigrant tribes.[40] Later, people from Darjeeling settled here as tea garden coolies, even the Oroans of Ranchi came and settled permanently as jotedars.[41] After working for some years, the migrated workers in the tea garden would buy land and settle in the district. [42] Tea gardens located at the hills were completely worked by Nepali labour, but as a whole, the Dooar tea garden is dependent on labour from a distance, the chief recruiting grounds being Chotanagpur and Santhal Pragana.[43] After the British occupation of the area, the society changed from feudal and theocentric to an imperial system, leading to various changes. In the Dooars Terai region, aboriginal Autro-Mundaric Adivasi people from Chotanagpur and Central India Deccan were introduced as labourers. During the Gorkha Shahi, the Nepali people entered into included parts of Darjeeling-Kurseong to work in the tea Garden. They also settled in Terai Dooars along with the Adivasis. They claim credit for introducing settled cultivation among the other hilly autochthones.[44] British Company and the British Raj encouraged both the civilians and native collaborators to establish tea estates in Bengal and Assam Dooars, as well as Darjeeling-Kurseong-Siliguri continuity. Tea estates, the new establishment of permanent cultivable grounds, and the establishment of the Forest Department brought a new kind of economy other than the previous forest-dwelling, shifting cultivation and transnational trade.[45] Rajbangsis, Koch

Rajbangsis, Bengali caste and Muslims from different parts of Bengal entered into the area along with the Adivasis, who introduced irrigation and settled way of crop cultivation rather than shifting cultivation and agroforestry.[46] Tribal people in the Dooars tried to develop a common language like the Sardi, Kamaptapuri and Nepali in western Dooars[47] and Goalporia and Bagania in the Assam Dooars.

The amalgamation of various cultures gave rise to new cultural heritage by providing a multi-coloured canvas to be the people. The co-existence of the forest, the tea garden and agricultural belts added to the complex thread of the culture. The area was full of ethnic people from Mech, Rava, Toto, Lepcha, Tamang, Limbu, Adivasi, etc.

A significant portion of the tribal people of the Dooars was the tea garden worker like the Oraon, Santhal Kharia, Mahali, Ho, and Kora communities who came from Chottanagpur, Orrissa, Kronjhar (Jharkhand) and Madras province. When they went to the Dooars, the first problem they faced was with the language they used because all were unfamiliar with the language of the other; as a means, there emerged a 'Lingua Franca'- The Sadri Language. The Adivasi tribe in the tea belt area primarily uses the Sadri language to communicate with other sects of their society.[48] Similarly, the Sherpas in the Dooars, including the Lepcha, Tamang, and Limbu, have their own dialect and speak Nepali.[49] Conversion to Christianity paved the way for wiping out many indigenous cultures. The change in lifestyle among the tribes is one of the major concerns for the deterioration of the culture. 'Linguistic imperialism is certainly causing the loss of many languages in the region.[50]

After the establishment of tea gardens and forest departments in the doors, many townships with urban features came into existence. Adivasi people, mostly from the

Chotanagpur plateau of the Jharkhand-Odisha region, hill people from the Himalayan country of Nepal and the foothill people of the Indo-Nepal borderland also invaded this place. Many caste Bengali and agrarian Rajbangshi also invaded the area in search of agricultural land. Agrarian tribes like Santhal and Oraon, as well as different caste groups from Adivasi-dominated regions of Central India-Jharkhand, were further attracted to this land due to job and business opportunities as well as availabilities of fertile land patches.[51] These diverse people belonging to so many communities had one thing in common: their settled mode of agriculture, which marginalized the Indigenous communities like Mech, Bodo, Rava, Toto, Koch, Garo, Tamnag, Subba and Lepcha. They mainly were shifting cultivators and produced different goods from the forest resources. In the colonial period, they gradually accepted settled agriculture and other alternative ways of living.

Tea, plantation formation, emigration and immigration from Nepal, Tibet, Bhutan and other states of India provided Dooars with a multicultural setup. Traditional transnational trade routes were replaced with inland connectivity between mainland India and North-East India. People with mainstream religious identities and coming from the Bengali business community have resulted in the flourishing of multiculturalism in the Dooars.[52] There have been cultural-linguistic identity movements based on common languages Sadri, Nepali, Bagania etc.[53] North Bengal pockets were also the origin of so many agitations with historical references like the demands of Gorkhaland By Nepali-speaking Gorkhas as well as Kamtapur or Koch Behar by the Rajbangsis.[54] Adivasis in Dooars, though had relationships with Nepalis and Bengalis, but the majority of them never made any demand for separate statehood; however, at times, they ask for Sixth Schedule under the

Indian Constitution or other safeguards.[55] The inter-cultural flow of suppression and rivalry among its various communities lead to the emergence of regional politics like Gorkhaland.[56] In the backdrop of the centre peripheries always being deprived, this area has so far witnessed socio-economic and political movements born of economic, political and cultural deprivations as well as ethno-economic and ethno-cultural identity crises.[57]

Conclusion

Thus the Dooars is certainly a transnational region of India made up of the Himalayan state of Sikkim, the Royal Kingdom of Bhutan, Tibet (China), the independent Country of Nepal, and the Northwestern part of Assam. From Tibeto-Kashmir, Tibeto-Himalyas, Indo-Himalayas, Sikkim-CHumbi-Bhutan, Frontier Bengal and North Bengal, continuity could be found upto North East India. Assam. It is this transnational multicultural situation that has developed here with a certain level of indigenousness. However, the region has now lost ancient trade and culture. Tribal communities like Mech(Bodo) Rava, Garo and Koch have been mostly incorporated into the wider category of agrarian Rajbangshis in Western Dooars, whereas the Immigrants like the Nepalis in Assam Dooars took to the Assamese identity and preferred to call themselves as 'Assamia Nepali'. Varendri caste group in the region speaks of their Aryan origin. A new form of the Indigenous Knowledge System has grown up locally that contains identity movements and multiculturalism. The indigenous communities have shifted from pre-agricultural to agricultural and post-agricultural stages; this alteration in their mode of production has had an impact on their social structure and even, to some extent, on their superstructure (magic, religion, values, art, law, belief, knowledge moral, norm etc.

There are forty different tribes in West Bengal. It is a matter of fact that almost all the tribes can be found in this Dooars of Jalpaiguri; many of them have been brought into service as the labour class in the tea gardens. These people have delivered a flavour of multiculturalism to the Dooars region and also formed human shields in this geo-strategically critical area. With the maintenance of the new weapons of British colonialism, like the tea industry and the railways, Dooars witnessed the emergence of diverse communities living side by side in this tract of land, which still continued even after 1947 and acquired a specific idea of identity, unlike the rest of India. After the partition of India in 1947, the significance of the Dooars has increased manifold, for the chicken neck of the doors is the only corridor of communication between India with its seven eastern states. Bounded by the international borders of Bhutia, Tibet part of China and Bangladesh, the strategic position of the Dooars is of paramount importance to the people speaking various languages and practising diverse religions; the Dooars of late has become a cockpit of identity politics and statehood movements.

Notes

1. David Field Rennie, *Bhotan and the Story of Dooar War,* Pilgrims Publishing, Varanasi, 2009, p.2.
2. Sailen Debnath, *The Doars in the Historical Transition,* N. L. Publisher, Siliguri, 2010, p.V.
3. Lakshmi Devi, *Ahom Tribal Relations*, Lawyer's Book Stall, Guwahati, 1992, p.249
4. The Bhutias, Lepchas, Koches, Bodos, Garos, Meches, Gorkhas and Totos.
5. Bhutan, Koch, Ahoms, Sikkim, and Nepal.
6. Nagendra Singh, *Bhutan: A Kingdom in the Himalaya,* Thomson Press Limited, New Delhi, 1972.

7. Nirmala Das, *The Dragon Country: The General History of Bhutan*, Bombay: Orient Longman, 1974.
8. Manorama Kohli, *India and Bhutan: A Study in Interrelations 1772-1910, Munshilal Manoharlal Publishers,* New Delhi, 1982.
9. Arabinda Deb, *Bhutan and India: A study in Frontier Political Relations: 1772-1855*, Firma KLM, Calcutta, 1976.
10. Madhu Rajat, *Indo-Bhutan Relation through Prism of History*, Manak Publication, New Delhi, 2011.
11. Joseph C Mathew, "Indo-Bhutan Relations: An Overview", *Indian Foreign Affairs Journal*, Vol 2, No. 1 (January-March, 2007), pp. 88-101.
12. Suranjan Das and Shantanu Chakrabarti, "India and Bhutan: A Symbiotic Relationship?", *Indian Foreign Affairs Journal*, Vol. 2, No. 3 (July-September, 2007), pp. 73-90 https://www.jstor.org/stable/45340663.
13. Heramba Kanta Barpujari, *Problem of the Hill Tribes of North-East Frontier 1822-42,* Volume I, Lawyers Book Stall, Guwahati, 1970.
14. Swarna Lata Baruah, *A Comprehensive History of Assam,* Munshiram, Manoharlal Publishers, New Delhi, 2015.
15. Pratab Chandra Choudhury, *The History of the Civilization of Assam to the Twelve Century A. D.*, Spectrum Publication, 1987.
16. Gunnel Cederlof, *Founding an Empire on North Eastern Frontier 1790-1840,* Oxford University Press, New Delhi, 2014.
17. Sailen Debnath, *The Dooars in Historical Transition,* N. L., Publisher, Kolkata, 2007.
18. Sanghamitra Mishra, *Becoming a Boderland: The Politics of Space and Identity in Colonial Northeastern India*, Routledge, New Delhi, 2011.
19. Shymal Chandra,"The Condition of the Tea Garden Workers of Jalpaiguri Distrcit in Colonial", *International Journal of Advance Research*, IJOAR.org. I (ijoar.org)

20. A. C. Sinha, *Bhutan: Ethnic Identity and National Dilemma*, Reliance Publishing House, New Delhi, 1998, p.50.
21. Sailen Debnath, *The Doars in the Historical Transition,* N. L. Publisher, Siliguri, 2010, p.5.
22. Lakshmi Devi, *Ahom Tribal Relations*, Lawyer's Book Stall, Guwahati, 1992, p.257
23. He was a Tibetan Lama belonging to the Drukpa sect and entered Bhutan having being forced out of Tibet by his rival. Manaroma Kohli, *op. cit.,* pp. 46-47.
24. Ajit Kumar Boruah, *The Koch Kingdom*, D. V. S. Publishers, Guwahati, 2011, p.39.
25. Nalini Ranjan Roy, *Koch Rajbangsi and Kamatapuri: the Truth Unveiled*, Vicky Publishers, Guwahati,2007, pp.95-96.
26. S. K. Chaube, *Hill Politics in Northeast India*, Orient Longman Limited, New Delhi, 1999, p.34.
27. Priyam Goswami, *The History of Assam: From Yandaboo to Partition, 1826-1947*, Orient BlackSwan Pvt. Ltd., Hyderabad, 2012, p.17.
28. Govinda Choudhury, "Land Tenure and Land Use in Sub-Himalayan Regions of Jalpaiguri Doors", *Journal of the Foundation for Agrarian Studies*, Vol. 5 No. 1, 2005, p.64. available at http://ras.org.in/land_tenure_and_forest_conservation_in_the_dooars_of_the_eastern_himalayas accessed on 02/08/2021.
29. Michael Hutt, *Unbecoming Citizens: Culture, Nationhood and the Flight of Refugees from Bhutan,* Oxford University Press, New Delhi, 2003, p.37.
30. Subhajyoti Ray, *Transformation of the Bengal frontier: Jalpaiguri 1765-1948,* Routledge Curzon, London, 2002, p.73.
31. D. H. E. *Sunder: Final Report on the Survey and Settlement of the Western Duars in the District of Jalpaiguri*, 1889-95, N. L. Publisher, pp.125-126.

32. *Ibid.* p. 208
33. Gurudas Das, *Border Trade North India and Neighbouring countries,* Akansha Publishing House, Delhi, 2000, pp.12-14.
34. Ashok Das Gupta "Indigenous People of Sub-Himalayan North Bengal with Special Reference to the Rajbangshis", International E-Publication, p.67. Microsoft Word - ashok_1_rechecked (isca.co.in)
35. *Ibid.*, p.73.
36. *Ibid.*, p.71.
37. Ray, *op. cit.*, p.73.
38. Hillol Kumar Chakraborty, *Economic Transformation of the Tribals*, Abhijit Publication, Delhi, 1994, p.41.
39. Debnath, *op. cit.*, p.45
40. Krishnopriya Bhattacharjee, *Silent Departure: A Study of Contemporary tribal Predicament in Bengal duar*, Papyrus, Kolkata, 2007, p.72.
41. Sender, *op.cit.*, p.80.
42. J. F. Grunning, *Eastern Bengal and Assam District Gazetteer, Jalpaiguri*, Pioneer Press, Allahabad, 1911, p.40.
43. *Ibid.*, p.42.
44. Das, *op.cit.*, p.54
45. *Ibid.*, p.54.
46. *Ibid.*, p.55.
47. *Ibid.*, p.56.
48. Sutradhar Samar, "Tribal Culture of the Doors: An Insight and Deteriorating Trends", *Research Review Journal*, ISSN 2455-3085, Vol-4, Issue 07, July 2019, p.36.
49. *Ibid.*, p.36.
50. *Ibid.*, p.36.
51. Das, *op.cit.*, pp.4-5.

52. *Ibid.*, p. 100
53. *Ibid.*, p. 101
54. *Ibid.*, p. 356
55. *Ibid.*, p.6.
56. Somoshree De, "Doors and its emerging identity", pp. 7-8 available at (PDF) Dooars and its emerging Boderland Identity | Somoshree De - Academia.edu.
57. Debnath, *op.cit.*, p.14.

18

Frontier Columns and Gurkhas: British Counterinsurgency Strategies in Northeast India

Bishnu Kumari Gurung

Introduction

> I feel that internal strife remains the greatest threat to our authority, and that it would almost certainly be the most difficult problem with which the Indian government would have to deal.
>
> — C. B. Pritchard in 1893[1]

C. B. Pritchard echoed the troubles of difficulties of the Colonial Government in maintaining internal peace and the need to focus on it to protect their interests in India. The British controlled the Indian subcontinent through political cooption and coercion. Due to pressure from the British-Indian military, indigenous social groups were sometimes obliged to comply with the colonial administration. As a result, the British-Indian Empire perimeter areas (North-West and North-East India) frequently 'rebelled', and this caused 'trouble' for the British internal security, to which the colonial government responded by launching a series of small wars. However, the military expeditions against the various northeast Indian tribes[2] are yet to be critically analysed.[3] Scholars of the region have not yet looked into the Anglo-tribal conflicts from the lens of small wars; instead, they choose to inherit the colonial appellation- 'punitive expeditions' and 'low intensity conflicts'. The problem with the use of inherited epithet is that it disguises the use and horrors caused by the naked Colonial power by labelling them 'low intensity conflicts' while also undermining the deaths that occurred during the conduct of small wars as 'punitive' (of both soldiers and members of tribes).Thus, this chapter explains how the Indian Army gradually developed the philosophy of small wars that offered a rough framework for conducting military operations against the 'rebellious' frontier tribesmen. The chapter is divided into three sections. The first section will introduce the readers to the theory of small wars in northeast India concerning the people's physical environment and socio-cultural dimension. The second section discusses the various groups of colonial units which were used as a tool to wage small wars in northeast India. This section will focus on the Gurkha soldiers as a part of the regular rifles (Gurkha Rifles) and military police (Assam Rifles) in carrying out the mission of 'civilising' and 'pacifying' the frontier tribes. In doing so, it will also provide a chronological overview of the various campaigns. The last section of the paper attempts to critically look into the broader debate surrounding the colonial use of 'minimum force' in the region.

The chapter makes use of primary and secondary sources from British colonial Indian governments, such as private and public letters, notes, government reports, field reports and telegrams, meeting minutes, and policy proposals, which are primarily housed in the National Archives of India, as well as secondary literature. These documents shed light on several factors leading up to the tactics of the small war in the northeast region and the motivation behindthe deployment of imperial soldiers in India's North-East frontier policy. The chapter intends to provide a partial overview of the region's history or conflicts.

Theories of Small Wars

In the mid-nineteenth century, British military officers developed complex ideas on the nature of conflict against 'rebellious' tribes. The colonial army was dubbed the small wars army in the early twentieth century because of the wars they were generally engaged in, most of which were irregular warfare. In 1896, British commanders classified irregular wars as 'small wars'. As mentioned earlier, Small Wars are now known as 'low-intensity conflicts', 'counter-insurgency campaigns', 'sub-conventional wars', and 'operations other than war'. During the *Raj*, most British officers stationed in India focused their small war approach on the Indus Frontier, while British officers stationed outside India attempted to universalise small warfare across Africa and Asia to build a coherent body of ideas. As a result, the northeastern part of India is mostly overlooked, despite the fact that it has its distinct geography, terrain, and society, all of which should be addressed separately.

It was Charles Callwell,[4] who pondered the nature of insurgencies which dealt with the theories of irregular warfare independently and not as an appendage to regular warfare. Many historians see his work as the starting point of the history of the British approach to counter-insurgency.[5] According to him, 'all campaigns other than those in which both opposing sides are made up of 'regular troops' are considered small wars. Here regular troops meant those equal in equipment, organisation and discipline. It includes expeditions by disciplined soldiers against irregular units, often considered 'savages' and 'semi-civilised' races, and campaigns to crush rebellions and guerrilla warfare in all parts of the world where organised armies fight opponents who will not meet them in the open field. The term 'small wars' has nothing to do with the size of a campaign but it simply refers to activities of pitting conventional troops versus irregular groups.'[6] Because of its asymmetrical nature, small wars were inherently attritional. He gives a general account of the theories and principles of small wars by citing historical references from all across the world.

Another Briton, Major George Younghusband, in *Indian Frontier Warfare*[7] focused upon the irregular wars fought along India's frontier regions in particular. Callwell's work is analogous to Younghusband's 'civilised' warfare. The latter writes that the norm in civilised warfare was to concentrate the attack on the escort when targeting a convoy. Yet, in small wars, irregular fighters tended to attack the convoy's weakest position, leaving the escorts as it was. This discussion clarifies that the regular and irregular forces are more or less stuck to a similar strategy. But the local conditions led to alterations in the tactical bearings of each campaign. Callwell and Younghusband harped on developing tactical skills where the commanders would lead the regular forces by dint of his boldness and acumen outwitting the opposition. Thus the purpose of these theories was to prepare the commanders for any challenge that they might face in the unknown territory so that they could take prompt decisions without losing their nerves. Callwell and Younghusband's theories of small wars relied heavily on tactical superiority gained through training and adaptation to the surroundings.

Violence in India's Margin: Geography as a Factor in Northeast Small Wars

The history of the northeast frontier of India can be called an example of the geography of violence. Callwell was correct in his estimation that more than enemies, the small wars were campaigns mostly against the nature of forces more often than not accustomed to the hilly and jungle-clad terrain in which they operated.[8] Stretching from Chittagong (at the seacoast) to Nepal (in the Himalayan highland), the Bengal and Assam plains bordered the mountainous country along its eastern borders. This mountainous region (part of the Himalayas) was the home of indigenous tribes who had traditionally depended on the products of the valleys adjoining their hills and marketed their produce. Border battles with the hill tribes erupted once the British colonial state arrived in the Bengal and Assam lowlands, owing to a clash of interests. The tribal 'raids' were met with military 'expeditions', sometimes annually.[9]

The small wars of northeast India included elements of both 'Hill War' and 'Bush Warfare'. The pamphlet of the military establishment (1903) in India titled *Bush Warfare* provided guidance to the troops deployed in northeast India, focusing on skirmishing skills required by the troops deployed in the region.[10] The harsh geography provided a safer haven to the 'rebels'against the state just as it provided a massive friction of terrain to the troops, often described as 'passing against the knife'. In the face of the harsh topography in the 'disorderly frontier', the weary soldiers naturally chose the shortest and most effective tactics ('moral effect' doctrine) to get away from the 'thankless job' assigned to them.

Following the various armed rebellions in India and the Amritsar incident (1919), the government and military adopted a new attitude towards using strength to suppress any form of revolt i. e., the 'minimum use of force'. However, one would wonder why, while the official policy was to go easy on the 'rebellions' or use 'minimum force,' however, violence still dominated colonial 'small wars' in northeast India. The answer lies in the mode of conducting warfare in the region. Both colonial troops and 'rebels' depended heavily on employing maximum or exemplary force during 'raids' and 'expeditions'. As a result, the hill 'raiders' raided 'plains communities, killed the residents, stole their heads, looted and burned their homes.' Normally, they would leave with human heads, hostages, and plunder. The heads/skulls created a precious prize on the hills to prove their prowess. It was a rite of passage for them as warriors. The authorities used various techniques to combat such raids, ranging from non-violent to violent. It usually began with the closure of frontier markets to 'rebellious' hill communities or tribes, followed by the establishment of military/police outposts in the foothills and the formation of local levies/ mercenaries to guard the border. In addition, initiatives such as arming frontier communities for self-defence and occasionally relocating friendly tribes to the border to operate as a 'buffer colony' were pursued.

As a result, one of the most crucial components of small wars was winning the hearts and minds of those who lived in the troubled area.[11] One of the fundamentals of conducting successful pacification operations, according to R.M. Betham, was to gain the trust and belief of the people who lived in the region that was constantly raided.[12] In extreme cases, military expeditions were sent into the hills.

Burning entire villages, including homes, property, and food grains, was considered one of the most efficient ways of punishing 'rebellious' hill villages. The army would frequently scout the woodland for 'secret granaries.' If the expedition team successfully arrested any (which was rare), they returned with captives who were usually tried and exiled for life or executed. In some circumstances, such a harsh policy kept the frontier calm for a while. Still, in the majority of cases, the techniques of indiscriminate violence resulted in more conflict. In the Naga

Hills, for example, it was determined that indiscriminate village burnings impacted even clans that were not initially involved or immediately associated with the conflict. Following that, these clans joined the 'enemy clans' in their fight against the government. As the 'enemy' gained strength, more and more expensive conflicts had to be waged. The boundary squabbles continued in this manner until the hills were placed under the direct rule of the British Government of India.

As previously stated, Northeast India's rough mountain landscape formed the 'geography of violence' there. Every expedition into this mountainous region was a major military undertaking that required the authorisation of the British Government. Even for the purpose of punishing the few settlements, a large military column was needed, which had to be aided by a larger group of baggage carriers (typically three times the number of the infantry) to transport all of the party's food and ammunition for a month or so. This was the bare minimum, as there was no food in the hills, even at high prices, and the imperial troops had to scale pathless, rough heights, rendering their beasts of burden useless. The arduous travel across the pathless mountains, which were densely forested, was a common occurrence in all border military operations. It shaped soldiers' behaviour in order to deploy the most effective method for 'punishing' the enemy at war. Aside from physical limitations, the forest contained other lethal elements such as hazardous diseases and insects, wild animals, and an ambuscade from the hill warriors. Every expedition party had to retrace their steps as soon as possible, with only enough food to reach the targeted village(s) and the risk of famine and death. All of these elements put the soldiers' lives in jeopardy. The exhausted soldiers had 'no choice' but to burn down the hillmen's villages and destroy their property, food grains, and cattle due to the gruelling circumstances described above. This only possible kind of punishment, involving 'barbarous expedient' tactics and causing 'contemptuous ruin,' to use Mackenzie's accurate words, was thought to have a moral effect narrative in the hills, leading the hillmen to refrain from invading the British settlements again.[13] The expedition records from the early colonial period in the region reflect this harsh terrain and the resulting military cruelty.[14]

Tools for Conducting Small Wars in Northeast India

According to numerous colonial documents on counter-insurgency, the imperial perspective in fighting small wars in the region was to 'civilise the savages' and 'pacify the tribes.' The observation of Major John Butler (1844)[15] and Colonel L. W. Shakespear (1929)[16] expedition's reports back up this claim. Several local levies (forerunners of paramilitary organisations) were raised to guard the North-East Frontier of India. Major General H.W. Norman recommended stationing regular troops in Assam in 1872, citing the region's proximity to the 'wild tribes'.[17] Senior British officers, however, agreed that dividing a regiment into multiple tiny detachments for an extended period of time in order to execute policing duties degraded regimental spirit and hampered unit preparation for 'conventional' operations (against a possible Afghan or Russian attack). As a result, the Army's regular battalions in Northeast India served as the last line of defence. The military police first guarded the posts, but if they failed, the local levies moved in. Regular army units were dispatched to save the situation if the local levies failed. The infantry unit was equipped with a couple of brass guns.[18] One Subedar, two Jemadar, seven Havildars, seven Naiks, two Buglers, one drill Instructor, and 160 sepoys made up the Assam Local Militia, which was established in 1827.

The Cachar Levy in Nowgang District was the first local levy established under Assam civil government in 1835 as a less expensive alternative to military deployments. The Cachar Levy man army was tasked with guarding the frontier and defending British properties, communities, and tea gardens from tribal raids. In 1838, the Jorhat Militia, established from local Shan, was founded to guard the Sibsagar-Naga frontier. This militia merged with the Cachar Levy in the 1860s to become the Frontier Police, which was formed to protect the frontier boundary from raids.[19] On Major Lister's recommendation, 200 Kukis were enrolled into the Kuki Levy in 1850 to aid the armed civil police in protecting the boundary and provide employment to Kukis living in British-Indian territory.[20] Another reason for the increase in local levies was that they were less expensive to maintain than the normal units. In 1861, the annual cost of sustaining the Kuki Levy was over Rs 17,708, although it was around Rs 13,404 for the Assam Local Militia.[21]

Under the Assam Police Frontier Regulation of 1882 and the Assam Military Police Regulation of 1890, the Frontier Police were reorganised into military police battalions. With more strength, the military was divided into four battalions, each allocated to the Cachar, Lakhimpur, Garo Hills, and Naga Hills districts. These levies were then reorganised to form the Assam Rifles. Its mission was to maintain law and order by dealing with "rioting and disorder," providing security for surveys and exploration, road extensions, and other infrastructure projects, assisting civil authorities during natural disasters, and continuing defensive operations along the border while largely leaving offensive campaigns to the regular military.[22] According to an 1892 report from the office of the Chief Commissioner of Assam, the principal benefit of utilising this force for minor disturbances was 'a great saving in expenditure as opposed to what a military expedition would have cost.'[23] When the Military Police could no longer handle the situation, the Military Regular Regiments were called for and were provided logistical support from the Military Police.[24] Their responsibilities included "acting as scouts, maintaining open communications, collecting information, and providing baggage and various other guards."[25] When the Indian Army was employed overseas during World War I in 1917, British authorities turned to the paramilitary units to help them fight Kuki clans in Manipur who were rebelling against British incursions into their area.[26]

Gurkhas in Small Wars of Northeast India

The army helped the Company to weaken the native ruling states' military and political authority, conquer the border tribes, and create a monopoly on power throughout India. Gurkha soldiers were part of colonial local levies, frontier police (Assam Rifles), and regular battalions (Gurkha Rifles). The first interaction between the Gurkhas in the region occurred in 1817 (two years after the Anglo-Nepal War) when 1,000 Hindustanis and Gurkhasoldiers served as soldiers of the Cuttack Legion in the Sylhet operations (later known as Assam Light Infantry).[27] Since the early nineteenth century, Gurkha soldiers have been involved in practically all important missions in the region. The 6th, 7th, and 8th Gurkha Rifles are the most active of all the Gurkha Rifles in the small wars.

The following elements contributed to Gurkha's success in the region: Firstly,being from Nepal's mountains and the region's proximity to their home country, they acclimatised and adapted to the northeastern region's surroundings and geography better than Hindustani soldiers; and secondly, the military recruiting policies of Northeast India were successful in absorbing the 'line boys' in its various units and managed to fill the gaps created by Local levies (Manipuris in particular) in the military system for wanting to join their own rulers rather than work under the British Government banner.[28] The impact of changes in military administrative practises on the makeup of Gurkhas in colonial regular and irregular forces was dramatic. By 1917, the fifth Assam Rifles, which had been formed by a significant influx of troops following the demobilisation of military formations at the end of the First World War, had a recruitment composition of 70% Gurkhas, 20% Garhwalis and Kumaonis, and 10% Jaruas, Lushais, Nagas, and Kukis (10 %).[29] As a result of the composition and strength in numbers among the Gorkha soldiers, the colonial army in the region gradually became 'gorkhanized'.Let us examine the role of Gurkhas in the British Empire's expansion and consolidation in northeast India.

Khasi-Jaintia

The Anglo-Khasi War, which lasted until 1833, was one of the major conflicts of the Sylhet Light Infantry (which eventually became the 1st Battalion of the 8th Gurkha Rifles, formed for the aim of guarding the Sylhet and Cachar frontier during the commencement of the First Anglo-Burmese War (1824-6)). The Battalion was dispatched to the Khasi hills in 1829 to revenge the Nongkhlaw massacre.[30] Alexander Mackenzie[31] chronicled the details of the mission against the Khasi. H.K. Barpujari also dealt with it.[32]

The Company was able to break the Khasis resistance by the end of 1829. David Scott, Agent to the Governor General of the Northeastern Frontier, negotiated an arrangement with the Khasi chiefs to seek 'pacification.' Most of their holdings were restored as a result of their dependency and recognition of the Company's authority. The British eventually recognised the presence of 25 Khasi chiefs who were, nevertheless, completely 'subservient' to them. The British did not annex the Khasi hills, but they did station a Political Agent at Cherrapunjee to manage relations between the Khasi Chiefs and the Company. With the expansion of military power, colonial officials and missionaries arrived, and Shillong, the Chief Commissioner's province headquarters, became equipped with administrative and structural accoutrements to strengthen colonial rule in Northeast India.

The Sylhet Light Infantry was also involved in the annexation of the Jaintia kingdom. Kidnapping and sacrifice of three British subjects by Chattar Singh of Gobha[33], a Jaintia dependent, was reported in 1832. The Jaintia ruler Ram Singh was entrusted with apprehending the criminals. When he died in November 1832, his nephew Rajendra Singh was forced to hand over the criminals, and the Company also wanted Rs. 10,000 annual tribute from the Raja.[34] In 1824, the Company made a formal alliance with Ram Singh as part of a defensive arrangement to protect the Bengal frontier from the Burmese threat. Ram Singh agreed to employ his troops to fight the Burmese in the War.[35] There was no mention of a tribute; therefore, the Company's demand was unjustified. In 1835, the Company took advantage of the situation and annexed Jaintiapur. Captain Lister and two companies of the Sylhet Light Infantry took official possession of Jaintiapur, the capital of the state of Jaintia, on the 15th of March.[36] The Raja declined to continue with his reduced allotment,[37] and Jaintia hills—the hill portions of Jaintiapur—became part of the Company's holdings. A unit of the Assam Light Infantry also took over the small chieftainship of Gobha, where the sacrifice had taken place. The conquest of the Kingdom of Jaintia placed an area of around 3850 square miles under the Company's control. From 1861 to 1863, the Sylhet Light Infantry, or 44th Native infantry in Cachar and Silchar, was once again used to put down the Synteng or Jaintia Rebellion.[38] Jemadar Kharang Sing Rana was promoted to Subedar and advanced to the Indian Order of Merit (IOM) for his valiant defence of the Jowai stockade.[39]

Naga and Lushai

During the nineteenth century, the Gurkha Rifles engaged in small wars to subjugate the Naga in order to control and 'punish' the hill tribes for their raids.[40] The Company deployed expeditions and promenades to North Cachar villages to control Angami Naga incursions. Seven expeditions were undertaken against the Angami Naga between 1839 and 1847. In early 1839, an expedition led by Mr Grange, Assistant Commissioner of Nowgong, was dispatched against the Angami Naga, which included 50 Assam Sebundy Corps sepoys. Several expeditions were led by Major Thomas Fisher of the 48th Native Infantry between 1841 and 1849.[41] Captain L. P. D. Eld led a party of Assam Sebundy Corps (which later became the second Battalion of the 8th Gurkha Rifles in 1861) into the highlands in 1844 and burned several Naga villages. Following the assassination of Bhogchand, Captain R. Campbell led another expedition and was sent to 'punish' the Angami Naga in 1849. Under the command of Major H. Foquett, a force of 500 men with three guns and two mortars was despatched to the hills in 1850. Several villages were set ablaze, culminating in the storming of Kekremah, a powerful Angami hamlet. A total of 300 Nagas were killed or injured.

In 1866, a major shift in the conquest of the 'border' resulted in the foundation of 'Forward Policy'[42] and the subsequent annexation of hill areas inhabited by different groups. As a result, the Naga Hill District was established in 1866, with its headquarters in Samaguting (near Dimapur), by combining the regions of North Cachar and Nagaon, as well as the Angami districts, and Lt. Gregory served as the Political Officer. Samaguting was too far from the core of Angami country to secure political authority and influence over the Nagas, particularly the Eastern Nagas, over whom strong control and influence was required due to the rapid expansion of tea plantations in the Sibsagar area. The Naga Chief District was transferred to the newly appointed Chief Commissioner of Assam in 1874.

In February 1877, the Cachari settlement of Gomaigaju was invaded, and six men were slaughtered by the Angamis of Mozema, who refused to pay any recompense. In the winter of 1877-78, Captain Brydon led a 196-strong contingent of the 2nd Assam Sebundy or 42nd Assam Light Infantry on an excursion to the Naga Hills. Aside from a few dwellings, the town was destroyed during the assault. Despite sporadic shootings and many night attacks, the people maintained their resistance. As a result, reinforcements from the 43rd Assam Light Infantry, led by Lt. Macgregor, were deployed to the Naga Hills. The community of Mozemah made overtures for peace when their food supplies were destroyed. The village was imposed a heavy fine of Rs 50 and surrender of their firearms.

In the winter of 1879-1880, one of the important small wars in the Naga Hills took place. This was in retaliation for the assassination of G. H. Damant, the Political Officer of the Naga Hills. The Angamis were enraged by Damant's demands for revenue, which they saw as a "symbol of authority" and a "disciplinary measure," as well as his meddling in internal feuds. The Angamis of the powerful villages of Khonoma, Mozema, Jotsoma, and some khels of Kohima were largely alienated by the return of the Headquarters to Kohima in 1878. Firearms were purchased, and the fortifications around villages were reinforced. On the 14th of October 1879, while on a surprise visit, Damant was killed by the men of Khonoma village, who also attacked his escort. Thousands of Nagas (about 6000 representing various clans and armed with rifles) assaulted the post of Kohima in an attempt to drive the British out of their hills. The situation for the British was hazardous for ten days. On the 27th, reinforcements were hurried in from Wokhs, and Johnstone, the Manipur Political Agent, came with a troop of 2000 soldiers from Manipur. The Nagas dispersed when they learned of his presence, and the siege was raised.[43] The re-establishment of British authority necessitated swift action against the Naga. The 44th Sylhet Light Infantry, led by Brigadier General Nation, and a detachment of the 43rd Assam Light Infantry, led by Major Evans, attacked the rebels during the cold season of 1879. Before the final attack on Khonoma, many 'hostile' villages were razed to the ground. On March 28, 1880, Khonoma surrendered. The Angami Naga resistance was shattered as a result of this. The British then expanded their territory to include the Ao and Tuensang areas.

Similarly, during the nineteenth century, the Lushais were also 'subjugated'. In 1844, the 8th Gurkha Rifles were sent for the first time.[44] In December 1844, Captain W. Blackwood led an expedition of Sylhet Light Infantry against the Lushais for the raid at Kochabari in Pratapgarh (16th April 1844), in which twenty people were slain. Chief Lalchokla's village was surrounded, his supplies were cut off, and he submitted himself on December 4th. He was put on trial and transported. Following repeated Lushai attacks on the Cachar Plains, Lt. Col Lister relocated to Silchar. Lister launched an expedition against the Lushai in 1850. This was, however, one of many little wars waged to bring the Lushais under control. The Lushai Hills District was established in 1889, with a superintendent in charge of administration.

As a result of the arrival of the East India Company and the British Indian Government in the Bengal and Assam plains, border warfare/small wars with hill tribes intensified. Between 1839 and 1850, ten military missions were dispatched against the Naga tribes.[45] In the years that followed, other expeditions were dispatched against them: 1873–1874, 1877–1878, 1879–1880, and so on. Expeditions were sent against the Kuki tribes in 1845, 1847, 1850, 1860, 1869–1870, 1871–1872, 1888–1893, 1910, and 1917–1919. Expeditions were also made against the Garos (1861, 1872), Khasis (1829–1833), Jaintias (1860–1862), Adis (1848, 1858–1859, 1911–1912), and other tribes on occasion. The Lushai Expedition (1871–1872), Chin-Lushai Expeditions (1888–1893), and Kuki Operations (1917–1919) were all directed against specific hill villages, but in some cases, such as the Lushai Expedition (1871–1872), Chin-Lushai Expeditions (1888–1893), and Kuki Operations (1917–1919), the operations were directed against entire tribes.[46]

The Gurkha soldiers were selectively recruited and employed by the colonial state to play a significant part in almost all of the small wars described above, owing to the spread of the 'martial race' ideology, in which they were depicted as a 'martial race'.[47]However, due to the limit of length of this chapter, not all the small wars in which the Gurkhasparticipated have been discussed.[48] The small wars discussed above were mostly carried out by the 8th Gurkha Rifles.

Conclusion

The human culture created tales about the kill in order to legitimise and rationalise societal behaviour. Certain wars had become 'fair' and 'civilised,'while others had degraded into ‘barbarism’ and ‘savagery,’ according to the ‘common civilisation' narrative. At the same time, certain wars were labelled as 'insurgency,' 'small war,' and 'counter-insurgency,' while others were labelled as 'law and order' issues. For being beyond the paradigm of 'regular war,' small wars have been exempted from the laws of 'civilised warfare,' which are thinly electrified by a nebulous concept of 'minimum force.' According to David French, the British justification for their action under the 'minimum force' theory was merely to mask the use of naked force under a carefully manufactured veneer of legality. In reality, he had pointed out; they frequently utilised widespread coercion to intimidate and close down civilians, including cordon and search operations, mass detention without trial, involuntary population resettlement, and the construction of free-fire zones.[49] This is evident in the expeditions that the Gurkhas carried out in northeast India as well.

Charles Callwell and Young Husband's theories of Small War were based on the dual doctrines of 'minimum force' and 'moral force,' which took the shape of a moral effect narrative in the colonies when counter-insurgency operations took place. On the other hand, they have urged that villages be burned, farms be destroyed, cattle be lifted, and indiscriminate animal slaughter be carried out to destroy the 'rebel' population's food supply. This is a duality that is highlighted in the numerous small wars conducted in the region that must be addressed in order to bridge the region's civil-military ties. Despite the Gurkhas' critical function as an arm of the colonial state and its broader societal impact, they remain marginalised in the region's existing historiography. This can be because of the present trend in historiography in the region, where interacting with military history, also known as 'war studies,' 'war and society,' and 'armed force and society,' has not been very popular among scholars of the discipline.

Notes

1. George White Collection, Minute by C.B Pritchard, Enclosure no. 2, IQ/14, 29 August 1893, MSS.EUR.F 108/24, IOR, BL, London.
2. For academics, defining 'tribe' poses both conceptual and empirical challenges. However, the tribals have now adopted this phrase of administrative convenience to refer to the region's dispossessed and destitute inhabitants. There is no claim to being the original occupants of the land, but there is a prior claim to the region's natural resources against outsiders and the ruling caste. The tribal identity now provides marginalised individuals pride and self-esteem. Virginius Xaxa, 'Tribes as Indigenous People of India', Economic and Political Weekly, Dec. 18-24, 1999, Vol. 34, No. 51 (Dec. 18-24, 1999), pp. 3589-3595, p.3589.
3. Marcus Franke analyses the political aspects of the colonial and post-colonial state's policy towards the Nagas in his *War and Nationalism in South Asia: The India State and the Nagas*, Routledge, London, 2009.
4. He served with General Redvers Buller's staff in South Africa during Ladysmith's relief and retired after the First World War.
5. Despite his prominence in the history of irregular warfare studies, Callwell's portrayals of "uncivilised" or "savage" conflict show that he was a product of his time. While he understood that victory in small wars was far from guaranteed, he lived during a time when regular armies were often victorious. Non-European foes were widely thought to be 'inferior' – or, at best, 'semi-civilised.' To explore the idea more, see Daniel Whittingham, 'Savage warfare': C.E. Callwell, the roots of counter-insurgency, and the

nineteenth century context' in *Small Wars & Insurgencies*, 23:4-5, 591-607, DOI: 10.1080/09592318.2012.709769, p.592.

6. Charles Callwell, *Small Wars: A Tactical Textbook for Imperial Soldiers*, Greenhill Books, London, 1896, (reprint 1990), p.21.
7. G. J. Younghusband, *Indian Frontier Warfare: The Military Methods of British Empire on the Sub-Continent 1878-1900*, Driffield, Leonaur, 1898 (reprint 2012).
8. Chales Callwell, *Small Wars*, *op. cit.*, p.91.
9. See Mackenzie, *North-East Frontier of India*, for many 'raids' and 'expeditions.' (Mackenzie's work was first published under the title *History of the Government's Relations with the Hill Tribes of Bengal's North-East Frontier*).
10. T. R. Moreman, *The Army in India and the Development of Frontier Warfare*, 1849-1947, Houndmills, Basingstoke, Macmillan, 1998, p.91. For the use of the Royal West African Frontier Force, a pamphlet titled *Notes on Training in Bush Warfare* was printed in 1922 and reprinted in 1930. Skirmishing, reconnaissance, and the use of machine guns were all covered in this leaflet.*Notes on Training in Bush Warfare*, Crown Agents for the Colonies, London, 1922 (reprint 1930).
11. Winning the 'hearts and minds' (also known as WHAM) of the people who live in the troubled region is a concept coined during the Cold War era when the West was fighting Communist insurgencies. WHAM's beliefs include using force exclusively against rebels and not the entire population, providing basic amenities to the people (running water, food, health care, etc.), and eventually granting land and political rights. The goal is to keep the insurgents distinct from the general public by avoiding unnecessary collateral damage and preventing greater alienation of the general public, which could lead to them joining the ranks of the insurgents. The British administrators and military officials in India did not use the word WHAM, but they did try to follow the concepts behind it in a primitive manner at times.

For a discussion on WHAM in modern counter-insurgency operations, see, Thomas R. Mockaitis, 'Winning Hearts and Minds in the 'War on Terrorism', *Small Wars and Insurgencies*, 14 (2003), pp.21-38; Gavin Bulloch, 'Military Doctrines and Counter-insurgency: A British Perspective', *Parameters*, Summer, 1996, pp.4-16.

12. "Introduction" by R.M. Betham in A.H.M. Simcox, *Memoir of Khandesh Bheel Corps: 185-91*, Thacker and Spink, London, 1912, pp.i-ii.
13. NAI, FP (A), December 1875, No. 92: Capt. John Butler, Political Agent, Naga Hills to H. Luttman-Johnson, Secy. to the Chief Commissioner of Assam, 30 April 1875.
14. Mountain fever, leeches, flies, and other insects posed a particular threat to troops and coolies, resulting in high casualties. One of the factors for such high casualties from diseases was the absence of medical treatment. Foreign soldiers were used to Western medicine, while the hillmen depended on traditional methods of healing.
15. 'The object of the expedition was to meet the Angami Naga chiefs and, by a conciliatory intercourse, to prepare them to cooperate with me in repressing their annual murderous and marauding incursions against our more peaceable subjects; to survey the map the tract of country in question, and to open a regular communication with Manipur and Nowgong, through the Angami country via Dimapur, Sumokhoo-Ting, Poplongmaee, and Yang, which would promote trade, ameliorate the status of the hill people, and ultimately lead to the abandonment of primitive habits and the peaceful and prosperous settlement of this barbarian tribe'. See Major John Butler, *Travels and Adventures in the Province of Assam during the Residence of Fourteen Years*, Munshiram Manoharlal, Delhi, 1855 (reprint 2004), p.12.
16. Colonel L.W. Shakespear reported in 1929 that British military activities against the Angami Nagas were attempts to stop slave

raiding in the districts of Nowgong and Cachar to restore peace to the borderland. See, Colonel L.W. Shakespear, *History of Assam Rifles*, Spectrum Publication, Gauhati, 1980, (reprint 1929).

17. Minutes by Major General H.W. Norman, 1863-76, Memorandum by Norman on the distribution of the Native Armies of India, 26th September, Bengal, Para 10, p. 320, National Archives of India, Delhi.
18. Lieutenant-Colonel B.N. Majumdar, *History of the Army Service Corps*, Vol. 2, 1858-1913, Sterling Publication, Delhi, 1976, p. 250.
19. Colonel L.W. Shakespear, *op. cit.,* p.9.
20. *Ibid.*, p.22.
21. Military Department Proceedings, October 1861, From Col. G. Balfour, Chief of Military Finance, to the Secretary to the Government of India, Military Department, 24th September 1861, p. 426, National Archives of India.
22. Colonel L.W. Shakespear, *op. cit.*, p.142, 188–189; DK Palit, *Sentinels of the North-East*, 1984, 98.
23. "Mr. McCabe"s Report on the Outbreak Amongst the Eastern Lushai Tribes in March 1892," 1892, 4.
24. "Kohima affairs.Murder of Mr. G.H. Damant, Deputy Commissioner, Naga Hills.Punitive Expedition against the Nagas," 1880.
25. Shakespear, History of the Assam Rifles, 1929, 72.
26. Guite, "Colonial violence and its "Small Wars," 2019; and "Report on the operations undertaken in connection with the disturbances on the AssamBurma Frontier during the season 1917–18," 1919.
27. Bishnu Kumari Gurung, 'The Gurkhas in the Non-Military Services in Colonial Assam' in *Proceedings of North East India History Association*, 39th Session, Shillong, 2018, p.301.

28 Imdad Hussain, 'Frontier Defence: Development of Local Forces' in H. K. Barpujari (ed.), *The Comprehensive History of Assam*, Vol. IV., Publication Board Assam, Guwahati, 2007 (Third edition), p.190.

29. D. Banerjea, Central Police Organisations, Part 2, Allied Publishers, Kolkata, 2005, p.185.

30. Two British Officers, LtsBeddingfield and Burlton, along with about 50-60 men, were killed at Nongkhlaw in retaliation for what the Khasi saw as an attempt by the Company, led by David Scott, the Agent to the Governor General of the Northeastern Frontier, to subjugate the hills under their control under the guise of road construction to link Sylhet and the Assam plains.

31. Alexander Mackenzie, *History of the Relations of the Government with the Hill Tribes of the North-East Frontier of Bengal,* Originally published in 1884, Mittal Publications, New Delhi, 2001 (Reprint), 2001.

32. For details, see H. K. Barpujari, *Problems of the Hill Tribes of Northeastern Frontier* 1822-44, Vol I, Lawyers Book Stall, Gauhati, pp. 51-52 and Tejimala Gurung's, 'Role of the 8th Gurkha Rifles in British Expansion in Northeast India' in *Proceedings of North East India History Association*, Thirty Seventh Session, Gangtok, 2016, p.383.

33. Bengal Judicial Proceedings, Nos. 29-30; 19 July 1827; P.R.T. Gordon, *The Khasis,* Macmillan and Company Limited, pp. 103-104

34. The tribute was paid in the hopes of ratifying the 1832 treaty with Raja Ram Chandra. 'The people of the territory might be 'timid and unwarlike,' but the Raja held besides the hills two fertile tracts on the north and south populous, well cultivated, and capable of yielding a revenue estimated at a lakh and half rupees sufficient to maintain four or five companies of sepoys or pay a subsidy equivalent to the cost of maintaining such a

body of troops... we have made a very unsatisfactory bargain,' writes Captain Fisher. Bengal Political Consultation, 1832, 14 May, No. 117, Private Letter, fisher to Jenkins, 16 April; H.K. Barpujari, *Problems of the Hill Tribes of Northeastern Frontier* 1822-44, Vol I, Lawyers Book Stall, Gauhati, p.89.

35. P. N. Dutta, *Impact of the West on the Khasis and Jaintias: A Survey of Political, Economic and Social Change*, Cosmo Publication, New Delhi, 1982, p.79.
36. Home Public No. 30 C; 3 July 1863; J.C. Haughton to the Secretary Government of Bengal.
37. *Ibid.*
38. Shobhan N. Lamare, *Resistance Movements in North-East India: The Jaintias of Meghalaya*, 1860-1863, Regency Publication, New Delhi, 2001, p.85.
39. Lt Col. H. J. Huxford, *History of the 8th Gurkha Rifles 1824-1949*, Gale and Polden, Aldershot, 1952, p.14.
40. Naga-a generic term for a composite of various tribes by which the Angami was the 'most' robust.
41. Lt Col. H. J. Huxford, *History of the 8th Gurkha Rifles 1824-1949*, Gale and Polden, Aldershot, 1952, p.14.
42. The word 'Forward Policy' gained popularity in the 1860s as a result of a well-known discussion between the two schools of thought over imperial policies in the North-Western Province. It meant the creation of administrative control over hill tribes in northeast India, as well as their constitution as an important part of the Assam province. In the 1870s, the strategy was first implemented in the Garo Hills and Nagas, and by the end of the century, it had spread to the Lushai Hills.
43. Alexander Mackenzie, *op.cit.*, p.135.
44. Colonel L.W. Shakespear, *History of Assam Rifles*, Spectrum Publication, Gauhati, 1980, (reprint 1929).
45. See Butler, Travels and Adventures in the Province of Assam.

46. For more details, see, Jangkhomang Guite, Colonial violence and its 'Small Wars': fighting the Kuki 'guerillas' during the Great War in Northeast India, 1917–1919' in *Small Wars and Insurgencies*, Vol. 30, No. 2, p.453.
47. Tejimala Gurung, 'The Making of Gurkhas as a 'Martial Race' in Colonial India: Theory and Practice', *Proceedings of India History Congress*, 75th Session, Aligarh, 2015, pp.520-529.
48. This is an area that the author is exploring in detail in her ongoing research programme.
49. David French, *The British Way in Counter-Insurgency, 1945–1967*, Oxford University Press, 2011; and Huw Bennett, 'The Other Side of the COIN: Minimum and Exemplary Force in British Army Counter-insurgency in Kenya', Small Wars and Insurgencies, 18:4, 638-664, https://doi.org/10.1080/09592310701778514.

19

Indigeneity and National Integration: A Semi-Biographical Account of a Jaintia Officer in NEFA

Geri Koyu

Since colonial times, North East Frontier Agency (NEFA) was one of the tribal areas of northeast India that had witnessed colonial influence. However, with the advent of modern administration in the twentieth century, the region experienced a wave of exploratory missions by explorers, military officials and modern administrators. These tours and explorations enabled the colonial officials to interact with local inhabitants and assert authority in the absence of direct administration. In the post-independence era, when efforts were undertaken to extend administration into the region, it ushered in a new era of frontier administration. The year 1953 saw the establishment of the Indian Frontier Administrative Service. However, the expedient of creating a distinct cadre for relatively restricted duty was ineffective since the new cadre had virtually no routes of proportion, which are dormant for labour.

As a result, the Indian Frontier Administrative Service and the Indian Administrative Service were forced to merge. Following that, the Indian government developed a distinct service cadre for the Union Territories to provide Frontier Service troops.[1] Most of the officers in the frontier service were selected from Assam's existing All India service cadres. In rare circumstances, Extra Assistant Commissioners of the Assam Civil Service were appointed as Political Officers or Assistant Political Officers. Thus, the administrative cadres were divided into two groups: Frontier Civil Service, which included positions such as Base Superintendent and Assistant Political Officer, and Indian Administrative Service, which included positions such as Political Officer.[2]

Most of these frontier officials were outsiders who endured living in the harshest conditions to carry on their administrative duty. The period of their stay and their work involved the technicality of integrating the region and people with the nation. In the process, they lost parts of their indigeneity in their association with the societies in the NEFA region. Among these officials was Harkom Scofield Pariat, who had served as a frontier official in NEFA. This paper presents his semi-biographical account and opens further scope for developing a new perspective on the history of the region by creating a prosopography of such frontier officials. The work is based on secondary sources, interviews and family records.

I

History is essentially the record of events where the participation of individuals is crucial, and a thorough understanding of those individuals creates more possibility of understanding the context and circumstances. Historically, every event is defined by the involvement of several individuals who played their roles. So biographical works bring up studies with detailed information that add significantly to historical traditions. In general, the boundaries of biography in history may be limited, but appreciating and remembering the vitality of the individual's works and the lives they lived or have impacted shed light on historical realities for all genres of history.

The role of an individual in history has always been a concern for historians. Biographers also had difficulties solving the puzzle of – do individuals shape events or do events shape individuals. For a long time, history has not been able to look beyond the throne or seat of power, and one must remember the contributors who worked to ensure that the power does not shake or fall. Therefore, contrary to the Marxism method of writing history, biography throws light on issues and information relating to events that may provide a new perspective on events and prominent figures, their lives and works. The Marxist claim that individuals cannot change the course of history at will, as it had been the collective efforts of a group of individuals which constitute a society or union that dominates the circumstances. Though this claim may be correct, this does not mean that individual lives and their contribution are unimportant. In many circumstances, the role played by an individual can have a lasting impact and can be decisive. Hence, this role deserves to be jotted down in the pages of history. Biographical works are significant in filling the gap in understanding the narratives from a closer range as they provide information that may have been neglected.

Marxist scholars and the Marxist method of historical analysis have largely dominated the post-independence historiography in India. The approach of historical materialism gave importance to the economy and society and/or economic development leading to other changes. In this exercise, one of the different methods of historical analysis is in which the role of an individual is assessed in the more significant historiographical construction/deconstruction. The historiography of Arunachal

Pradesh is also a victim of this trend. Another problematic area of the historiography of Arunachal Pradesh has been tribe-wise or ethnocentric studies. Scholars studying the history and culture of a particular tribe, too, ignored the role of individuals in the history of Arunachal Pradesh. From the late 1950s onwards, the Department of Research of NEFA, under the leadership of Verrier Elwin and L. N. Chakraborty, to mention only two besides others, initiated the research in this area. They laid the foundation of ethnographical and/or historical studies, and the tradition continues even in the twenty-first century. They also have not highlighted the role of an individual in the historical progress of Arunachal Pradesh. Another problematic area in the historiography of Arunachal Pradesh is the lack of biography of individuals who contributed to the developments in the State. This paper attempts to go beyond the established norms and pattern of history writing of Arunachal Pradesh. It is an attempt to critically evaluate the contribution of an individual who worked against all odds to improve the life of the people of Arunachal Pradesh.

II

There is a genre of books that provide us with the perspective of important individuals who served in the frontier regions of NEFA. Ursula Graham Bower's work, *The Hidden Land*[3]. is a journal account of the author and author's husband, Lt. Col. F. N. Betts, who was the first Political Officer of Subansiri region. It provides a good insight into the life, activities and duties of a frontier official in the area during the 1940s, which in hand helps the researcher to get a proper idea of the dynamics of exploration and administration in the region. This perspective is further enriched by Nari K. Rustomji's book *Imperilled Frontiers: India's North-Eastern Borderlands*[4] and *Enchanted*

Frontiers: Sikkim, Bhutan and India's North-eastern Borderlands.[5] Rustomji was the District Commissioner of Lakhimpur in the later 1940s, later assumed the post of the advisor to the Governor of Assam for the tribal regions, and later became the first Chief Secretary of Meghalaya. His writing adds richly to the perspective and information of an administrator who always worked closely with the region.

Verrier Elwin's books, *A Philosophy for NEFA*[6] and *Democracy in NEFA*[7] are the product of the data and information acquired via touring frontier officials and their tour diaries. The book is the guiding principle for policies that were adopted for NEFA. It was also a guide for the frontier officials, which provided them with the philosophical dimension of how the government must approach the tribes of the region. Another work of Elwin, *India's North-East Frontier in the Nineteenth Century*,[8] is a compilation of several accounts of the colonial period on tribes of Arunachal Pradesh. These works provide much information about the region during the twentieth century.

B. B. Pandey's book, *Arunachal Pradesh Village State to Statehood*,[9] is one such book that deals with Arunachal Pradesh's historical, administrative and societal aspects. The book deals in detail with the interaction process between the state and society and outlines the emergence of Arunachal Pradesh from the nebulous assortment of self-contained autonomous villages into its present identity and position in the country as a state. Another book which deals with the same aspects of Arunachal Pradesh is J. N. Chowdhury's book *Arunachal Pradesh: from Frontier Tract to Union Territory* Cosmo Publications, New Delhi, 1983.[10] The book chronologically studies the region's growth from a frontier tract to a union territory. M. L. Bose, *History of Arunachal Pradesh*,[11] tries to provide a comprehensive history of Arunachal Pradesh, starting from the British annexation of Assam in 1826 to the end of British rule in 1947. It provides an understanding of the development of this region through the British period. The book also provides the historical developments dealt with during the post-independence time.

Berenice Guyot-Rechard's article, 'Tour Diaries and Itinerant Governance in the Eastern Himalayas, 1909-1962' (2017),[12] presents us with the state-making process by examining its material and communicative culture embodied in tour diaries. The article argues that touring and tour diaries exemplified a certain form of frontier governance, marked by itinerancy and personalisation. The paper helps to understand the importance of touring and itinerancy of the officials, which was the key that gave birth to a frontier. Guyot-Rechard's book *Shadow States: India China and the Himalayas, 1910-1962*[13] deals with the Indian government's actions towards the region in the post-independence era. It discusses how the Indian government expanded its administration into the area was earlier outside any formal administration and made efforts to make the tribes realise that they are the benevolent government. The chapter talks about the birth of NEFA up to the 1962 Chinese aggression when the region became a tension zone.

III

In the post-independence era, NEFA was included in the state of Assam under the new constitution. It was specifically stipulated that its administration was the responsibility of the President of India and that the Governor of Assam was the President's agent for the discharge of this responsibility. It was also laid down that, in carrying out his agency powers, the Governor would act at his discretion rather than on the advice of his ministers. The reason for adopting this approach towards the region was to foster further interaction of the tribes under NEFA with the rest of the northeast region and the country.

During British rule, the importance of constructing outposts up to the McMahon line had been acknowledged, and a step in that direction had been made in the 1930s, but with the onset of the war, priorities were re-adjusted, and men could not be spared for what was then regarded a low-priority border tract. Despite this, several outposts were established during the winter months, when the hill tracks were navigable, and supplies for their upkeep could be sent up. However, during the monsoon, when severe rain made the tracks unusable, such outposts had to be removed.[14] Subsequently, the Chinese invasion of eastern Tibet in 1950 signalled that the NEFA could no longer be ignored. The Chinese confrontational stance resulted in the northern border becoming a live and sensitive territory, and the concerns of the frontier tribes had become a subject of national concern, which is why the central government chose to take direct and complete responsibility for the tribes and their region.[15] These things demanded an immediate effort to extend a formal modern administration into the region along with a need to intensify the process of national integration in the region.

The immediate response of the government towards this effort was to intensify the efforts to integrate this frontier region and its people with the nation, thereby introducing a modern administration. For this purpose, the government established a single-line administration in which the Deputy Commissioner is the chief administrative authority within the district and is not only the District Magistrate and Collector but also the head of all district-level offices. As the locals of this area were not trained enough to function as officials in modern administrative machinery, most of the frontier officials inducted by the government were outsiders. Further, the frontier officials posted to NEFA were not only trained to carry administration in this rugged region but also to integrate the region and the people into the newly independent nation.

While carrying out their duty of integrating the region and people with the nation, some of these frontier officials lost parts of their indigeneity in the process. One such case is of Harkom Scofield Pariat from Jaintia Hills of Meghalaya, who came to NEFA as an Agriculture Inspector in 1954 and retired as an Extra Assistant Commissioner (EAC), a mid-level position in the NEFA civil service in 1989.

Harkom Scofield Pariat was born in 1928 in a Jaintia tribe of Meghalaya. He was the first person from Meghalaya to graduate in agriculture from Assam Agriculture University, Jorhat, in 1953. Pariat was a very adventurous person. Growing up in Jowai in West Jaintia Hills District, he admired forests, mountains and rivers more than towns from a very young age. He had an immense enthusiasm for trekking, touring, fishing and all the adventurous stuff that a place like NEFA offered.[16] Hence, he had an apt attitude of a frontier officer.

Around the same time as his graduation year, a new discourse in NEFA about farm improvement and food self-sufficiency took root. Therefore, when the time came, he applied for the frontier service and young Pariat got inducted as an Agriculture Inspector in the Tirap Frontier Tract of NEFA in 1954. During his time as Agriculture Officer, he married a woman named Swisly Lyngdoh, whose father, Lipong Phawa, was also serving in NEFA as VLW (Village Level Worker),[17] the post is now known as AFA (Agriculture Field Assistant) in Tirap Frontier Tract.

Pariat served as an Agriculture Inspector till 1962-1963, when the Sino-Indian war broke out. After the war, Special

Service Bureau (SSB) was established in 1963 after the Sino-Indian war to strengthen India's border areas against enemy operations. So, after receiving his training at Mahabaleshwar, Maharashtra, he joined the SSB in NEFA as a Sub Area Organiser (SAO) in 1963-64. He was posted in the Subansiri Frontier Division. During his time at SSB, he served in places like Koloriang, Sarli, Yinkiong, etc.[18]

During the period after the Sino-Indian war, the subject of the frontier region's integration into the country gained further traction, and the frontier region's administration was to be reinforced to speed up the process. Hence, a *Single Line* system[19] of administration that was introduced in 1954 was further amplified. The roles of Circle Officers, Extra Assistant Commissioners, and other officials were expanded under a single-line administration. They now served as local heads for all development programmes in their jurisdictions, including community development schemes, people's socio-cultural activities, supervision and authority over technical departments like schools, hospitals, roads, agriculture, and so on, as well as law and order and revenue work.[20] This resulted in a need for an increase in the number of officials in the administration.

Pariat was one such individual who filled this increasing demand for more administrative officials in NEFA. After serving in SSB till the late 1960s, he took up the post of Circle Officer (CO) of Chowkham in 1970-71. After Chowkham, he was posted to Hayuliang. He was promoted to the post of Extra Assistant Commissioner (EAC) in the year 1975 at Hayuliang. Next, he held the position of EAC at Pasighat in the years 1977-81.[21]

During his time as an EAC, due to some official misconduct of his inferiors, he was demoted and was posted to Mariyang in the year 1981 as a Circle Officer. After Mariyang, he was posted to Geku in the year 1982 and then to Khonsa in 1984. It was during this time that he was cleared of the official misconduct that led to his demotion, and he was again posted to Namsai as an EAC in the year 1987. Unfortunately, during his time at Namsai, he met with a road accident that led to paralysis. He took voluntary retirement in the year 1989. He passed away aged 72 on April 16 2000, at Wahiajer village, West Jaintia Hills District, Meghalaya.[22]

Integrity and loss of indigeneity

The frontier administration envisioned neither assimilation nor isolation for the tribes but rather a middle ground that would bring the best of the modern world to them while not destroying their traditional way of life but rather activating and developing all that was good about it. Within these broad guidelines, the government was to promote material and social growth by promoting economic and agricultural self-sufficiency, establishing law and order, and promoting a renaissance of art, music, beauty, and the pleasures and graces of life.[23]

The attainment of freedom did not just imply the end of colonial control; it also included unleashing creative forces and establishing an equal society in preparation for a reformed Indian country; for this, the state's role in the growth of nationalism was seen as crucial.[24] The official goal of welfare, development and cultural protection was to help the NEFA tribes feel at home in India and to show them that they are a valuable part of the country. The idea of progress as a path to Indianness was part of a 'developmental nationalism'[25] philosophical genealogy in which country, state, and development were all connected. So the frontier officials were to work in tune with this idea, and they became the core element for integrating the tribes into the nation. Pariat's case is no different; he was one among many officials who worked to integrate the tribes through a notion of 'developmental nationalism'. But what makes his case unique is that he lost parts of his indigeneity while carrying out his duty of integrating the region and people with the nation.

Soon after his marriage, his father-in-law was murdered in 1958 at Yumchum village, Changlang, which made him take full responsibility for his wife's family which also settled in NEFA.[26] Later, Pariat and his wife had three sons (Late Dowin Scofield Pariat, Late Airman Scofield Pariat and Waterman Scofield Pariat) and three daughters (Rilomina Pariat, Late. Tiny Pariat and Jennifer Pariat). Swisly's family and their six children spent their whole life in the remotest regions of NEFA, where ever Harkom was posted.

At that time, Pariat and his family lived in the extremely inhospitable terrain of NEFA. In its primitive, underdeveloped form, NEFA's overall food output was barely enough to feed its sparsely distributed people. Its economy was designed to suit just the most basic needs of a primitive community. Outsiders were not enticed to pursue their life's work in a location of dense woods and rugged mountains where food scarcity was a serious issue.[27] Furthermore, there was not even a rudimentary network of hill paths across the area. Thus getting from one location to another took days to months.

All of this did not break Pariat's will to work at NEFA but it secluded his family far from their homeland. His long service as a frontier official in NEFA led to such large implications in his life that he and his family started losing parts of their indigeneity. Starting from their surname, their children adopt Pariat's surname and not Swisly's surname 'Lyngdoh' even though they came from a matrilineal society of Meghalaya where lineage is traced from a mother. This could be seen as the very onset of how they were getting far from their indigenous custom and becoming more attached to NEFA's patriarchal society.

Spending their whole life at NEFA meant that Pariat and his family got better accustomed and versed to NEFA's tribal ways rather than the place from where they belonged. His family got well versed in tribal customs, tradition and tribal language, especially Adi and Galo. His service's implications were so high that when one of Pariat's daughters passed away in 1979, they could not even take her to their place and her mortal remains were laid to rest at a church cemetery in Pasighat.[28]

Later on, two of Swisly's sisters were married to a Galo and an Adi, respectively, and two of Pariat's children, Waterman Scofield Pariat and Jennifer Pariat, were married to a Singpho girl and a Galo, respectively. Subsequently, Pariat and his family, who had come to NEFA due to his frontier duty, never left. In the process of 'Indianising' the tribes as part of Pariat's frontier service, they became a part of this society and embraced it.

Conclusion

The British government had trained a few Indian officers with frontier expertise, and when the decision was taken to expand administration in the hills after independence, these trained officers came in useful.[29] The tribesmen themselves showed a willingness to cooperate and offered no substantial objection to the administration's progress. They could already see the advantages of administration at this point. Even as early as the 1950s, a few NEFA tribesmen with the necessary skills stepped up to share administrative tasks with officials from throughout the country. There were even more competent tribal individuals available for absorption in border duty from other tribal regions in North-East India. As a result, tribesmen made up a sizable portion of the middle-ranking officers. These individuals formed the nucleus of a devoted political team that sprang into action when the government decided to unite the furthest reaches of the frontier tracts under one administrative umbrella.[30]

The case of Harkom Scofield Pariat is one of many frontier officials who came to the tribal society of NEFA and became a part of it. This could be seen as an example of many frontier officials who lost portions of their indigeneity while carrying out the task of integrating the region and people with the country. This itself was a sacrifice they made for their duty, and it stipulated a new perspective of looking towards the region of Arunachal Pradesh and its administrative history. The development of such a perspective may result in the development of a prosopography of such frontier officials, which would contribute largely to the historiography of the region. It would also enrich the administrative history of the region by creating a history not from the state's perspective but from the perspective of the administrators who did not just bring changes to the region but were primarily a part of those changes.

Notes and References

1. Nari K. Rustomji, *Imperilled Frontiers: India's North Eastern Borderlands,* Oxford University Press, Delhi, 1983, p. 238.
2. M. L. Bose, *History of Arunachal Pradesh*, Concept Publishers, New Delhi, 1997, p. 238.
3. Ursula Graham Bower's work, *The Hidden Land,* John Murray, London, *1953.*
4. Nari K. Rustomji, *Imperilled Frontiers: India's North Eastern Borderlands, op.cit.*
5. Nari K. Rustomji, *Enchanted Frontiers: Sikkim, Bhutan and India's North-eastern Borderlands*, Oxford University Press, London, *1974.*

6. Verrier Elwin's books, *A Philosophy for NEFA, 1957.*
7. Verrier Elwin, *Democracy in NEFA,* North-East Frontier Agency, Shillong, 1965.
8. Verrier Elwin, *India's North-East Frontier in the Nineteenth Century,* Oxford University Press, London, 1959,
9. B.B. Pandey, *Arunachal Pradesh Village State to Statehood,* Himalayan Publishers, Delhi:Itanagar, 1996.
10. J. N. Chowdhury, *Arunachal Pradesh: from Frontier Tract to Union Territory,* Cosmo Publications, New Delhi, 1983.
11. M. L. Bose, *History of Arunachal Pradesh*, Concept Publishing Company, New Delhi, 1997.
12. Guyot-Réchard, Bérénice. Tour Diaries and Itinerant Governance In The Eastern Himalayas, 1909–1962, *The Historical Journal,* 60. 1-24. 2017. 10.1017/S0018246X17000073.
13. Guyot-Rechard's book *Shadow States: India China and the Himalayas, 1910-1962* Cambridge University Press, Delhi, 2017.
14. Nari K. Rustomji, *Enchanted Frontiers: Sikkim, Bhutan and India's North-Eastern Borderlands*, Oxford University Press, Mumbai, 1971, p. 115.
15. Nari K. Rustomji, *op.cit.,* p. 96.
16. Jennifer Koyu, about 47 years old, daughter of Harkom Scofield Pariat, held a scheduled interview on March 15, 2022, at 06:28 pm. (referred to as JKI)(*Jennifer Koyu Interview*).
17. Waterman Scofield Pariat, 53 years old, son of Harkom Scofield Pariat, held an unscheduled interview on March 25, 2022, at 03:00 pm. (referred to as WSPI)(*Waterman Scofield Pariat Interview*).
18. JKI.
19. Verrier Elwin, *A Philosophy for NEFA,* Directorate of Research, Itanagar, first published in 1957, Fourth Reprint 2012, p. 4.

20. J. N. Chowdhury, *Arunachal Pradesh: from Frontier Tract to Union Territory*, Cosmo Publications, New Delhi, 1983, p. 264.
21. Rilomina Negi, aged about 58 years old, daughter of Harkom Scofield Pariat, held a scheduled interview on April 20, 2022, at 8:00 pm. (referred to as RNI) (*Rilomina Negi Interview*).
22. JKI.
23. Berenice Guyot-Rechard, *Shadow States: India China and the Himalayas, 1910-1962,* Cambridge University Press, United Kingdom, 2017, pp. 129-130.
24. *Ibid.*, p.146.
25. *Ibid.*, p.145.
26. WSPI.
27. Rustomji, *Imperilled Frontiers, op.cit.,* p. 108.
28. RNI.
29. Chowdhury, *op.cit.,* p. 255.
30. *Ibid.*, p. 255.

20

The Lone Figure of a Woman: Reflections on Khasi Society

Christine Zenith Mylliemngap

Humans are social beings; they cannot live in isolation except in rare cases. In their love for the company, humans communicate with each other through the medium of language. While communicating, views, opinions and ideas of all kinds are exchanged. Communication is also a mode where knowledge from the past is carried on to the present in all societies, albeit those with written or unwritten histories. In the case of tribal communities, which have no written records that will help communicate ideas from one generation to another, oral transmissions are paramount in disseminating such ideas. But it is significant to point out that oral discourses are firmly dependent on the community's collective memory for knowledge of the past to be carried on in the present and retained for future generations. Oral transmissions of knowledge in a tribal society include folk narratives- like folktales, legends, myths, proverbs, rumours or tall tales, fairy tales, animal stories, riddles, children's stories, urban legends or contemporary legends. As such oral transmissions are highly dependent on what is commonly called 'Stories'. Because every storyline is not conceived in a vacuum but has its settings in historical time and space, and thus much can be gleaned from the collections of tales that are reflective of a society's evolution at a particular time

Story tellers everywhere have always found avid listeners. Tales of various kinds are loved by all listeners, be it stories of the remote past- like myths and legends; or tales of the recent past or a well-crafted piece of fiction and the like. People have always satisfied their longings for entertainment, freedom from boredom and gathering information by listening to stories told by the avid story teller.[1] One such story that will be discussed in this paper is a popular contemporary legend that was circulated in the recent past. This Contemporary legend is closely linked to the rapid strides of development in the newly formed state of Meghalaya, which came into being in 1972. Before delving further into the paper, it is imperative to understand the meaning of Contemporary legend.

A Contemporary legend is a genre of folklore that focuses on tales or narratives that are 'believable as well as unbelievable'. Quoting Emili Samper, 'Contemporary legends are known by a variety of names. They have been labelled "extraordinary stories", "rumours", "contemporary legends", "urban legends", "apocryphal anecdotes", "modern myths", "credible stories", "legendary stories of today", "repulsive legends" (for those that deal with a particular theme), "contemporary myths", "urban tales" or "FOAF legends". Urban legends belong to the sub-class of folk narratives, legends that –unlike fairy tales are believed or at least believable and that –unlike myths are set in the recent past and involve normal human beings rather than ancient gods or demigods.[2]For this paper, both the terms will be used interchangeably, for both have the same meaning and connotation.

This paper discusses the contemporary legend of the vanishing female hitchhiker that is believed to be frequent at night in particular spots along the Gauhati- Shillong road (NH 40).[3] The rumour that eventually developed into a tale of human encounters with the ghostly female figure who performs the peculiar action of 'hitchhiking' for a ride from unknown drivers travelling to Shillong via the Gauhati Shillong road is a popular one. The legend can be traced to have originated after the construction of the Gauhati Shillong road. Hence its emergence only after this period is significant for it showcases the pace of infrastructural developments that was accelerated in the Khasi and Jaintia hills, especially after the achievement of statehood.

Associating this popular genre of folklore like the contemporary legend or urban legend in a historical study is significant because such contemporary legend of the vanishing female hitchhiker reflects the socio-economic and cultural-traditional belief systems of any society at a given time. Scholars in recent years have come to an agreement, that folklore possesses historical potential. Folklore was a social phenomenon, as it expresses the 'shared experiences' of people particularly at a time when their history has not been written.[4] Before delving into the legend of the vanishing hitchhiker, let us focus first on Meghalaya's economic and social transformation as the background against which the legend is set.

Economic and Social Transformation of Meghalaya

The formation of the new state of Meghalaya in 1972[5] was not only a joyful event for the people, but it also heralded a change in this quaint little hill station of Shillong, the capital of the newly formed state and former headquarters of the British Raj. It ushered in a phase of rapid transition not only in the political sphere; but also in the economic, social and cultural life of the Khasi, Jaintia and Garo people belonging to the state. The metamorphosis of Shillong is seen right from 1866 when the British administration transferred the administrative headquarters of Assam from Cherrapunjee to Shillong; the latter was merely a village. The village grew in size and significance, and its facelift continued unabated.[6]From 1972 onwards, Shillong has overgrown its rural past. It is now a populous and proliferating city, besides being the headquarters of the State Government; a national highway also connects it. This is one of the important factors responsible for its urban growth.[7]

New opportunities were opened up in the new state, particularly in the government sector. Gainful employment came into the hands of the educated middle class amongst the people. The economy grew rapidly; the educational sector also considerably progressed by expanding existing schools and colleges and setting up new establishments. Politically the state of Meghalaya was also making rapid inroads with the legislation and execution of administrative reforms for the welfare of the state and its people. The pace of development in the sphere of roadways is particularly noteworthy. Right from the British period, roadways were constructed; initially, they were kaccha roads that later on became tarred roadways. These roads served as lifelines connecting the erstwhile Khasi and Jaintia hills of the *British Raj* with the province of Assam and Sylhet, and later on, after Independence, these roads connected Shillong township with Assam and the rest of India. The year 1906 should serve as a landmark in Assam's transport and communication history. This year, the first passenger bus plied between Shillong and Gauhati.[8] As mentioned earlier, the importance of these roads lies in the fact that they are the lines of sustenance of the economy of the newly formed state. They help transport goods, services and the mobility of people (from the rural to the urban areas). With the subsequent improvement in transport facilities, people from outside started moving into this area.[9] Road connectivity is, therefore, a useful indicator of the development process and, perhaps, reaches of the market as well.[10] Four National Highways in the state have a total length of 706.56km.[11] In the context of this paper, we will study one such National Highway connecting the state of Meghalaya with that of Assam, the present Guwahati- Shillong road. The construction of this road was first taken up during 1927-1929.[12] The road length per hundred square kilometres increased in Meghalaya from about 22.5kmsin 1981 to 28.9 kms in 1991 and 37.8 kms in 1997.[13] The public transport services have a sufficiently broad coverage linking the crucial places within the state and with areas in the neighbouring states.[14]

The 1970s marked the period of rising business households in Shillong, significantly contributing to state political formations. These businesses were led by individuals with money power earned to a certain extent from their endeavours in transporting goods and commodities to and from the state. Special attention has been paid to the development of transport and communication in the area after the nationalisation of these services in 1938.However, the state government have allowed private owners also to ply their vehicles to a limited extent on selected routes. In Shillong city, they plied 75 vehicles. The owners and workers are mostly Khasis. Initially, the State transport started operating on particular routes with its fleet of 150 vehicles. It has, at present, a much-expanded operation along a network of roads throughout the state, covering about 3000 kilometres (1,900 kms in the plains and 1,100 kms in the hills) and has a fleet of 730 buses. The movement of goods has also been nationalised on the Shillong Guwahati and Shillong- Aizawl routes.[15] The improved transport facilities have accelerated the contact between the Khasis and the non-Khasis and provided them with opportunities to come into close and intimate contact among themselves. The process of urbanisation has received a considerable fillip.

The economic transformation in the new state of Meghalaya has brought about social changes, too; men and women alike joined the workforce in huge numbers earning their livelihoods in different ways. Many depended upon the government sector, while others ventured into entrepreneurship of various kinds. It is significant that in the Khasi and Jaintia hills, women in the past and present times have always been active participants in economic enterprises; many of them often tending as breadwinners to their families. This is particularly evident in families with an absent father figure. A significant part of the female workforce among the Khasi Jaintia women includes 'women entrepreneurs'. Khasi Jaintia women are enterprising and very laborious. They are endowed with an innate power that can make them successful entrepreneurs. As entrepreneurs, Khasi women often initiate, organise and operate a business enterprise representing a fundamental part of the society and the economy by contributing to the source of economic growth. This is one of the important activities carried out by women in the economic sphere by engaging in diverse forms of income-generating activities, which include micro and small enterprises. They are involved in different agriculture-based entrepreneurial activities and have played an important role in developing various sectors, including businesses, contractual works and shopkeepers in the market.[16]

Not only are Khasi and Jaintia women entrepreneurs, but they also follow other occupations- many of them work as teachers, employees in the government sector, medical professionals, farmers and domestic workers. The matrilineal social systems of the Khasi and Jaintia people have given its womenfolk huge familial responsibilities which somehow they are bound to undertake. Women's participation in entrepreneurship may be seen as an indicator of their position in society. It was found that most of the Khasi women took up entrepreneurship because of poverty and the need to support the family.[17] It is against this economic and social backdrop that the paper seeks to address the contemporary legend of the vanishing female hitchhiker, the tale making its early rounds as an unverified local event of a supernatural nature that is accepted as a believable as well as unbelievable true tale; and then deriving its form as a popular contemporary legend with the passage of time.

This rumour based event or alleged event developed into a popular story or what is termed as a 'contemporary legend'or an 'urban legend'. It has a recurrent theme but with several variants. The core of this urban legend is as follows:

> One night a truck driver[18] on his return journey from Gauhati reached the Barapani[19] area (popularly called dam site). Upon crossing the bridge after a few minutes, he sees a woman 'ordinarily dressed'. She signals for the truck driver to stop, which he does. He lets her inside the truck and makes her sit at the back. He then carries on some conversation with her, but she keeps quiet the whole time, and the driver thinking that something is amiss, views the rear glass to look at the woman, but instead, he sees a skeletal frame in place of the woman. His truck swerves on the road bringing the driver to a near-fatal accident. He survives and lives to tell this horrifying tale to his friends and acquaintances.[20]

Similar tales/rumours on the same theme have spread with variations.[21]

In one instance, the lady hitchhiker is seen carrying a baby on her back; in this case, she asks for a ride from a doctor. The unsuspecting doctor takes her in his car and drops her off. While she gets off his car, he sees a strange sight 'of the woman's face melting in thin air'. Another narrative is that the 'face becomes distorted', and the figure vanishes at sight. The location of this tale, however, is at a different place in the Ryngain area.[22]

In another variation of a similar tale,

> A group of men travelling from Gauhati via the G S Road see a woman alone waving for a ride at a lonely spot next to the 'infamous' Ryndangbriew area.[23] They accommodate a seat for her at the back of the car; she then asks them to stop at a particular spot in Mawiong rim[24] called 'Nan Ka Brin', and as she gets down, she turns off to walk towards the wooded area that has a small pond, and it was then that the men saw a strange sight of the woman's feet abnormally twisted with the heels at the front and the toes at the back.[25]

The legend of the vanishing female hitchhiker, as narrated popularly by people living in Shillong, has established its stage along the national highway via the Guwahati-Shillong road; at the same time, similar such legends are staged on different roadways, for instance, in this paper a similar narrative is said to have occurred in the Pynursla-Dawki road.[26] The contemporary legend of the vanishing female hitchhiker is popular in folkloric studies, particularly in American folklore. Significantly, such legends are not alien to indigenous culture and have been disseminated worldwide. One such example is its spread in an area specific to the Khasi Jaintia hills of North East India. In comparison to the American one, this urban legend has been indigenised; one of the probable reasons could be that the conveyors and listeners of such tales could believe in them only when they have been truly localised to suit the socio-economic environment they belong to. Thus the vanishing hitchhiker of the Khasi and Jaintia hills is narrated as a female figure cutting a sordid sight, who is seen either alone or with a child on her back or walking alongside the mother. The physical appearance of the hitchhiker is not striking, and she is always described as ordinarily dressed and not particularly beautiful. The intentions of the drivers who stop their vehicles halfway are always questionable. However, according to the informants, it is 'always sympathy for the poor woman and her child in the middle of the night by the roadsidethat has motivated the drivers to stop their cars to pick them up.

With roadways connecting people and places, transportation of goods and commodities, a resurgence in economic enterprises, rising businesses, the sight of a woman late at night, either alone or in tow with a child, was neither a suspicious nor surprising scene for it was something commonly seen all the time among the women folk of the Khasi Jaintia community. The desire of the drivers to help the poor helpless woman is always questionable, but whatever their real intentions of offering the woman a ride, the idea that they accepted a woman travelling on her own/ or accompanied by a child shows an inevitable reality of the position of women in Khasi Jaintia society.

In the socio economic milieu of the Khasi Jaintia people, women as the repositories of familial welfare is a long accepted fact that has often times been taken for granted. Matriliny in Khasi -Jaintia society has not only given its women the right of inheritance and the carriers of the family name; but it has also accentuated the female's sense of responsibility for herself and for the well being of her family. Khasi Jaintia women are viewed as the upholders and caretakers of their families. Thus by conferring the right of descent on the mother, Matriliny places a heavy responsibility on women for raising of their children[27] as well as even sustaining their well being by providing for them. What may perhaps seem unlikely is the fact that a woman dared to ask for a ride in the middle of the night from an unknown stranger. The stranger's stopping may be questioned, but the woman's hitchhiking alone at night in itself was a strange phenomenon unknown to Khasi Jaintia cultural ethics and practices where women would generally be fearful of unknown men, who may turn out to be 'nongshohnoh'..[28]Hence, logically speaking, Khasi people are generally apprehensive of giving or taking rides from unknown people. Therefore this contemporary legend is divergent from the general practices of the Khasi Jaintia populace. Here we see the dissemination of the idea of hitchhiking from Western contemporary/urban legends to a society with no concept of such a practice.[29] This story of the vanishing hitch hiker as spread in the Khasi Jaintia hills amply reflects the gender dimension and social relations of men and women in Khasi society. Women travelling at nightis a common scenario among the Khasi Jaintia people. The women belonging to lower income groups particularly have to move from one place to another on their own for the purpose of work.Therefore many of them are largely independent and mobile. Most Khasiand Jaintia women not only earn their own livelihoods to sustain themselves and their families butare also the guardians of their children and grandchildren in a largely matrilineal social setup.

What is relevant in this contemporary legend is that it is set against the backdrop of newly developed roadways, rising business enterprises and the use of the motif of the 'vehicles' in most cases 'trucks' carrying sack loads of rice returning from Guwahati or 'jeeps' and 'ambassador cars' is resonant of popular vehicles in the 1970s in Meghalaya. This legend is important because it was popularly known and disseminated far and wide at a certain point. Recording them is necessary because with the passage of time they may no longer be told, as they will be replaced with other newer contemporary legends befitting the time and age. Another reason of the importance of the legend of the vanishing hitchhiker is the fact that in all vanishing hitchhiker's tales related to the Khasi and Jaintia hills it is always a 'woman' asking for help and never a 'man'. The gender paradigm is to be looked into it, for why would revenants or ghosts choose to be female and not a different sex. Answers to these questions could be found on the general perspective of society about women as being vulnerable or members of the 'weaker sex'. As such even in a matrilineal society like that of the Khasi Jaintia society, there is a dichotomy in the contemporary legend of the vanishing hitchhiker. On the one hand, the woman's role as a worker, a mother, a poor pitiful woman needing help stranded at night alone or with a child is accepted. She is given help by a man, who himself is part of the matrilineal society and who perhaps has subconsciously accepted this role of the Khasi Jaintia woman without any second thoughts. His motives for picking the woman up will always be questionable. It may be in his kindness or his quest to take advantage of a needy woman's vulnerability he gives her a ride. In either case, it does not bode well for the driver here, whose story ends in trauma that will probably last for a lifetime. On the other hand, the woman's turning into a ghost could be a part of her revenge on society in general for harbouring her with responsibilities and difficulties which she could not muster on her own.

Notes

1. Desmond L. Kharmawphlang, *Folklore Imprints in North East India*, Don Bosco Publications, Shillong, 2017, p. 9.

2. Jan Harold Brunvand, *The Vanishing Hitchhiker: American Urban Legends and their Meanings,* University of Utah, New York, 2003, p. 3.
3. It starts from Jorabat (Assam) and terminates at Tamabil (Dawki) in Meghalaya, covering a distance of 163.00 kms. This highway consists of two sections, namely Guwahati -Shillong (GS) section and the Shillong-Tamabil (ST) section.
4. Soumen Sen, *Between Tradition and Change A Perspective of Meghalaya*, B R Publishing Corporation, Delhi,1988, p. 1.
5. S. K. Chaube, *Hill Politics in North East India*, Orient Longman Limited,1999, p. 145.
6. P. R. G.Mathur, *Khasi of Meghalaya Study in Tribalism and Religion*, Cosmo Publications, New Delhi,1979, p. 5.
7. *Ibid.*, p. 6.
8. *Ibid.*, p. 11.
9. *Ibid.*, p. 12.
10. P. Nayak and E. D. Thomas, *Human Development and Deprivation in Meghalaya*, Akansha Publishing House, New Delhi,2007, p. 77.
11. *Ibid.*, p. 157.
12. *Ibid.*, p. 11.
13. *Ibid*, p. 78.
14. *Ibid.*, p. 157.
15. *Ibid.*, p. 12.
16. For details, see Tiplut Nongbri, *Gender, Matriliny and Entrepreneurship The Khasis of North East India,* Zubaan publications, New Delhi, 2008.
17. Lanukumla Ao (ed.) *Historical Development in North East India Trends and Perspectives,* Research India Press, Don Bosco College, Kohima, 2021, p. 93.

18. Name withheld as the informant is no longer alive, but he told this tale to others (friend of a friend).

19. Approximately 72.0 Kms Gauhati -Lad Umroi (Barapani) Shillong

20. As told to the writer by Mrs R.Mylliemngap, Mr. Lambok Mylliem, Mr. Teilang Mylliem and other family members of a local businessman Late Mr. Modrick Nongkynrih. The informants heard this tale from one of the truck drivers of (L) Mr. Modrick Nongkynrih, (L) Mr. Croswell. The story was believed as a true strange tale witnessed by the driver himself in one of his late night return journeys to Shillong via the G-S Road.

21. As told to the writer by Mr. Jansing Tynsong, Mr. West Mylliem, Mrs Banti Mylliem. This was a famous tale known to many; it made the rounds in the villages of Mylliem, Laitlyngkot, Pomlum and Lyngkyrdem and was supposedly told by Dr. Dohkrut, who was serving as a medical doctor in these villages. The incident happened to the doctor while journeying towards Pynursla during one of his medical visits.

22. Located at less than 30 km or less than 18.5 miles approximately from Shillong. This site is infamous for many gruesome accidents. The deep gorges known as the Riat Ryngain or Ryngain Valley are the scene of many such horrible accidents.

23. Shillong to RyndangBriew 12 Kms.

24. Shillong to Mawiong Rim 10kms.

25. As told to the writer by Ms. Saphimosha Blah War, it was an incident that happened to the informant's brother and his two friends.

26. Pynursla-Dawki road 35 Kms.

27. *Ibid.*, p.3.

28. According to Auswyn W Japang, 'Nongshohnoh' implies a cut-throat responsible for catching a human and extracting blood

or other items, which are then used as a commodity of exchange between the keeper family of U Thlen and U Thlen itself. This explanation has been given in *U Thlen and the Nongshohnoh: Folklore, Experience, and Reality* LITERATURA LUDOWA. *Journal of Folklore and Popular Culture* vol. 66 (2022), no. 3Polskie TowarzystwoLudoznawcze Polish Ethnological Society.

29. See Margaret Lyngdoh, "The Vanishing Hitchhiker in Shillong: Khasi Belief Narratives and Violence Against Women", *Asian Ethnology, Vol. 7,* No. 2, 2012, pp.207-224, accessed from Academia online journal downloaded on 5-06-2020.